Disturbing the Peace

Disturbing the Peace

A History of the Christian Family Movement 1949–1974

JEFFREY M. BURNS

University of Notre Dame Press
Notre Dame, Indiana

Copyright 1999 by
University of Notre Dame Press
Notre Dame, IN 46556
All Rights Reserved
Manufactured in the United States of America

Library of Congress Cataloging-in-Publication Data

Burns, Jeffrey M.
   Disturbing the peace : a history of the Christian Family
Movement, 1949–1974 / Jeffrey M. Burns.
      p.   cm.
   Includes bibliographical references and index.
   ISBN 0-268-00889-2 (pbk. : alk. paper)
   1. Christian Family Movement—History.   I. Title.
BX2347.8.F3B88   1999
267'.182'09—dc21   98-35634

∞The paper used in this publication meets the minimum requirements
of the American National Standard for Information Sciences—Permanence
of Paper for Printed Library Materials, ANSI Z39.48-1984.

Contents

Foreword

The Christian Family Movement changed the lives of the couples who participated in it and changed the lives of their children. The discipline of meeting every two weeks and using the Observe-Judge-Act technique provided a formation in social awareness and a deepened knowledge of the Gospel.

This book is a tribute to the thousands of married couples in each city and country who devoted themselves to seeking out what role the Gospel message should play in their lives and who made CFM what it was; to the chaplains who guided us and patiently listened to the stories of our lives as parents; to the members of the Program Committee who spent endless hours planning the annual inquiries; to those convention presenters who helped us understand how the Church's social teachings related to our daily lives; to the liturgists whose spirit-filled liturgies opened up a way of worshiping not known to us before.

For these and many other blessings, especially for our spouses, Pat, Ralph, and Dan, we are thankful. We hope this book will be welcomed by the many friends formed because of the Christian Family Movement.

PATTY CROWLEY,
REGGIE WEISSERT,
AND ROSE LUCEY

Preface

This is a story about people who gathered in one another's living rooms. So it is fitting that the proposal to create a history of the first twenty-five years of the Christian Family Movement was made in a living room—specifically, like so much else about CFM, in the Crowley living room. A living room, to be sure, without Pat Crowley, deceased for more than twenty years, but inspirited by Patty, now in her eighties but possessed of the mind and will of a person far younger.

Patty was passionately convinced of the need to record the history of CFM's early years before it became too late to capture the recollections of that period's "alumni." Those she drew together on that January evening in 1994 were an informal group of veteran members and chaplains, who shared her conviction that such a project was important, not only for those who were part of it but even more for those who were not.

They share her hope that someone seeking effective ways to bridge the all-too-common gap between faith and everyday life will one day find in this history the inspiration to create anew a movement for their own time. Our faith is that new leaders for new times will adapt the methods and catch the fire that made CFM a potent force in the community and in the Catholic Church (and in other Christian churches as well) in the quarter-century after World War II.

This original group identified some points they saw as essential to a worthwhile CFM history. First, it must be an authentic history—not a puff piece, not a venture in hagiography. Second, it must resonate with the voices of many leaders, who would speak for the diverse and even conflicting views of CFM's mission. Third, it must aim for a good geographical spread—from many parts of the country and from other countries—which would, again, reveal the diversity of thought and action from place to place, within a single program.

That same weekend, a small group set out to create the working conditions for meeting these criteria. After combing the planners' address books, they mailed out a letter/questionnaire that asked:

—Did the couple (chaplain) agree that a CFM history was needed? (There was, after all, the possibility that we were trying to throw a party that no one would come to.)

—If they did agree, alumni were asked to give their own evaluation of CFM's impact—on them, on their community, on their parish/diocese—and to report significant accomplishments.

—Finally, these veterans were asked to identify other leaders who should be queried as we cast a wider net.

The response was an enthusiastic Yes. And the names and addresses that poured in were the foundation for a file that grew finally to hundreds of names.

Next came a sortie to the University of Notre Dame in South Bend, Indiana, the repository for the national (and to a considerable extent international) CFM archives. Our goal was to satisfy ourselves on a critical point. Was there a body of organized material adequate to sustain not just a book of memoirs but a book of record that would be both reliable and objective? We found voluminous correspondence; complete files of annual programs, organized around major themes; more than twenty-five years of *ACT,* the national newsletter; successive editions of the introductory *For Happier Families,* and a cluster of commissioned surveys that gave readings on the nature and state of CFM. This last resource turned out to be important.

Our hostess, Reggie Weissert (who, with her husband, Ralph, was one of South Bend's earliest members) gathered up other interested local members, including the revered Father Louis Putz, C.S.C., to hear their comments. Should we develop a CFM history? If so, how should we go about it? After quick endorsement of the idea, the discussion about *how* produced a consensus that a professional historian was needed, to do justice to the task. The suggestion came that we consider Jeffrey Burns, whose doctoral thesis had dealt with CFM as part of a wider treatment of Catholic Action.

The idea immediately clicked. His insight into the meaning as well as the workings of the movement had already impressed us. The reason was not far to seek. When we asked Jeff to take on the assignment, his first words were, "My parents were CFMers." (Parenthetically, Rose Lucey's *Roots and Wings* is filled with accounts of how CFM's spirit was transmitted to the children of CFMers.)

When we noted that we wanted the account to be based on interviews with large numbers of alumni as well as on the written record, Jeff clinched the match by telling us that he was both experienced in and enthusiastic about using oral history as a data base. Jeff currently serves as archivist for the Archdiocese of San Francisco and teaches college courses in U.S. Catholic history.

This book is also a story about friends. About the lifelong friendships forged in the pressure cooker of shared risk, shared action. About the readiness of old friends of CFM to support this project. ACTA, a Chicago-based foundation created by a group of Chicago priests, all CFM chaplains, has provided two generous grants, the first of which has already underwritten the costs of travel and telephone for interviews and for planning and editing sessions. The second will support efforts to assure widespread distribution. Another staunch friend, the University of Notre Dame, home of CFM conventions for many years and now home to CFM's archives, is once again allying itself with CFM: Its press is the publisher of this book.

There has to be some disappointment that CFM didn't grow and grow forever, some disappointment that dissension and disaffection eroded the membership and the influence of CFM, but facts are facts and Jeff faces them. We think he is right about why CFM lost membership and influence, why CFM is very different today than it was in its first twenty-five years. We ourselves can only say that CFM declined for the right reasons. Though individual CFMers may not have been able to accept challenging programs on race relations, CFM insisted on addressing the issue. CFM could not ignore the question of world peace, even though international affairs seemed to be remote from one's own family and neighborhood. CFM could not refuse to be ecumenical, though its efforts to be ecumenical put it into conflict with the institutional church.

After you read this book, you may well have in mind the same question that many of us have had. Can something like the CFM of old ever exist again? Was it a passing shadow on the screen of history? Certainly the Church—whether Catholic, Episcopal, Lutheran, or UCC—is not the same as it was fifty years ago. Marriage is not the same. Society is profoundly different; but the problems that CFM addressed are still with us.

It is some forty-five years since we met in our living room with our first action group. The gender referencing of the closing prayer at the end of every CFM meeting may have a dated flavor; the essence of the prayer is dateless:

> Almightly and eternal God, may Thy grace enkindle in all men love for the many unfortunate people whom proverty and misery reduce to a condition of life unworthy of human beings.
>
> Arouse in the hearts of those who call Thee Father, a hunger and thirst for social justice and for fraternal charity in deeds and in truth. Grant, O Lord, peace in our days, peace to souls, peace to families, peace to our country, peace among nations.

The human condition has not changed. The need to remedy its ills has not abated. Nor has the need for people to change what is wrong about the world diminished.

CFM, with its method, with its people, with its committed couples, with its thoughtful and comprehensive program, played its role on the stage of history.

And some day, we are convinced, a transformed CFM will come again.

JOSEPH AND MADELYN BONSIGNORE

Acknowledgments

My introduction to the Christian Family Movement began many years ago. On a personal level my own parents were members of CFM. I am deeply indebted to my father, Edwin Burns, and my mother, Mary, for their extraordinary parenting. Typical of a CFM family, our home was always open to neighbors and guests from around the world. One summer we entertained students from Mexico, Japan, Nicaragua, India, and Australia. My parents taught me the true meaning of family.

One of the great joys of this project has been the opportunity to meet so many members, past and present, of the Christian Family Movement. Old or new, what distinguishes true CFMers is their hospitality. I especially want to thank Reggie Weissert, who opened her home to me during my two summers of research at the University of Notre Dame and made me feel like a part of her family. Her generosity far exceeded what was necessary. I feel blessed to know Reggie, whom I consider a good friend.

Special thanks to Patty Crowley. Without her drive and enthusiasm this project never would have been completed. She is one of the most gracious people I have ever met, and is a model of grace and dignity.

I am deeply indebted to Madelyn and Joe Bonsignore, who edited and reedited every page of this manuscript for me. Their incisive minds and broad vision have greatly improved this book. Still, the shortcomings are my own, not theirs. Any grace or elegance the text has is a result of Madelyn's efforts.

During the course of this project I have developed a tremendous respect, even awe for Reggie, Patty, Joe, and Madelyn, who have provided such a marvelous model of lived Christianity.

Thanks to Sharon Sumpter and the staff at the Archives of the University of Notre Dame for their tremendous assistance.

Thanks to Father Gerard Weber and ACTA, who provided two grants to support the research and writing of this study. Thanks also to the Cushwa Center for the Study of American Catholicism at the University of Notre Dame for providing a most appreciated travel grant.

Thanks to all the CFMers who shared their experiences with me. My apologies to the many CFMers who deserve to be in this history but whose names do not appear here. It is their efforts that provided a story worth telling at all.

Finally, thanks to my wife, Sabina, who patiently supported me during the long travail of writing this book. And special thanks to her first-graders, whom she constantly had praying for me to complete my "holy book." Without their prayers who knows when this book might have been finished!

ONE

Introduction

Mike and Muriel Dumaresq had just returned home from a pleasant evening out, playing bridge with friends. The time: shortly after World War II. The place: a suburb of Montreal. The Dumaresqs were typical of a new breed of young Catholic couples emerging in the United States and Canada. Unlike most of their forebears in the faith, they were professional, well-educated, and suburban. Mike was a veteran of the war, currently working selling insurance. The Dumaresqs and their four children had recently moved to the area. On this night, as they prepared for bed, Muriel asked Mike, "Do you remember one significant thing that was discussed all night?" Mike could not. They had had a good time, but it had all been rather trivial. The late evening reflection intensified within the Dumaresqs the feeling that had been recently gnawing at them: There had to be more to life than this. The following day, they received a call from a friend inviting them to join a new group that was forming—the Christian Family Movement. They went, they joined, and their world was changed forever.[1]

At the midpoint of the twentieth century something curious was beginning to happen on the periphery of Catholic parishes in the United States and Canada: Young couples like the Dumaresqs began meeting in one another's homes to discuss their lives and their communities in light of the gospels. The effect was exhilarating. Couples whose lives had been dominated by an ethos that extolled material success began to see that there had to be more.

Young professional couples were learning that the blessings of suburban, middle-class life were not enough. These young couples soon found that the newly created Christian Family Movement gave them a tool with which to transcend and transform not just their own family life but their culture. As an early CFM editorial in *ACT,* the movement's newsletter, declared, "You are in the Movement because you are dissatisfied with materialism and secularism. You want to live your life close to your God. You want Christ to have a place in your community and you want your community to be the kind of place where Christ may dwell in peace."[2] Over the course of two and a half decades, tens of thousands of couples discovered in CFM a means of integrating their faith with their daily lives, a means of satisfying their yearning for meaning in their lives.

Though the phrase "integrating their faith with their daily lives" seems simple enough, in actuality it was profoundly transforming. Once CFM was encountered, life could not go on as before. Veteran CFMers Bill and Laura Caldwell once observed, "Fourteen years ago when we read in *For Happier Families* [CFM's introductory booklet] that CFM would require a few pleasant hours a month, we didn't realize where it would lead us."[3] It led beyond the family to intense involvement with the neighborhood, the parish, the community, the world. CFM family after CFM family repeated the same story—what began as a mere diversion that might enhance one's own family became a transforming experience that drew the couple and their family into a lifetime commitment to make the world a better place for families to live.

CFM began simply enough, but even the first simple actions such as introducing oneself to one's neighbor required a bit of courage. Other acts took more than a little courage: A South Bend CFMer decided to eat lunch with an African American in his factory. Others delivered clothing and food to sections of town they ordinarily avoided. In an era in which conformity was sanctified and rejection dreaded, CFMers opened themselves up to rejection and failure.

CFM thrust its members into ever greater involvement in their communities. Many, perhaps most, CFMers began to serve in community groups, and their exposure led many of them, including many women, to run for public office. One veteran CFMer observed, while running for county supervisor, "It is because of involvement in CFM that I got my real start in community and civic affairs and ultimately into the political arena."[4] And a veteran CFM chaplain noted that CFM converted people "to a new way of life. . . . I should say that in Oklahoma (where I speak most experientially), whenever you go to NCCIJ [National Catholic Conference for Interracial Justice] meetings or political or social meetings, percentage-wise the greatest number of Catholics will be CFMers. The grass roots support for interracial justice will be given by CFMers. The laymen pushing the liturgy, Cana conferences, couples retreats, lay school boards, adult education classes, YCS groups, are CFMers to a significant degree."[5] Similar statements could be made for virtually every city in which CFM was established. CFM changed the life of the CFMer and CFMers changed the communities of which they were a part.

At the heart of CFM was a meeting held every two weeks. At these meetings six couples gathered together to examine their lives, their neighborhoods, their world, using the Observe-Judge-Act formula for Catholic Action developed by Canon Joseph Cardijn. The formula not only drew the couples into the world, it also had the effect of creating a tight bond between them. Since the typical CFMers were young married couples, just beginning their families, mostly professional and suburban, they were largely cut off from the extended families that so characterized Catholic urban parish life. CFM came to serve as an extended family. CFMer after CFMer can recount the close friendships that originated with CFM, life-long friendships which remained strong long after the couple had left the movement. One couple noted in a 1953 report that "our last accomplishment . . . is the feeling that we have developed towards the other couples in the group . . . a mixture of trust and affection, as if a close relationship existed between us."[6] A close bond *did* exist between CFM couples. Over the years they shared with one another all the joys and sorrows of family life—births, weddings, deaths, illnesses.

CFMers particularly acted as extended families in times of crisis. CFMers provided sustenance to families that had lost their sons in the Vietnam War. In countless cities, CFMers provided support and consolation for families who suffered the death of a young child, a spouse, or another loved one. When accident or illness struck, CFMers rallied behind their friends. CFMers were not just a family movement. CFMers were family.

CFM'S UNIQUE CONTRIBUTION

The Christian Family Movement changed the Church in the United States and Canada and improved the quality of life for countless families and communities throughout the world. Though its membership never exceeded 50,000 couples in the United States, the movement's impact far surpassed its numbers. Beyond sustaining member couples, CFM challenged families. It refused to allow couples to be content with their lives as they were and insisted that families take responsibility for their Church and world. As national Chaplain Reynold Hillenbrand put it, "We aren't in the world just to do comfortable things. We are here to do what our Lord directs us to do."[7] And what the Lord directed Christians to do, according to Pope Pius XI, was to "restore all things in Christ." Nothing less than that should satisfy the CFM family. CFM trained its members to be active participants in the world, "apostles," not merely wallflowers or cheerleaders, and their mission was the transformation of the social order.

CFMers displayed an élan that transmitted a special spirit to the rest of the Church in the United States and Canada. They perceived themselves to be an avant-garde with a mission to bring the American church into the modern world. Within the Church, CFMers were at the forefront of liturgical renewal. Long before the Second Vatican Council, CFMers regularly celebrated the dialogue Mass. Long before Vatican II, at the 1959 national convention, Mass was said with the altar turned around and the celebrant facing the people. The liturgical innovations gave CFMers the sense that they were at the forefront of the future Church that was in the process of being born.

CFMers were disturbers of the peace, not content with the status quo. Their actions often brought them into conflict with the powers that be. One pastor remembers, "CFM, as I encountered it in the early 1960s, had become pretty critical of everything the pastor was doing, so some of the pastors did not like them for that reason. They had enough trouble keeping morale up without them criticizing everything."[8] Having been trained to be apostles, CFMers were not content with the traditional role of the laity to "pay, pray, and obey." Their independence made them a challenge for many pastors and bishops.

CFM was, after all, born in an era that had just emerged from more than fifteen years of depression and war. The United States was embarking on one of its longest periods of sustained growth and prosperity. Militarily and economically, the United States was the supreme world power. American Catholics were equal beneficiaries of America's success. Postwar benefits, such as the GI Bill of Rights, sped up the slow immigrant evolution into the middle class, creating a substantial Catholic middle class for the first time in U.S. history. The church that had for more than a century so valiantly provided for wave after wave of Catholic immigrants was now ripe for change. It was a heady time for Catholics who sought to take their place in American society.

Not all was sweetness and light, however. Real problems confronted America. Despite its successes, many felt the United States had broken free of its spiritual moorings; despite material success a vacuum existed at the core of American life. An early editorial in the newsletter, *ACT,* lamented, "The moral confusion of the U.S. grows deeper each day." Nor were Catholics immune. Countless Catholics, the editorial continued, "[t]heir social senses . . . blunted . . . have reduced their religion to something that goes on in the pew for an hour each week on Sundays. Many have developed a schizophrenic quality to their faith, which permits them to pray one minute and to be anti-Semitic and anti-Negro the next." A recommitment to the Catholic way of life was necessary; it alone could lead the United States out of its current morass. "We know that Catholicism is a way of life, which, if pursued, can bring peace, and dignity and justice to all mankind. The answer to the weakness of Catholics is more Catholicism."[9] And the way to generate more Catholicism was through Catholic Action.

Of particular concern to thoughtful people, Catholic or not, was the plight of the family. Concern for the family was nothing new in American history. Throughout the nineteenth century, Americans fretted about the state of the family. By the early twentieth century the notion that the family was in "crisis" was firmly entrenched in the American mind. A plethora of organizations, studies, and agencies arose to assist the family. These concerns escalated after the dislocation of World War II. The skyrocketing divorce rate of 1946 was only one symptom. Yet more organizations and programs designed to solve the "family crisis" came on the scene. But of all the family organizations to emerge in the postwar world, the Christian Family Movement was by far the most dynamic and innovative, both within the Church and in the wider community. From many directions, CFM pushed the Catholic Church in the United States toward renewal and revival, presaging in many ways the reforms of the Second Vatican Council.

Start with the fact that CFM was a *lay* movement in a church that was overwhelmingly clerical. It was a *couples* movement in a church that traditionally separated organizations into male and female groups (e.g., sodalities). In contrast, the couple was the basic unit of CFM. Not only that, in CFM the man and woman were equal. In a church predominantly male-directed, CFM encouraged women to become leaders. CFM was primarily a *suburban, middle-class* movement in a church that had long been urban and working class.

But the more significant difference was this: Unlike many other family organizations, the focus of CFM was not solely on the well-being of one's own family. It was not enough to reflect on the husband-wife relationship or on that of parent and child (though some reflection was necessary). Nor was the focus solely on the CFM "family." It was not even limited to Catholic families. The focus was on nothing less than the total environment in which families live. CFM's reasoning went like this: Families are not isolated islands, they are located in the midst of society. To improve family life, the environment in which the family found itself must be made more nurturing, more Christian. The goal of CFM was to create a social order in which it was easier for families to be good, human, and healthy.

Without a reform of the social order the best efforts of the family would go for naught. As Hillenbrand observed, "God has planned that man . . . is going to do all things within the framework of institutions. . . . The welfare of the individual and society is dependent on the health and good order of the institutions which exist to serve them. That is the way we find man and find families—steeped and governed by a host of institutions. . . . For better or for worse, as institutions go, so go people. Always there is free will but seldom do we expect to find that free will pulling in a direction counter to the drift of the great mass of secular institutions. . . . Institutions are habits or accepted patterns of society that form people's attitudes and influence their behavior. We want to construct a social order that is human and Christian, where institutions help persons form Christian mentalities, giving them a more Christian, human destiny, and helping them gain their eternal destiny with God."[10] In sum, the family apostolate could not simply focus on the family; it had to focus on the social order and its institutions if family life was to be improved.

The theology that informed the movement contributed to this outlook. CFM was one of the earliest Catholic groups to vigorously popularize the concept of the Mystical Body of Christ and to push it to its logical conclusion. Given authority by Pius XII's 1943 encyclical on the Mystical Body, the concept introduced a new model of the Church. In Paul's metaphor, the Church is a living body, of which Christ is the head and the faithful are the members. This was heady stuff for the laity, who were now being told that they were the Church. If Christ's redemption of the world was to be completed, it was up to the laity. Hillenbrand captured this best in what became a standard and often repeated CFM slogan, "We are the hands of Christ in the most noble sense, where we work, Christ works. We are the feet of Christ in the most noble sense, wherever we go, Christ goes. We are the heart of Christ, wherever we are the love of Christ is found. We are the lips of Christ, whatever we articulate we are articulating for Christ."[11] In place of the meaninglessness of the modern world, CFM offered ultimate meaning: Each member was indispensable to the work of Christ; without the individual, the work of Christ could not proceed and the expansion of the Kingdom of God would be stymied.

Beyond giving the laity a new sense of responsibility, the concept of the Mystical Body suggested a new approach to relationships within the Church. Rather than reinforcing the traditional hierarchical structure of the Church, the Mystical Body instructed that each person was responsible to and for other members of the Body. These insights matched the CFM's social-action thrust. As the "Notes from the [CFM's]President's Desk" reminded, "We should be mindful that we are the Church."[12] Clearly anticipating Vatican II, CFM dispatched old notions that the clergy were the "Church teaching" and the laity the "Church taught." If the world was to be restored to Christ, it was up to the laity to do it. Family life, work life, civic life, cultural life—all of these areas, largely inaccessible to the priest, were the domain of lay people. As an editorial in *ACT* observed, "We must move into places forbidden . . . to bishops and priests. . . . We must grapple with the problems of the marketplace."[13]

Simultaneously, the concept of the Mystical Body undercut the individualism of modern American society, undercut selfish concerns about one's own success and one's own family. Nor could the individualistic concept of salvation that had crept in since the Reformation be accepted. CFM taught that salvation was not simply an individual matter between God and the person. Salvation was communal. The person's purpose in life—to know, love, and serve God—could be worked out only within the context of the human community. As one chaplain asserted, "The Catholic view is that we are saved only through incorporation into a family, into the family of God, the Mystical Body."[14] Citing French poet-philosopher Charles Peguy, the 1954–55 program booklet instructed, "We must save ourselves together. We must not arrive and find God one without the other. We must all come home together to our Father's house."[15] Salvation could only be achieved with the aid of the other. This communal notion of salvation rejected the Protestant notion of individual salvation that had increasingly taken hold in the Catholic Church since Trent. The person, then, was dependent not only upon God, but also upon his or her brother and sister. Together they were responsible for God's world and for the well-being, spiritual and material, of one another.

Besides making rich and fruitful use of the grand image of the Mystical Body, CFM also put to work on behalf of family renewal the innovative Cardijn technique. The Observe-Judge-Act technique characterized what came to be called "specialized Catholic Action" (to distinguish it from more general forms of Catholic Action in the United States). It was a technique that CFM shared with its U.S. counterparts, the Young Christian Workers (YCW) and Young Christian Students (YCS), which had been using it since the 1930s. CFM's special role lay in adapting it to the family apostolate.

The introduction of specialized Catholic Action to the United States in the 1930s and 1940s initiated a debate between the long-established Social Action Department of the National Catholic Welfare Conference (NCWC) and these upstart groups over what constituted *real* Catholic Action. The NCWC and its departments, including the Family Life Bureau, opted for a general organizational setup, placing special emphasis on "social education," which was to be effected through "study clubs." Rather than adopting an aggressive policy of action aimed at converting American culture, the U.S. Bishops chose instead to create a number of "sanctuaries"—updated versions of the old Catholic ghetto—which would inform Catholics about, and also safeguard them from, the radical and subversive influences of the predominantly non-Catholic culture. To the advocates of specialized Catholic Action, this method seemed woefully inadequate. Such a policy implied that Catholics should seek only to save themselves and forsake the responsibility of converting American society as a whole.

In sharp contrast, CFM, YCW, and YCS expressly called upon Catholic organizations to "penetrate" all aspects of modern life and to place a truly Christian imprint upon them. To effect such an impact, their brand of "specialized Catholic Action," not traditional organizations devoted to study, were needed. Social action, not social education, action cells, not study clubs, were essential to this approach. Protective sanctuaries were no longer enough; American Catholics had to find effective ways to engage the world and so create "a real renaissance, a renovation, a spiritual revolution."[16] The different strategies sponsored by the NCWC and CFM created a tension between the two groups that was never fully resolved, although in 1960, CFM did affiliate with the NCWC's Department of Lay Organizations.[17]

Of course, CFM was not alone in its analysis of the ills besetting modern American society. The standard Catholic bogeys of materialism and secularism were denounced and CFM joined the chorus in bemoaning the effects of the Reformation, the Industrial Revolution, and Planned Parenthood, as had untold Catholics before them. CFM was unique, however, in that it generally accepted the modern world. The CFM strategy was not to reject the world or abandon it, flee from it or scorn it, but mold it so as to bring it closer to the mind of Christ. CFM rejected the romantic image of the Middle Ages that prevailed among many Catholics.[18] As one CFM chaplain put it, "The Middle Ages were not all sweetness and light . . . we do not expect or desire a return to the Middle Ages." Nor did CFM urge a radical rejection of the workaday world in the manner of St. Francis. In the CFM world vision, the best days of Christianity lay ahead and were to be ushered in by a "well-trained, thoroughly Christian and fully responsible laity."[19] Lay people were to undertake their duty right where they were. As the initial issue of

ACT noted, Catholic Action "does not require a change in what a man does so much as a change in the way he does it and the motive which impels him. He is not asked to leave his home or his job."[20] CFMers were to improve the world of which they were a part. They were to be saints in the marketplace.

In fact, the eminent theologian Bernard Haring referred to CFM as "the great order of the Church in modern times." At different times in the Church's history, he noted, orders had arisen to respond to the special needs of that era. According to Haring, CFM was "essential to the needs" of the new era.[21] A lay couples' movement addressing the needs of the family was precisely what the modern world required.

MR. AND MRS. CFM

As had been the case with past religious orders, a charismatic leader arose to forge the new movement. In this case, the "leader" was a married couple—Patrick and Patricia Crowley, or Pat and Patty, as they were known in the movement. Born in Chicago in 1911, Pat graduated from the University of Notre Dame in 1933, and received his law degree from Loyola of Chicago in 1937. He worked as a lawyer the rest of his life, taking care of the his family's businesses. Patty was born in 1913 in Chicago into the well-to-do Caron family. In 1936, she graduated from Trinity College in Washington, D.C., where she had been exposed to the progressive Catholic social thinker Monsignor John Ryan. On October 16, 1937, Pat and Patty were married in Chicago. Together they would raise five children of their own, act as guardian to close to a dozen foster children, and host more than forty foreign students in their home. Together they formed one of the most significant lay couples, if not the most significant, in the history of the U.S. Catholic Church. Former University of Notre Dame president, Father Theodore Hesburgh, C.S.C., is fond of saying that, if they ever canonize a married couple, it should be the Crowleys.

Together they forged a movement that was one of the most dynamic in the U.S. church during the 1950s and 1960s. Though there is some debate as to who should be designated founder of CFM (see chapter 2), there is no doubt that the driving force behind the success and spread of CFM was the Crowleys. Rightly, they have been called Mr. and Mrs. CFM. Father Louis Putz, of whom more will be said later, observed in 1961, "The Crowleys exemplify CFM and its ideals. It seems to me that if you did not have any literature at hand, but could observe them as they extended themselves to their personal family which includes many more than their own children, the way they demonstrate hospitality, the way they are bighearted to embrace all the nationalities and races of the world, you would have an idea of the Christian Family Movement."[22]

In addition to epitomizing the CFM ideal, the Crowleys were significant in that they were the U.S. Catholic Church's first leadership *couple;* that is, they led CFM as a couple, not as individuals. Many people have commented on how well Pat and Patty complemented each another. Patty was noted as "the energizer, the organizer, the motor. More efficient, more intense . . . far shrewder and more profound."[23] Pat was more enthusiastic, more affable, more political and with a wonderful sense of humor that defused many tense situations. Pat also provided the optimism. As he once observed, "You can spend your life fighting those who want to tear down or you can spend your life building up. I believe it is better to build."[24] Together they formed a dynamic, brilliant couple who guided and shaped CFM for more than two decades.

CFM, then, was a unique contribution to the Church in the United States. It changed that Church and improved the quality of life for countless families and communities throughout the world, far out of proportion to its numbers. The growth, trauma, and travails that beset the Church in the United States during this era is reflected in the history of the Christian Family Movement.

TWO

The Origins of the
Christian Family Movement
1943–1950

The Christian Family Movement had its roots in the Jocist movement begun by Canon Joseph Cardijn of Belgium in the 1910s. As a young man Cardijn watched his father die at the premature age of 43. Cardijn later recalled, "I vowed at his deathbed to consecrate myself to the salvation of working youth and the working class. The vow became the guiding motive of my life."[1] In 1913, Cardijn began organizing workers between the ages of fourteen and twenty-five into a junior trade union. Gradually this group evolved into the apostolic movement that came to be known as "Jeunesse Ouvriere Chrétienne" (translated by its American counterpart as "Young Christian Workers" or YCW).

Cardijn's genius lay in developing leaders by forming and motivating small groups. He organized the workers into small groups or "cells" (later called sections in the U.S.) of ten to twelve people. The cells were made up of people of the same occupation, gender, and age. Ministry was to be carried out on a like-to-like basis: worker to worker, student to student, farmer to farmer, and so forth. Using these cells, Cardijn developed his trademark "Observe-Judge-Act" formula for Catholic Action. Notably missing from the formula were the formal, top-down trappings of most meetings: presidents and chairs, motions, minutes, and *Robert's Rules of Order.* Instead, the members of the cell were to *observe* their environment carefully, assembling facts about the world around them. They were then to put on "the mind of Christ" and to *judge* whether what they had observed was in keeping with the teachings of Jesus. Judgments

13

were to be grounded in concrete reality. Finally, cell members were to *act* to decrease the distance between what they observed and what Jesus intended.

The Jocist method, as it came to be called, expanded slowly. It quickly drew criticism from many who feared that the organization of young workers would be too radical, that such an organization would foment revolution. In 1924, the cardinal archbishop of Brussels, reacting to the criticisms, condemned the movement. Undeterred, Cardijn appealed the archbishop's decision directly to Pope Pius XI, the pope who came to be known as the Catholic Action pope. Pius overturned the condemnation and wholeheartedly embraced Cardijn and his movement. "Here at last is someone who came to talk to me of saving the masses."[2] And concluded, "We shall make the movement our own." The following year, 1925, the movement held its first national congress in Belgium, and from that point it spread quickly. By 1937, membership included more than 85,000 workers from more than twenty countries.

YCS COMES TO THE UNITED STATES

The movement was brought to the United States in 1938 by Father Donald Kanaly, a priest from Ponca City, Oklahoma, who encountered Cardijn while studying at the Louvain in Belgium. He quickly became convinced that Cardijn's method was precisely the tool needed to bring the American working class back to Christ. Upon his return to the United States, he spoke to a gathering of priests at the Catholic School of Social Action in Chicago, providing the first widespread exposure to Cardijn's program. Preaching the Jocist gospel of action, Kanaly stressed that "only actions will make apostles," and that the movement was necessary "to save America from communism."[3] Kanaly continued to present the Jocist vision: an authentic apostolic movement had to grow from the bottom up, from the grass roots. Any system imposed from the top was destined to failure.

Shortly after Kanaly's presentation, Australian activist and writer Paul McGuire was brought to the United States by the Knights of Columbus to give a series of talks on Catholic Action. McGuire had previously written a Catholic Action handbook with John Fitzsimons, national YCW chaplain in England, entitled *Restoring All Things*. McGuire's talks were met with enthusiasm everywhere he went. Through Kanaly's and McGuire's efforts, Cardijn's movement became known in the United States.

One of those who took their message very much to heart was Chicago priest Reynold Hillenbrand. It was Hillenbrand who became the prime mover behind specialized Catholic Action in the United States. Hillenbrand or "Hilly," as he was affectionately called, was born in Chicago in 1904 and grew up in the German parish of St. Michael's. Hillenbrand studied at the archdiocese of Chicago's Quigley Preparatory Seminary, and later at St. Mary of the Lake, the archdiocesan seminary, before being ordained a priest in 1929. Shortly thereafter, Hillenbrand spent a year in Rome studying at the Gregorian University. While there, he was exposed to the latest thinking in the liturgical movement and in Catholic Action. He was to devote the rest of his life to the advancement of both causes in the United States.

Upon Hillenbrand's return to the United States in 1932, he was assigned to teach at Quigley. In 1936, in a bold move, Cardinal Mundelein appointed Hillenbrand rector of St. Mary of the Lake Seminary. In introducing Hillenbrand, Mundelein allegedly said, "I know the seminary can be a dull place, so I have brought you a man with imagination."[4] Over the next eight years, a whole cadre of dynamic young priests emerged from the seminary bearing the designation "Hilly's boys." As such, they were deeply committed to liturgical renewal, to the ecclesiology of the Mystical Body of Christ, and to Catholic Action. In 1944, Hillenbrand was removed from the seminary for becoming too involved in the local labor struggles (he was stridently prounion) and was named pastor of Sacred Heart parish in suburban Hubbard Woods. As one early CFMer remembered, "He was sent to a rich man's parish to cool off."[5] Hillenbrand was not the type to cool off, however. Sacred Heart became a showcase for the latest liturgical developments, and Hillenbrand threw himself ever more vigorously into developing the lay apostolate.

Hillenbrand became the first national chaplain of the Christian Family Movement in 1949, but even before he received this designation he was the driving intellectual force behind the movement. Pat Crowley simply referred to him as "our idea guy." For CFM's first decade and a half Hillenbrand placed his distinct stamp on the movement. He brought to the movement passion, drive, and commitment, and he repeatedly pushed, scolded, cajoled, and counseled the leadership of CFM to bring forth a new order . He made it clear that it was not his own personal program he was advocating: it was the papal plan for the reconstruction of the social order. Hillenbrand was intensely loyal to the authority of the pope and his teaching. Restoring all things in Christ meant, for him, bringing the world into accord with papal teaching. As early CFM chaplain Dennis Geaney, o.s.a., observed, "The genius of the rector seemed to be his abiding conviction that when the pope speaks, it is the voice of Christ we hear."[6]

At the heart of the papal program, according to Hillenbrand, was the concept of the Mystical Body of Christ as articulated by Pope Pius XII in his 1943 encyclical *Mystici Corporis Christi*. Equally as important were the famous social encyclicals *Rerum Novarum,* by Leo XIII, and *Quadragesimo Anno,* by Pius XI. All papal teaching stressed the need to undo "the corrosive effects of liberal individualism."[7] As such there was a need to return a "corporate" sense to the liturgy, which would then seep into the secular social order. Hillenbrand wrote that the purpose of the Mass "is to restore the corporate sense and corporate action . . . to learn our oneness at the altar and to bring that oneness to the other relations of life. This oneness must be brought to our homes . . . to our political life . . . to our economic life . . . into working life . . . to our international life."[8] For the Hillenbrand agenda, liturgical renewal, especially the promotion of the active participation of the laity in the liturgy, was of paramount importance.

Hillenbrand found a kindred spirit in Kanaly, whose vision of the church clearly meshed with his. Before the Second National Catholic Social Action Congress, held in Cleveland in 1939, Kanaly and Hillenbrand met for dinner to discuss the lay apostolate. The meeting proved to be historic. While discussing the areas upon which lay leadership should focus, Kanaly took a holy card out of his breviary and wrote on the back of the card the words "domestic," "economic," "political," and "international."[9] (Hillenbrand later added "leisure," "education," and "parish" as appropriate areas of lay concern, though the latter two were shared with the clergy. These areas became the basis for CFM's annual inquiry programs). As historian Dennis Robb summarized, "They agreed, then, that specialized movements should treat every problem of social life."[10]

The third major clerical figure to contribute to specialized Catholic action in the United States was a young Holy Cross priest from Bavaria named Louis Putz, who came to the United States in 1923 to study for the priesthood at the University of Notre Dame. After graduating in 1932, he returned to France to the seminary of Le Mans, where he studied with theological giants Jean Daniélou, Yves Congar, and Henri de Lubac, who helped to lay the groundwork for the Second Vatican Council. Putz was ordained to the priesthood in 1936, having the year before become chaplain to a Jocist cell in the "red zone" of Paris, where he learned the Jocist technique. In 1939, with the outbreak of World War II, Putz was forced to flee to the United States. He returned to Notre Dame, where he began teaching in the theology department. In 1940, approached by four graduate students, Putz began Notre Dame's first Jocist cell, originally called Catholic Action Apostles, later known as the Young Christian Students (YCS).

The same year, Putz was introduced to Hillenbrand by Chicago priest and Catholic Action enthusiast Father Charles J. Marhoefer. Hillenbrand, impressed by Putz's practical knowledge of and experience with the Cardijn method, invited him to speak to the deacon class at the seminary. In addition, Putz was invited to speak at various gatherings of priests. By 1941, Putz and Hillenbrand were collaborating to forge a national specialized Catholic Action program (YCW/YCS). They agreed that what was needed was a uniform program and a national spirit of unity. Putz began working on a five-year plan of social inquiries; Hillenbrand began organizing a national study week. Both men supported the publication of material that would connect cells across the country.[11]

By 1943, the efforts of Kanaly, Hillenbrand, and Putz had firmly planted Cardijn's method of Catholic Action in American soil. It was soon to blossom into its most successful manifestation—the Christian Family Movement.

FOUNDING THE CHRISTIAN FAMILY MOVEMENT

The question of who founded the Christian Family Movement remains controverted and difficult to ascertain. Quite remarkably, the movement sprang to life simultaneously in at least three different cities: Chicago, South Bend, and New York. Since Chicago emerged as the headquarters of the movement, CFM's early history is often attached only to that archdiocese, but legitimate claims can also be made for South Bend and New York, and even for Paris, France. Regardless of where the idea of a couples' movement using the Cardijn method originated, Chicago became the driving and unifying center of the movement, and the Crowleys became the movement's chief evangelists. And it was certainly the case that Chicago and the Crowleys were responsible for the rapid expansion of the movement to other locales.

The mythical beginning of Chicago CFM took place in the Loop law offices of Patrick Crowley's father. At the instigation of Paul Hazard (a former seminarian) and Frank Crowe, six young businessmen began meeting weekly in 1943 searching for a way to restore all things in Christ. As the initial issue of *ACT* observed,

"Society appeared to them to be on the road to its doom."[12] They all agreed something needed to be done, but what form should it take? With the help of their chaplain, Father Marhoefer, unofficially appointed by Hillenbrand, the group came to adopt the Cardijn Observe-Judge-Act method of Catholic Action. But the group faced a basic problem in adopting the Cardijn method—if "like" was to minister to "like," how could they fit in? "Vocational specialization," thought to be essential to real Jocism, was absent. Their group consisted of two lawyers, an insurance salesman, a statistician, an investment counselor, and a newspaperman. The second cell that formed in Chicago was equally diverse, made up of a salesman, a plumbing inspector, a teacher, a punch press operator, and a few business executives.[13] The initial cell came to refer to itself as the businessmen's cell, but the second group did not even have that generic designation to bind them together. The groups began to be referred to as Adult Catholic Action.

These early groups expended considerable energy investigating topics for social inquiries and checking out other formats and bases for organization. Several from the businessmen's cell explored the Third Orders of St. Francis and St. Dominic. Several became Oblates of St. Benedict, attached to St. John's College in Collegeville, Minnesota. Newspaperman Clem Lane, an early recruit, advised the group "not to waste their time" with these explorations and pieties.[14] Accepting his and Marhoefer's advice, the group abandoned its experimentation and its members committed themselves to the Cardijn method.

But the problem arising from diversity remained. Happily, another early recruit, Joe Joyce, pointed out the one experience they shared: The men were all young fathers. (Many had been spared the rigors of World War II to take care of their family responsibilities.) Joyce suggested that family life was and should be the "area of common experience and concern."[15] Pat Crowley later recalled, with his usual jocularity, "We decided . . . that we'd straighten out marriage and then move on to something serious."[16] The group's first inquiry looked into the problem of divorce, and the resulting action was to create a list of family experts which they provided to the Chancery Office to assist couples in trouble. The men then forged ahead to other family issues. Patty Crowley later reflected somewhat sarcastically, "It was absolutely ridiculous. These men were never at home and they were talking about marriage."[17]

Shortly thereafter, the men happened onto an action that intensified their commitment to the family as their focus. Jesuit John P. Delaney of *America*, had been pioneering days of recollection—"family renewal days"—for married couples, an idea he had picked up while in France. (Fellow Jesuit Edward Dowling of St. Louis later changed the name to "Cana Conferences," and the Cana Conference movement was born.) In 1944, Mr. and Mrs. Edward Kerwin of Oak Park, Illinois, invited Delaney to conduct a family renewal day in Chicago, which he did. (Mrs. Kerwin was an officer in the Archdiocesan Council of Catholic Women). Several weeks later another conference was held at Sacred Heart Convent in Lake Forest, followed by another at Barat College in Lake Forest. Members of the businessmen's cell attended this third family renewal day.

The men were deeply affected by the conference and enthusiastically endorsed the movement. From that day on, the men adopted the promotion and sponsoring of what came to be called Cana Conferences as their primary action "and gave it its first citywide impetus."[18] As the newsletter for the Cana Conference in Chicago later recorded it, "Out of this grew the organization of the Cana Conference of Chicago."[19] By 1945, a distinct organization had emerged, with members of the men's cells, Edgar Beaumont, Fred Becklenberg, and John Grimes, directing Cana under the watchful eye of Father James Voss, the unofficial chaplain of the Cana Conference.

As Cana prospered, so did the expansion of the adult men's cells. By 1946, six had been formed. In 1944, several of the wives of members gathered to form a married women's cell. One of the earliest was formed by Patty Crowley in suburban Wilmette. Father Gerard Weber served as the group's first chaplain. The married women's group represented something of a breakthrough. According to Crowley biographer John Kotre, Catholic women were "talking to each other for the first time in their lives about something serious."[20] As many of the women were college graduates, it is unlikely that this was the first time they had discussed serious issues, but it may well have been the first time they discussed serious issues in a Catholic group. Like the men, the women employed the Cardijn technique.

One of the earliest actions of the women's cell was generated by the forthcoming marriage of Patty's sister in 1946. At the time, Catholic marriage preparation was a rather inexact art, if it existed at all. Generally it devolved upon the pastor to give the young couple a cursory introduction to marriage. Patty thought it would be wonderful if the young couple could experience the benefits married couples were receiving from the Cana Conference. So she and the women's group invited Father Dowling to give a day of recollection for engaged couples. Patty remembers the difficulty of gathering enough couples to attend. "Another woman and I went around to about ten parishes, trying to get the names of newly married or engaged couples so we could invite them to the first Pre-Cana. Most of the pastors threw us out of the rectory."[21] When enough couples finally committed, the first Pre-Cana Conference, as they came to be called, was held at Mallinckrodt High School in Wilmette on April 16, 1946.[22] The married women's cell continued to support and promote Pre-Cana and Cana as their major actions. By the end of 1946, four married women's cells were operating in Chicago.

The year 1946 was a pivotal one in the development of the Christian Family Movement in Chicago. Soldiers were returning from World War II to marriages often hastily entered into and strained by years of separation. The ensuing rise in divorce was alarming. The 1946 divorce rate was the highest of any year during the period 1940 to 1960. The need for a family movement seemed paramount. By 1946, the married men's cells had developed to the point that they established an archdiocesan federation (a term that was adopted for all diocese-wide CFM structures) for adult Catholic Action, with Clem Lane, city editor of the *Chicago Daily News*, elected as chairman. The group began publishing *ACT: A Quarterly of Adult Catholic Action,* a newsletter designed to promote the movement and to serve as a national clearinghouse for adult Catholic Action cells, which were springing up throughout America. In the same year, Cardinal Samuel Stritch gave official recognition to the movements by appointing two full-time chaplains to Chicago Catholic Action. Father William Quinn was appointed chaplain for the Catholic Action movements in Chicago—YCS, YCW, and Adult Catholic Action. Father John J. Egan was appointed chaplain of the Cana Conference. The two major figures in the early development of these movements, Fathers Voss and Marhoefer were passed over in favor of the younger men, a decision which deeply wounded the two priests.

By 1946, adult Catholic Action in Chicago was firmly established, and was firmly committed to its focus on the family.

FORMING A COUPLES MOVEMENT

As of 1946, most adult cells were still separated by gender. Experiments in which married women's cells and married men's cells had met together had been tried, but they remained the exception rather than the rule. In 1944, Burnie Bauer and his wife, Helene, had attempted a married group in La Porte, Indiana, but it did not last. In December 1946, Clem Lane and the Evanston-Wilmette cell conducted a series of social inquiries on the family and family life, in which the members of the men's cells invited their wives to the meetings.[23] They met for four consecutive weeks, before returning to their separate cells. Mixed groups were still not thought to be appropriate for the Cardijn method. When the subject of mixed groups was presented to Hillenbrand, he responded, "That is not the Jocist way."[24] Nonetheless, the notion of a couples' movement was gaining momentum. The concept of a family movement that kept husband and wife separate was not destined to last.

By 1948, the trend toward combining the men's and women's

cells had become inexorable. In June 1948 the Chicago federation began planning a set of common inquiries for the men's and women's groups. Lorraine Dix chaired a program committee that developed a set of inquiries on the parent-child relationship. In addition, the federation scheduled a family picnic to be attended by both groups. In September, a joint meeting of the men's and women's federations was held to discuss the coming year's program.[25] Spouses, whether they were members of a cell or not, were invited to the meeting. By the time of the meeting, several groups were operating as couples' cells.

By January 1949, Pat Crowley could write, "Gradually our 'Sections' [cells] are being made up of husbands and wives, and our present aim is to set ourselves up as spokesmen for Christian families in the United States."[26] By September 1949, Patty Crowley, who had never been an enthusiast for separate groups, wrote a letter to Hillenbrand—perhaps to allay his fears—describing the benefits of couples meeting together. Patty wrote, "Our experience is that couples groups are wonderful. . . . Pat and I have thought alike for a long time, but each meeting brings us closer together. I hear other couples say the same thing all the time."[27] According to several accounts of early members, the evolution toward a couples' movement was a natural and gradual one.[28]

Other CFM veterans claim a different beginning for the couples' movement. Both Father Louis Putz and Burnie Bauer claim to have initiated the concept of couples meeting together. According to Putz, the idea of a couples' movement originated in France. In 1946, an international meeting of student unions was to be held in Prague, Czechoslovakia. Renowned Jesuit John Courtney Murray believed it was important that the United States participate, and since Putz's YCS group at Notre Dame was one of the most viable student groups in the United States, he asked Putz to attend. While in Europe, Putz visited his old Jocist groups in Paris. Following World War II, many of those in his old cells had married, but wanting to continue in the Cardijn movement, they began meeting as couples. Out of this emerged the Mouvement Populaire de Famille.[29]

When Putz returned to the United States, he introduced the couples concept to his South Bend groups, and to Pat Crowley's businessmen's cell in Chicago, with which he had been meeting on a monthly basis. According to Putz, "I suggested that the two groups [men and women's cells] merge and meet in one another's homes. And lo and behold the Christian Family Movement was born."[30]

Interestingly, the Mouvement Populaire de Famille was discussed at the Fifth Annual Catholic Action Study Week for Priests, held at Notre Dame, August 4–8, 1947. By that time a couples group was already meeting in South Bend under the leadership of Burnie Bauer and his wife Helene, with Putz as chaplain. However, at that time no consensus had yet emerged on this point. At the Notre Dame meeting it was suggested that it was desirable for husbands and wives to meet together but not necessary.[31]

Providing yet another view of the origins of CFM is Burnett C. Bauer, one of the original members of Putz's Catholic Action Apostles at the University of Notre Dame. (The Apostles' major achievement was to integrate Notre Dame racially.) After graduating from Notre Dame, Bauer married a St. Mary's College (Indiana) professor, Helene Cryan, in 1941, and they settled down in La Porte, Indiana. Burnie attempted to establish YCS among local high school students and a YCW among local workers. His efforts kept him away from home for long periods of time. Growing increasingly annoyed by his disappearing act, Helene asked him to explain what he was doing. He explained that Catholic Action was a way "to solve the problems of contemporary society in a Christian way," to which Helene replied, "Well, we have problems of our own right within our family, you know, and if that technique is as effective as you say it is, why not apply it to our own family?"[32] Together they attempted to start a couples group, but their effort was short-lived. They resurrected the idea in 1947, and successfully began the first couples group at Little Flower Parish (though the initial group was interparish) in South Bend. On March 17, the Bauers hosted Fred and Dorothy Govern and Fred and Grace Honold, and the CFM in South Bend was born. The couples started meeting in one another's homes. Soon Brooks and Florence Smeeton and Ralph and Reggie Weissert joined the group. After several meetings, Bauer invited Putz to become chaplain, and Putz developed a series of social inquiries for the group. At this point, the Weisserts broke off and started a new group. By 1949, six groups were operating and the South Bend–Mishawaka Federation was established.

On this basis, Bauer insists that he should be designated at least cofounder of the movement. Again, according to Bauer, it was he who introduced the couples concept to Pat and Patty Crowley at the annual Cana Conference meeting held in Chicago in 1948. Both the Crowleys and Bauer were on the program, and in informal discussions the Crowleys became excited about the concept of couples meeting together.[33] It is unlikely, however, that this was the first time the Crowleys had encountered the notion of couples meeting together, considering the experiment of Clem Lane's group in Chicago and the discussions of the MPF from France at Notre Dame in 1947. Still, it does appear that the South Bend group was the first cell to meet regularly as a couples group. If so, Chicago quickly followed suit. Bauer wrote the Crowleys shortly after their meeting in Chicago, "As yet there seems to be only your group and ours that are operating by couples according to the inquiry technique (which is real Catholic Action as you know)."[34]

While it is difficult to sort out all the details as to who exactly started CFM as a couples movement, several things are clear. First, the time was ripe for a couples movement that focused on the family. In many cases YCW and YCS members who had grown older and had married were looking to continue their involvement with specialized Catholic Action. CFM seemed a natural progression for them. Twenty-four percent of YCW members later became involved in CFM.[35] This is precisely what happened in New York City.[36] A group of veterans who had returned from World War II began a YCW cell in 1946. The following year, after a number had married, they formed a married men's cell. Their inquiries focused on (1) work, and (2) the home and family environment. Under the leadership of Father Declan Bailey, O.F.M., the group moved toward the

CFM model, or what he called "YCW for married people."[37] As such, New York can also claim a share in founding CFM. In any case, the ground was fertile and the movement spread quickly. Second, while it is impossible to pinpoint one "founder," it is clear that the credit for the development and achievement of CFM falls on many shoulders, especially those of Reynold Hillenbrand, Louis Putz, the Crowleys, and Burnie Bauer. They set the movement on its path and provided it with a firm foundation.

SPREADING THE MOVEMENT

The movement spread rapidly in the years 1946 to 1949, largely through the efforts of the Chicago and South Bend groups, particularly through the personal contacts made by the Crowleys. In 1946, an adult Catholic Action group was begun in Fond du Lac, Wisconsin, by former Chicago businessmen's cell member George St. Peter, with the assistance of Father Rudy Bierberg, C.P.P.S. Similarly, groups were begun in Minneapolis and St. Paul by former Winnetka cell member Michael Putnam in 1947. By the end of 1948, the Twin Cities had twelve adult cells operating. Both Putnam and St. Peter kept in close contact with the Crowleys. By 1949, St. Paul had decided to "follow the Chicago example and recognize that the field of adult cells had best be the immediate environment of the home."[38]

In 1947 another adult group was begun in Encino, California, a suburb of Los Angeles, by former Chicago cell member Mrs. Robert (Kate) McMahon. Following the typical early pattern, separate men's and women's groups were formed and their initial inquiries were on marriage and the family. Soon they were sponsoring Cana Conferences. In the summer of 1947, the group was visited by Father Putz, who suggested that they merge the groups to form couples groups. They took his advice and CFM was born in Los Angeles.[39]

From 1944 to 1948 adult Catholic Action groups of married

men and married women were also developing with no direct link to Chicago. We have already mentioned New York. Burnie Bauer introduced adult Catholic Action to Milwaukee, while Woonsocket, Rhode Island, seems to have been influenced by specialized Catholic Action in Canada. Woonsocket was one of the more interesting efforts. Groups were begun in 1944 with members primarily among those of French Canadian heritage. By 1949 eight active cells were operating and another nineteen were "in formation."[40] Under the leadership of Armand Beausoliel and Arthur Fortin these groups were aggressively working-class and prolabor. They decried the "long history of exploitation from the textile industry"[41] in the region, and their inquiries and actions were directed at distinctly working-class family problems. The cells developed and implemented plans for cooperative housing, assistance to families whose mothers had fallen ill, and a camp to make family vacations affordable. The Woonsocket group was driven by the usual Catholic fears of communism and a disgust for the practice of contraception, both of which, they believed, were in large part a result of an unjust economic order. As of 1949, Woonsocket maintained separate men's and women's groups and was quite resistant to the notion of bringing husbands and wives together.

A significant movement had developed in Cleveland as well, with eight married cells in operation by 1948. The groups "followed Chicago" in terms of focusing on the family, but Cleveland did not exclusively use the Cardijn method. Instead, greater emphasis was placed on education; thus the groups operated more as study clubs than action groups. As such, *ACT* referred to the Cleveland groups as a "pre-Catholic Action" organization.[42]

By February 1949 adult Catholic Action was operating in twenty cities in the United States—New York, Cleveland, Minneapolis, St. Paul, Cincinnati, South Bend, Milwaukee, Fond du Lac, Wilmington, Del., Providence, Woonsocket, Little Rock, Toledo, Indianapolis, Encino, San Carlos, Calif., Detroit, Nutley, N.J., Nashville, and, of course, Chicago. Holding the movement together were the extraordinary personal efforts of the Crowleys. As hundreds of letters began to pour into Chicago concerning adult Catholic Action, it was the Crowleys and a devoted team of workers who saw that this correspondence was answered. Equally important was the Crowleys' personal touch. They made frequent use of dinners at their home to bring together leaders from around the country to entice them to become involved in the movement. As the 1947 *ACT* opined, "All roads lead to the Crowleys."[43] In 1948, no less a personage than Canon Joseph Cardijn himself dined at the Crowleys' home, extending his personal blessing to their efforts. The Crowleys also traveled extensively promoting the movement. Pat used his work with the family businesses, the Caron and O'Brien companies, as an excuse for travel, but his real concern was the expansion of the movement. In 1947, when Father Bailey contacted the Crowleys about what he called adult YCW, the Crowleys traveled to New York to meet personally with Bailey. This pattern, established in the late 1940s, intensified during the 1950s with more dinners, more correspondence, and greater travel. In 1951, Patty Crowley could write, "We have been traveling the country from stem to stern."[44] More than any other element, the personal contact and efforts of the Crowleys assured the expansion of the movement.

FORMING A NATIONAL ORGANIZATION

By 1949, the blossoming of married men's and women's groups across the United States led to growing concerns about how to unite the disparate groups. In addition to the Crowleys' networking, the 1947 national convention of the Family Life Bureau of the National Catholic Welfare Conference in Chicago in March, at which the married men's and women's groups had been asked to work, gave many of the group leaders a chance to meet one another. The following summer many of the couples met again at the second annual Cana study week in 1948. Out of these contacts came a meeting in Chicago in January 1949 attended by couples from Chicago, Wilmette, Winnetka, Cleveland, South Bend,

Milwaukee, and Fond du Lac.[45] The meeting produced a call for a summit to be held at Childerly Retreat Center, just outside Chicago, in June 1949, to promote "greater unity" and "more effective organization" in the effort to restore the family in Christ.[46] On June 17, fifty lay delegates and twelve priests from eleven cities met to create the first national structure for what was to become the Christian Family Movement. Those who gathered were quite young—the average age was less than thirty-five.

After three days of lively discussion and, at times, disputes, the first national meeting of Catholic Family Action came to a close. One participant later recalled, "We all talked at once . . . which has been characteristic of CFM ever since."[47] This was to be no mere paper organization. Two operating mechanisms were set in place, both of which were to prove durable and effective. The convention created a national Coordinating Committee, which included a representative from each federation, and an Executive Committee of five. The group also determined that *ACT* was to be the official publication of the movement, and Chicago would serve as the movement's headquarters. These significant decisions were made on a trial basis for one year. They were to be reevaluated the following year at the second annual national meeting. Couples movement or not, both founding committees were made up solely of men. The Coordinating Committee consisted of Michael Putnam (Tennessee), Pat Crowley (Chicago), York McDonnell (Cincinnati), James J. Roche, Jr. (New York), George St. Peter (Fond du Lac), Eugene Lawler (Milwaukee), Michael Assalone (Tennessee), Armand Beausoleil (Providence), Burnett C. Bauer (South Bend), Earl J. Smith (St. Paul), and Carl Marterseck (Cleveland). The Executive Committee consisted of Crowley, Bauer, Lawler, Beausoleil, and Marterseck with Crowley chosen as the executive secretary.[48]

Beyond creating the incipient organizational structure, the convention sounded a number of themes that were to become basic to the movement. South Bend pioneer Grace Honold, who spoke first, stressed the centrality of the social inquiry, defining it as "a scientific method which becomes a way of life."[49] Armand Beausoleil articulated what was to become an ongoing struggle of purpose within CFM. He argued that CFM was not a "family" movement per se, nor was it a movement designed solely to assist the individual's spiritual life. The focus of the movement had to be the environment, or "milieu," in which the family was located. The environment had to be Christianized. By Christianizing the environment, members—and others—would find it easier—"normal"—to act as Christians, and thereby "we will Christianize individuals."[50] Patrick Crowley brought the three days of discussion to a conclusion with this statement of goals: The movement was, "to serve, educate, and represent the families of the community, in which we live, and of the larger community, the republic."[51] In other words, Catholic Family Action cells would act as pressure groups on behalf of families. Crowley's statement was a close adaptation of the stated aims of YCW, as applied to the family. Thus, as couples departed from the first national meeting, they had resolved several issues: Cardijn's social inquiry method would be the formal basis of the movement, and the focus of action was to be the environment in which the family was located, not just internal family concerns.

Several points of tensions remained. First, what would the movement be called? Chicago called itself Catholic Family Action; South Bend and Woonsocket went by the Christian Family Movement, and others called it Christian Family Action. The following year, all groups agreed to the name Christian Family Movement. The adoption of "Christian" rather than "Catholic" indicated the movement's desire to have a broader appeal and suggested its early commitment to ecumenism.

As noted before, the Cardijn social inquiry technique was adopted as the method of the movement: Observe, Judge, Act. However, other points of friction turned out to be much harder to resolve. There was some dispute as to the nature of the actions the groups should pursue. Several groups, most notably South Bend, pushed for continuing actions; that is, one topic and action should be focused on over an extended period so that CFM could have a major impact on the environment affecting family life. In opposition to this was the Chicago model articulated by Hillenbrand and the Crowleys. They argued that the movement was essentially a movement to form apostles, not necessarily to bring about major changes in its own name. According to this view, actions should remain small because the action was not as important as its effect on the actor. Simply put, "formation comes through action."[52] The Chicago model ultimately triumphed as the program booklet developed by the Chicago group, *For Happier Families: How to Start a Catholic Family Action Section,* was selected as the movement's introductory program (see below). Burnie Bauer's *Blueprint for Christian Family Living,* based on the South Bend model, was considered but not adopted.

Of greater concern was the gap in worldview between the more well-to-do, professional suburban Catholics as represented by the Chicago group, and those cities with greater working-class concerns, such as Cleveland and Woonsocket. The latter groups pushed for working-class actions such as cooperatives and housing. According to John Kotre, the working class was overruled by the "businessmen and professionals, who were 'footing the bill.'"[53] Feeling neglected, these CFMers eventually abandoned the movement. Difficulty in recruiting working-class members would remain a constant problem throughout the movement's history. At one point Hillenbrand lamented, "The movement was lodged in the middle class and would not take root among workers and non-whites."[54] The movement would make repeated attempts to recruit the working class and minority groups, but despite achieving some notable exceptions, it was never very successful in this regard.

EARLY INQUIRIES

Of immediate concern to the movement was the need to provide uniform inquiries. Since the earliest days of the movement, each group had developed its own inquiries, as the meeting outlines were called. Many sections mimeographed their inquiries and circulated them to other groups.[55] Most groups followed the same general meeting format: Gospel Inquiry, 15 minutes; Liturgy Inquiry, 15 minutes; and the Social Inquiry, 45 minutes. The Gospel and Social inquiries were to result in actions.

The earliest actions were quite simple. As Pat Crowley observed, "It's the little actions that are the lifeblood of the movement."[56] Many of these early actions were distinctively Catholic. One group's action was "to interest Protestants in watching Bishop Fulton Sheen,"[57] while another resolved to "accept for the sake of Christ, such slights and insults as may arise."[58] Several groups decided to try to get Catholic children currently in public schools to enroll in Catholic schools. Other groups encouraged members to invite a non-Catholic friend to a parish mission. Special attention was paid to Catholic reading habits (or the lack thereof). As *ACT* reported, "The judgment is that a diet of books with a complete lack of Christian principle, in which sin is glamorized, in which lewd or profane passages are too detailed or occur too frequently, is unhealthy, does not foster our spiritual or mental growth, and may be an occasion of sin."[59] Many groups concurred in this judgment and acted to correct it. Many groups established parish libraries to ensure good Catholic literature was available, or installed pamphlet racks at the backs of their churches.

Though most of the early inquiries and actions were simple, local, and Catholic, many also reflect a response to the practical needs of young families in the neighborhood and the community. Many groups established baby-sitter services for young mothers, who had little free time. Newcomer services were set up to welcome new families to the neighborhood. Groups were established to help families when members were sick. Many other services were inspired by CFM cells—sewing clubs, youth clubs, clothing drives for the needy, and assistance for the Catholic foreign missions. The list is long.

FOR HAPPIER FAMILIES

Very soon after the first organizing meeting, the Coordinating Committee, as noted earlier, chose *For Happier Families* as the basic CFM program booklet. Even before the 1949 convention, the Chicago Catholic Family Action Federation had organized a committee, chaired by Clem Lane, to create a common program. The result was *For Happier Families,* published in 1949. According to Gerard Weber, who advised the committee, most of the initial inquiries were written by Edwina Hearn, president of the YCW, though "Clem Lane did most of the phrasing of the book, although a great many people in fact wrote it."[60] The driving force behind the completion of the booklet, as always, was the Crowleys. Weber observed, "The Crowleys, of course, were the pushing force behind it and I mean 'pushing.'"[61] Pushing equally hard was Hillenbrand, who advised, "whether it's good or not, get it out."[62] Get it out they did, and by the end of 1949 2,300 copies had been distributed.

The first edition of *For Happier Families* came out in 1949 in a gray cover, but subsequent revised editions in 1950 and 1952 were published with the yellow cover that earned *FHF* the affectionate title "the little yellow book." It was this book that introduced thousands of couples to the movement.

FHF stressed the virtues of "neighborliness" in its fourteen meeting outlines. Each meeting began with a Gospel inquiry in which the group reflected on some aspect of Jesus' life. The group then reflected on some aspect of Pope Pius XII's encyclical on the Mystical Body of Christ, which in many ways was the Magna Carta of CFM. These first two sections emphasized that CFMers must know the life of Christ and the mind of the Church if they were to make valid judgments in the third, Social Inquiry, segment. The Gospel inquiries encouraged members to see in Christ someone who loved totally and took risks to act. The discussion of the concept of the Mystical Body was a mind-expanding experience for most, a chance to see the Church not just as a place or a building, but as a living community in which each person has a necessary job to do. With amazing speed, most CFMers came to see themselves in a new light; they *were* the Church in the world, ordained to bring Christ into daily life.

The heart of the meeting remained the Social Inquiry. *FHF* presented twelve inquiries and two "check-up" sessions. The first four inquiries were devoted to the neighborhood—getting to know one's neighbors and the problems of the neighborhood. Pioneer CFMer George St. Peter remarked that the primary duty of the first meetings was "your duty to know your neighbor."[63] The next four meetings focused explicitly on family problems—children within the home, children outside the home, the parent-child relationship, and the family obligations of the father. The last four inquiries dealt with the parish and the community—newcomers, housing, making the community a better place for the family to live, and the parish.

FHF provided an excellent indoctrination into the concept of the Mystical Body of Christ, and in the Cardijn method of Catholic Action. By 1952, 12,000 copies had been distributed. But a major problem remained—what to do once *FHF* was completed. Pat Crowley observed in early 1949 that "uniform inquiries are desirable . . . possible, and necessary."[64] The Chicago group began work on a set of new inquiries under the chairmanship of Paul Hazard. Patty Crowley and Edwina Hearn helped to develop a new set of inquiries during the summer, and in the fall Lorraine Dix prepared a series of inquiries on the parents' responsibility in the education of children.[65] These inquiries were circulated locally, but a national program was desired. This issue was addressed at the second annual national meeting.

THE SECOND NATIONAL MEETING

In the summer of 1950 the movement gathered at St. Procopius Benedictine Abbey in Lisle, Illinois, just outside of Chicago, for its second annual national convention. According to the lore of the movement, holding the convention at the abbey was somewhat ironic—the men and women were not allowed to sleep together. The women had to stay at nearby Sacred Heart Convent. The result was both men and women were kept awake all night, the men by their snoring and the women by the many among them who were pregnant and kept getting up during the night to use the ladies' room. Despite the inhospitable living arrangements, the St. Procopius meeting produced several significant results. First, the movement officially adopted a name—The Christian Family Movement—subsuming all other titles under this one. Patrick Crowley was elected president of the Executive Committee, removing the temporary designation of the previous year. Crowley, Bauer, Jim Dockery of Davenport, Iowa, Beausoliel, and John McCue of New York were named to the Executive Committee. And finally, the purpose of CFM was clearly enunciated: "To promote the Christian way of life in the family, in the families of the community, and in the institutions affecting the family by serving, educating, and representing the family."[66]

The convention also addressed the relationship between CFM and the Cana Conferences. Since the inception of Cana, CFM had been its most significant promoter. However, tension always existed between the two movements, largely as a result of their different goals. Cana chaplain John Egan explained to the convention that while CFM's task was to serve, educate, and represent the family, Cana's sole purpose was education in marriage and family life.[67] In a sense, the two groups should work hand in hand. CFM would be the natural follow-up to Cana. Despite such logic, and the ideological clarity of definition, the two movements often came into conflict.

The most important outcome of the St. Procopius meeting was the acceptance of a common set of inquiries for groups that had completed *FHF*—another step toward a coordinated national movement. The theme selected for 1950 was "The Economics of Family Life." The series of social inquiries that resulted included such topics as "Economizing on Food Expenditures," "The High Cost of Living," "Ability to Save," "Credit Buying," and "Housing." Several inquiries dealt with noneconomic topics—"The Family in the Parish," "Loneliness in the Family," "Prejudice," and "Religious

Education in the Home." In all, thirteen inquiries were produced, which were to be used by all the CFM sections throughout the United States. The sections were warned not to follow the manual slavishly, but to adapt the inquiries to their local circumstances. After using the national inquiry program, local sections were also encouraged to create their own inquiries, and many did.

By the end of the convention, all of the major components for CFM were firmly in place. The movement had an effective executive council, headed by Pat Crowley. A national program had been initiated. And the national meeting had now become an annual occurrence. All differences had not been resolved, but most conflicts were controlled and did not particularly inhibit the spread of the movement. The struggle between the approach of South Bend and the Bauers and that of Chicago and the Crowleys remained. In March of 1950, the Crowleys wrote to Hillenbrand, commenting on a set of inquiries created by Bauer, "We disagree on a few points, at least we in Chicago do not work the same way. Their inquiries in our opinion are not very good. They do not have the meetings laid out the way we have in ours, and from experience we think [they] must."[68] Burnie Bauer later reflected, "Pat's strong conviction of the family's essential place in all national and international considerations was back of the long arguments we had in determining what kind of yearly program CFM should adopt in those early years. While many of us pushed for local self-help programs like cooperative clothing exchanges, and neighborhood recreation, and parish get-togethers with inquiries aimed at benefiting immediate members of the group, Pat wanted to push on to more educational and social awareness programs that would give families a better understanding of other peoples' needs by studying civil rights, labor unions, urban problems, the UN, and national and international policies, etc. All agreed both aims were good, but we disagreed on priorities. Mostly he won, but often we compromised."[69] The tension between Chicago and South Bend, and the Crowleys and the Bauers remained a feature of CFM throughout the first decades of the movement.

BURNIE BAUER AND CFM IN SOUTH BEND, INDIANA

One of the most dynamic and successful CFM foundations of the early 1950s was Bauer's South Bend CFM groups. Despite its successes, Bauer has always felt his role in the foundation and growth of CFM has been neglected in movement histories. As early as 1953, Bauer wrote the Crowleys to refute the publicity brochures which stated that the Crowleys were the CFM's founders. He reminded them that he was the one who had started the notion of a couples movement.[70] Bauer's frustration increased over the years. In almost every policy decision his position lost out to that of the more popular Crowleys. Despite his disappointments, publicly Bauer supported the Crowleys and the national movement, though he referred to himself as the "loyal opposition."[71] Occasionally his frustration boiled over: he wrote on a copy of a CFM circular, "Crowleys ask for ideas (even if they won't accept them)."[72] While Bauer's ideas may have lost out, any authentic history must acknowledge the significant contribution he made to the movement and its success. He is clearly one of its founders and one of the early giants.

The beginning actions of South Bend CFM were similar to those of groups elsewhere; Cana and Pre-Cana Conferences were sponsored, as were family recreation nights, a monthly potluck dinner, a baby-sitter service. Bauer, however, disagreed with the Chicago method of planning a yearly program. Rather than jump from one topic to the next, he believed that groups should stick to one topic until their plan of action could make an impact on the community. He wrote, "Our Social Inquiries must be penetrating and persevering enough to occasion the setting up of *new* institutions. . . . Let each Social Inquiry be stuck to until somehow the families of the members of the group are in some way relieved of the social pressures that press on them from their environment and we will attract the masses."[73] Ultimately, national CFM would offer exactly this option to experienced "third-stage" groups that chose to stay in CFM rather than disperse into roles in the general community, as originally intended.

South Bend CFM did successfully sponsor a number of major actions. They began a preschool Sunday School at Little Flower Parish. At McKinley Terrace, a community swimming pool was built. The city established a Fair Employment Practices Commission. An inquiry on nutrition inspired the purchase of a flour mill and the creation of a co-op to provide fresh-ground wheat to the community. Ultimately, the House of Bread, "A Christian bakery using only whole ingredients," was opened in 1952.

South Bend CFM's most lasting accomplishment was the creation of Logan School for the education and training of mentally retarded children. The seed for the school was planted when it was discovered that one of the members of Bauer's group had a child with Down Syndrome. During the 1940s, relatively little public assistance was available for such children, and most families had to fend for themselves. The group decided to do an inquiry into mental and physical retardation. The action: a series of lectures by child psychologist Father James Smythe to educate the community as to the problem. The program quickly expanded beyond CFM. Other religious and community groups joined in creating the St. Joseph County Council for the Retarded Child, which called for the creation of a school and center. Through the efforts of CFM members and others, Logan School was created and currently serves more than a thousand children with a budget of close to $5 million. Typical of CFM actions, CFM's job was to get the ball rolling, then allow others (i.e., experts) to run the day-to-day business.

Throughout the 1950s and 1960s South Bend continued to play an important role in the national movement. And, Bauer continued to express himself forcefully, although often his pronouncements were not well received.

THREE

The 1950s
Forging a National Movement

The movement spread rapidly during the 1950s. By 1952, CFM was established in 97 cities, with a membership of more than 2,500 couples nationwide. By the following year it had expanded to 181 cities with more than 5,000 couples. Groups had also been established in 21 cities outside the United States including cities in Mexico, Canada, Japan, England, the Philippines, Uruguay, Argentina, Denmark, and Germany. More will be said of international CFM later, but by 1953 it was already an international movement. By 1955, CFM was flourishing in more than 330 cities with over 16,000 couples, and by 1957 the number of couples had doubled to more than 32,000. Several cities in particular stood out. As might be expected, Chicago was always the leading city, boasting more than 2,700 couples. But other cities were prospering as well— San Francisco, Denver and Joliet had 550 couples each, South Bend 507, Buffalo 450, Toledo 334, and Los Angeles 248. The explosive growth of CFM during the 1950s made the movement a significant force within the Catholic Church in the United States.

Several factors converged to produce CFM's amazing growth. As mentioned earlier, the Catholic Church in the United States, traditionally a working-class church, developed its first substantial middle class in the 1950s. Coupled with this was a new-found aggressiveness. The Church was no longer content to be a defensive or ghetto-bound Church. It now sought to break free of the ghetto and change American culture. CFM was at the forefront of this development. As an apostolic movement, CFM gave the newly

39

emerging professional and middle-class Catholics a means to put their faith into action. CFM was the right movement at the right time.

Several practical forces also contributed to the rapid spread of CFM, not the least of which was the high mobility that characterized postwar America. Quite simply, the movement was spread by CFMers who moved. When CFM couples were transferred, many promptly established CFM in their new locale. For instance, when the Robert McMahons landed in Encino, California, from Chicago, they immediately set out to create a CFM nucleus in their parish. Second, despite being a lay movement, many groups were initiated by priests, who saw the possibilities of renewal and action offered by CFM and the Cardijn technique. Many of these priests were younger clergy, such as Father John Coffield in El Monte, California, or Father Peter Sammon, a young high school teacher in San Francisco. Finally, and most significantly, the Crowleys tirelessly carried the word about CFM across the country and eventually throughout the world. In 1951, they were in California meeting with priests, seminarians, and lay couples. The following year they were in Denver, where CFM was begun after the Crowleys visited their friends in that city. That year the Crowleys visited forty cities in nineteen states and two provinces of Canada, all the while preaching the movement.[1] They continued to be the single most important force behind the expansion of CFM.

STRUCTURAL DEVELOPMENTS

As the movement grew, so did the national structure, though its very existence was always a source of unease. After all, even those directly involved in national roles agreed that CFM was a grassroots movement, one defined by what happened in thousands of living-room discussions, not by national rules and bylaws. If there was one dogma that everyone agreed on, it was that too much structure would rob the movement of its vitality. Repeatedly, members expressed fears of "too much superstructure." Two CFM pioneers, the James O'Shaughnessys, withdrew from the movement because of CFM's emphasis on a structured program.[2] Still, some structure was necessary if the movement was to be national in scope.

The Crowleys remained the executive couple throughout the 1950s; however, the Coordinating Committee (CC) took on more and more responsibility for guiding CFM as a whole. The CC consisted of a representative of each diocese in which CFM was present. The main tasks of the CC, which met twice annually, were to serve as a center and exchange of information for CFM, to produce an annual program, to oversee the publication of *ACT*, and to plan the yearly convention. The semiannual meetings became heady affairs with lively interchanges.

By 1956, the job of turning out an annual national program of social inquiries had become so time-consuming that the CC established a separate committee to carry out this essential work. To ensure that control of policy stayed with the CC, the Program Committee was required to submit a program outline to the CC for its final approval. The first chair couple for the new committee was Jim and Peg Cockrell of Tulsa, Oklahoma. Providing intimate direction and exercising ultimate editorial control was Monsignor Reynold Hillenbrand.

By 1957, the explosive growth of the movement made the Coordinating Committee increasingly unwieldy. That year it was decided to form an Executive Committee to be made up of twelve couples, plus the Crowleys, selected geographically. Their task was to make interim decisions between the semiannual meetings of the CC, but they were not to establish policy. They were to make long-range recommendations to the CC, and they were to cooperate with area chaplains. The initial Executive Committee consisted of the Crowleys, Charles and Kathleen Connolly of Toronto, Dan and Helen Heyrman of La Crosse, Bob and Charlotte Hogan of Detroit, Ted and Lory Lathamer of Denver, John and Corintha McCarvel of Great Falls, Montana, John and Kay McCue of New

York, Bill and Kay Morhard of Richmond, Dr. and Mrs. Francis O'Grady of Chicago, Jerry and Barbara Ryan of Pittsburgh, Ed and Cassie Schuman of Louisville, and Joe and Kay Trumble of Tulsa, Oklahoma. By 1959, the EC had expanded to twenty-one couples, as the movement had divided the United States and Canada into twenty areas, with a couple from each area serving on the Executive Committee.

CONCERNS ABOUT STRUCTURE

As the national structure developed, so did concerns that the national structure was violating the genius of the movement. As early as 1954, the O'Shaughnessys cautioned, "Executives (at the national and federation levels) should be administrators, not policy makers." Each local section should remain "autonomous."[3] By 1960, the Crowleys themselves were expressing concerns over the "bureaucratizing tendencies" of the CC. In a letter to the CC, they asserted, "We are going to cut down, if not out, the details of business and stress the subject of the laymen's role in the Church and the work of CFM."[4] In 1963, one of the movement's more flamboyant couples, Estelle and Mario Carota, sent an extraordinary letter to the CC, containing this caution, "The work of the movement is not to have committee meetings, publish programs and put on national conventions." Nor was it wise to "concentrate the guiding spirit of the movement into the hands of a few couples." The movement's genius, they argued, lay in its grass-roots approach. "We must work hard to find ways that will allow each and every couple in the movement . . . to put their hand to the wheel and not just be an oarsman that is given orders by a captain who in many cases doesn't even know the way or the water."[5] When the Carotas spoke, others listened. The couple inspired awe when they arrived at national conventions with their seventeen children—many adopted—stowed in their camper bus. Their authority stemmed also from the fact that they lived as they preached, spearheading a number of innovative projects including missionary trips to Mexico and to poverty-stricken areas of rural California. The following year, at the Co-ordinating Committee meeting, Bill Caldwell stated what he saw as the basic principle of the movement: Because the organization was built on "individual responsibility," its structure should not be "rigid, precise, or specific," and it should remain responsive to the local level.[6] In essence, Caldwell agreed with the Carota critique. Making it a reality was somewhat more difficult.

The struggle against excessive structure combined with the need for a national structure that gave attention to finances, expansion, and other practical matters remained a creative tension in the movement throughout its first twenty-five years.

This extended discussion of structure and the leaders' worry over it might easily lead the observer to picture a bloated bureaucracy. In reality, until 1961 the movement operated out of the Crowleys' home in Wilmette. The official address of the movement was that of Pat's law office at 100 West Monroe Street in downtown Chicago. Correspondence was sent to the office, then taken to the Crowley home, where Patty and a devoted crew answered the letters and sent out countless programs, booklets, and other materials. The correspondence was then stored in the Crowley garage. Patty's assistants included Lois Heidbrink, Helen Fagan, and Helene Bauer. Together they answered thousands and thousands of inquiries.

In 1961, the movement was able to move to more substantial quarters. In that year Bolton Sullivan and SKIL Corporation donated a two-story building at 1655 W. Jackson Street in Chicago. The building became the movement's headquarters, which it shared with the YCS and YCW movements.

By 1960 the structure of the movement was clearly in place.

- The basic unit of CFM was the *action group*, which consisted of six couples and a chaplain and was generally organized on a parish basis. This group met every two weeks.
- The leaders of an action group belonged to a *section*, which was made up of leader couples from each action group in a

parish. It, too, generally consisted of six couples and a chaplain. Active parishes had more than one section. The section was the "local coordinating group," whose members would meet with the chaplain to prepare for the upcoming action group meeting. General problems were discussed and background information was provided.

- All the sections and action groups in an area combined to form a *federation,* whose boundaries generally coincided with a diocese or archdiocese. Extremely large federations might be broken into smaller *regions.* The federation served as a communications center, published a newsletter, took care of local public relations, and where necessary coordinated the projects of local groups. It planned diocesan-wide events such as study days, conventions, family gatherings, and other events that went beyond the power of local groups.
- All the federations were part of a larger group known as an *area.* The CFM in the United States and Canada was divided into twenty areas.
- The president couples of all the federations made up the *National Coordinating Committee,* which met once a year to discuss policy and other issues.
- The president couple of each area served on the *National Executive Committee,* which met twice a year. This committee prepared proposals for consideration by the larger body, made interim decisions required by so large a membership, and maintained continuous contact with the Coordinating Committee.[7]

THE NOTRE DAME CONVENTIONS

Just as important as the national leadership cadre and structure in building a national spirit were the annual conventions. After the uncomfortable experience at St. Procopius, the movement looked to the University of Notre Dame. Pat Crowley was not only an alum-

they listened to such speakers as Philip Berrigan, s.s.j., Senator Eugene McCarthy, Archbishop Joseph Rummel of New Orleans, John Thomas, s.j., Joseph Fitzpatrick, s.j., Russell Barta, Bishop Loras Lane of Dubuque, Monsignor Joseph Munier, Monsignor George Higgins, Karl Stern, Bernard Haring, c.ss.r., Bernard Cooke, s.j., George Shuster, Walter Imbiorski, Charles Curran, Catherine de Hueck Doherty (the Baroness), Jerome Kerwin, Joseph Fichter, s.j. and Louis Twomey, s.j. This exposure to the latest thinking gave CFMers a sense of their specialness. Of course, a regular convention speaker was Monsignor Hillenbrand. Though he was not an electrifying speaker, the profundity of his words made a deep impression. One couple referred to the "wisdom-studded exhortations"[10] of Hillenbrand. Not all the talks were deadly serious—even as profound a speaker as Monsignor Joseph Munier could become playful. On a day marred by 100-degree temperatures and thunderstorms, Munier pulled out an immense thesis that he said he planned to read. To the audience's amusement and applause, Munier ripped the thesis up, and spoke note-free. Convention-goers felt especially honored to be addressed by Father Theodore Hesburgh shortly after he was named to head Notre Dame in 1952. His choice of CFM as the first group for him to address publicly as president seemed appropriate, since Hesburgh had served as a Catholic Action chaplain in "Vetville," as housing for married students was called at Notre Dame following World War II.

Equally as important to the conventions were the remarkable spirit-filled liturgies. Here again CFM was in the forefront. Hillenbrand was one of the most highly regarded liturgists of his era. As a result, CFM convention liturgies, though tame by current standards, became showcases for the latest in liturgical thinking. The convention-goers sang the mass, including one celebrated at the Notre Dame grotto to Our Lady. The dialogue mass was used, as were Gregorian chant and leaflet missals. At the 1957 convention, the Great Amen, Et cum spiritu tuo, Kyrie, Sanctus, Benedictus, Credo, and Gloria were all sung. At the 1959 convention the sung mass was celebrated with the altar facing the people.

All these elements were designed to impress upon the laity that they were to be actively involved in the Church's common worship. The Notre Dame liturgies were the best liturgies most CFMers would attend all year: Exquisite singing, powerful sermons, and a sense of unity created a euphoria seldom duplicated at the parish level.

Other devotions were also employed—singing Compline, saying the rosary, and candlelight processions. All contributed to what one report noted as "the feeling of the presence of the Holy Spirit."[11]

That spirit spilled over into the rest of the convention activities. CFMers from different parts of the country and different parts of the world excitedly exchanged ideas and experiences. Some exchanges took place in convention workshops, where members shared ideas about "How to make a good observation" or "How to be a good leader." More important, perhaps, were the informal discussions that took place at meals, over coffee, between talks, during walks around the campus. What the conventions did was expose CFMers to other dedicated, faith-filled apostles, working just as they were to restore all things in Christ. The result was electric and uplifting. As one CFM couple put it simply, "The convention tied us all together."[12] After the 1957 convention, 96 percent of those responding to the survey rated the convention as either good or excellent. The report further noted, "A good many remarked on the inspiration received from meeting . . . enthusiastic and friendly CFMers."[13] And after the 1965 convention, the summary read, "The outstanding feature of the convention was the enthusiasm and Christian spirit and fellowship by so many people from so many distant places."[14]

Each convention seemed to surpass the previous one. Of the 1958 convention a ten-year veteran observed, "I have never seen anything like it."[15] The 1959 convention was the last annual convention. Beginning in 1961 the annual Notre Dame convention became an every-other-year event. On the even years, the areas held regional conventions, some of them as ambitious as earlier national conventions. This change was made in the hope that more people could attend the regional conventions than could travel to Notre Dame. It proved to be a valid hope. In 1960, the Chicago area's convention drew more than a thousand couples from a five-state area. Nonetheless, Notre Dame remained a great source of unity for the movement and inspired CFMers to greater commitment to the movement.

THE NATIONAL PROGRAM

Beyond the Notre Dame conventions the annual social inquiry program provided the movement's basic common bond. Early on, the leadership of the movement decided that CFM would take no national stands on issues, unless directed to do so by the American hierarchy. Nor were local federations to use the CFM name to endorse any local issue. CFM leadership sought to avoid polarizing members over political issues—the movement was to form leaders, not advocate political policy. Still, some dimension of national unity was desired, and the annual inquiry became the basic tool in achieving it.

Hillenbrand pushed hard for the adoption of a national program. In 1953, he stated, in regard to the national program, "Cooperation by all CFM federations should enhance the unity, coherence, and emphasis so needed in our efforts."[16] Nonetheless, the disparate nature of the CFM structure insured that the autonomy of local sections would be jealously guarded. As the Coordinating Committee carefully pointed out, what was wanted was "unity, not conformity."[17]

Hillenbrand also saw the national program as a tool that would enable the movement to make a greater impact on the social order. The cumulative effect of the many individual actions, so ran his reasoning, would be much more powerful if all the action groups were addressing the same topic. Beginning in 1950, then, the movement produced an annual program that all groups were supposed to use, once they had worked through *For Happier Families*.

The annual program reflected the concerns of CFM on a national level. As one later publication observed, "The Program has always been the Christian Family Movement's most basic expression of philosophy."[18]

Until 1956, the yearly program was developed at the meetings of the national Coordinating Committee, drawn from suggestions sent in from all over the United States and Canada. Democracy at work in the Church, one might think. Reality was different. Monsignor Hillenbrand was the driving and ruling force behind the national program. It was he who defined the purpose of the movement: to "form lay apostles among married people,"[19] or to put it another way, "to form people to be instruments of Christ."[20] And that formation, as Hillenbrand repeatedly stressed, was to be effected through action. CFM was to be an action movement, not a study club. These fundamental beliefs influenced the development of the annual inquiry programs. Though the constellation of themes varied a little over time, the mix never strayed far from the outline that Kanaly and Hillenbrand sketched on that restaurant napkin in 1939.

The topics selected for the first six years are as follows:

1950: The Economics of the Family
1951: Social Pressures As They Affect the Parent-Child
　　　Relationship
1952: Civic Responsibility—Work—Recreation
1953: Social Responsibility—Family Finances—Education
1954: Community
1955: The Layman's Role in the Church

As the first cycle of annual programs indicates, nothing was to be alien to the CFMer. The movement was not just limited to the family, but to everything that affected family life. Chaplain Donald Kanaly told the Coordinating Committee that "the CFM is the university of Catholic mothers and fathers. You are educators, and it is your lifelong vocation to develop the mind of Christ in its totality.

In doing that you are the reformers of all things. You are the puri-fiers of art, literature, drama, economics, recreation, marriage, and family."[21] Hillenbrand reiterated Kanaly: "We must, in humble atti-tude, learn what our Blessed Lord has to teach us about working life, about industrial life, about economic life, because nothing is alien to the Mystical Body in human life."[22] The Mystical Body was to permeate every aspect of life, and if it was to do so, it was up to the lay members of the Body to neglect no aspect of human life. This philosophy directed the annual programs.

From the beginning, many CFM groups experienced problems with the program. Some were group dynamics problems. Distinctive personality types might derail a meeting's focus. Small wonder that leadership training became a perennial concern of the movement. Two other problems—lack of good observations and the failure to act—plagued enough groups to warrant constant concern. As pio-neer chaplain Gerard Weber observed, "We should constantly be looking for methods of obtaining facts, for once we have good ob-servations, action follows easily."[23]

There was yet another source of worry to leaders, which Hillenbrand defined as the "lack of discipline" in the movement.[24] Translation: Many groups were not following the national program. This was always a point of tension; though all groups were told not to follow the inquiry booklet slavishly but to adapt it to their local needs, they were instructed not to abandon the emphasis of each program-year entirely. The local group was expected to respect the general format as adopted by the national Coordinating Committee. That was a necessity if the movement was going to have any sort of unity and if it was to make an impact beyond the local scene.

The apparatus for creating the inquiry books was elaborate. As noted earlier, in 1956 the Coordinating Committee decided to es-tablish a Program Committee to develop the annual program. The committee would submit their work to the Coordinating Com-mittee for approval. The first Program Committee consisted of nine couples from eight different federations: Jim and Peg Cockrell of Tulsa, Oklahoma (chair couple), Don and Aileen Trudhope (Toronto), Bob and Jo Noonan (Buffalo), "Drape" and Mary Fran

Draper (Joliet), John and Dorothy Evans (Fort Wayne), Bob and Dottie Anderson (San Francisco), Bob and Alma Lee Hargan (Louisville), Jack and Agnes Gerber (Chicago), Dick and Elizabeth Ormsby (Chicago). Also included were Hillenbrand as the national chaplain, the Crowleys as the executive couple, and Father William Nerin of Oklahoma. The theme or themes for the year were set by the Coordinating Committee, (usually, as time went on, as recommended by the Program Committee). A committee of six priests was also established to prepare the Scripture and Liturgy inquiries. Father Dennis Geaney, o.s.a., who "preached the Gospel" of lay leadership in such books as *You Are Not Your Own* and *You Shall Be Witnesses,* soon became a strong presence on this committee.

Despite how it looked in theory, the dominant force in determining the content of the social inquiries remained Hillenbrand. In the first year of the program committee, Hillenbrand suggested sixteen of the thirty-two meeting topics—the other sixteen coming from suggestions from around the country. The following year Hillenbrand's control of the movement was made explicit as he laid out a five-year cycle of themes (the napkin memo again). Five areas were distinctly lay areas of responsibility—family life, economic life, political life, international life, and social life (e.g., race, immigration, recreation). Two areas were shared by laity and clergy—parish life and education. Hillenbrand presented a plan by which one or two of these seven areas would be examined each year, providing the movement both focus and depth. CFM covered the seven topics over the course of the next five years:

1956: Social Harmony (race and youth)
1957: Parish Life—Education
1958: Family Life and Economics
1959: Political Life and the Christian Family
1960: International Life

Hillenbrand's influence went beyond the choice of theme. Each program book was submitted to him before publication. Besides making sure the text was theologically sound, Hillenbrand exercised

ferocious editorial control as well, tightening up the language, structure, and content. Each year as he wielded his blue pencil from his
Wisconsin vacation retreat, he imperiled the copy deadline that
would permit printing in time for distribution at the late-August
convention. Hillenbrand also saw to it that each program received
the *nihil obstat* and *imprimatur* before he allowed the program to
be published. Though CFM was a lay movement, at the program
level it was clearly under the control of Hillenbrand, who, for the
1950s, was a brilliant, progressive cleric. He pushed the movement
toward greatness.

HILLENBRAND'S VISION OF CFM

While the Crowleys personified the movement in action, Hillenbrand personified the movement in thought.[25] Though nearly killed
in an automobile accident in Oklahoma in 1949, though autocratic,
ill at ease with women, and at times downright cranky, Hillenbrand
provided the intellectual underpinnings for the first two decades of
CFM. More than that, his passion and conviction drove CFM
through the 1950s. Typical of the era, Hillenbrand saw the world in
black-and-white terms. There were answers to problems, Catholic
answers, and these answers could be found in the papal encyclicals.
Doubt was for the weak; Catholics knew. Their job was to learn the
principles, and then apply them to the social order. The Cardijn
method was aptly suited for this endeavor.

Above all, the Cardijn technique was *the* method for training lay
apostles, which was, after all, the ultimate goal of CFM, according
to Hillenbrand. He asserted that four to five years of training were
necessary if the lay person were to become an effective apostle, to
put on the mind of Christ. "The social inquiry is summed up in
Christ. The observation of the problem is seeing the world as Christ
saw it—seeing an evil, therefore, as Christ saw it. The judgment is
putting on the mind of Christ. The action is the apostle's love of
Christ through loving others."[26]

The Cardijn formula kept the action group firmly rooted in real life. The group was to observe a problem in the daily life of the family, the parish, or the community. The observation forced the CFMer away from vague generalizations and opinions and toward clear and accurate statements of fact that were necessary for sound judgments and effective action. Hillenbrand argued, "The slightest observation accurately made is better than the most valid generalization."[27]

The judgment required that the couple "uncover the mentality of Christ and apply it to a specific problem."[28] The judgment served as a transition from theory to action. As Hillenbrand instructed, "the judgment should be, as far as we can make it, a precise formulation of the principles to be applied to the observation."[29]

The final and most important step was the action. Hillenbrand insisted that each meeting result in an action. Formation occurred through action. If the Cardijn formula was adhered to, real apostles would be created.

Training was particularly necessary to overcome what Hillenbrand called the "double conscience" that resulted from the modern world's separation of life from religion. Thus, one could be a good practicing Catholic, a daily communicant, and still be a racist, still be anti-Semitic, still be unjust in business dealings. As Hillenbrand noted, "the social teachings of the Church frequently conflict with the social, political, and economic thinking we have picked up along the way."[30] CFM, then, had to purge the prevailing cultural outlook from the CFMer's way of thinking and, in its place, inculcate the teachings of the Church. "The major job of CFM is to teach this doctrine [the Church's social teaching] to people and translate it into apostolic action."[31]

Central to this endeavor is the belief that the Church had clearly defined teachings in most areas, particularly in social doctrine. As Hillenbrand noted, "There are many clear and definite answers that the Church has given to the economic problem."[32] The task of the apostle was to learn these doctrines, then conform his or her life to them. The CFM program provided the basic training to accomplish this through the discipline of the Observe-Judge-Act method. The task of the CFM was not to challenge or question Church teaching. According to Hillenbrand, "the doctrine of the Church, which is enshrined in an encyclical . . . may not be challenged by a Catholic, even if he is a trained theologian. . . . When we hear the Pope, we hear Christ."[33] The task of the apostle was to learn the Church teachings and then apply them. As Hillenbrand asserted, "The Movement must be doctrinally strong."[34]

Hillenbrand was equally clear in his definition of lay and clerical roles. Lay people were not to be "little religious"; that is, they were not to try to duplicate the life of a religious. Lay people had their own calling, their own sphere, and their own spirituality. The spirituality of the lay person was based on action in the world, not on contemplative retreat. "The essential characteristic of a layman's spirituality is to take action in the areas of life allotted to him in the division of the redemptive work."[35] Nor was the priest to usurp the role of the lay person. The priest's main task was to help form apostles to work in the lay apostolate. He was not to take the layman's place.

Hillenbrand clearly articulated the areas of lay responsibility. In an oft-repeated statement he stressed that, "The Layman's task concerns the ordinary human relations and the communities which stem from these relations. The first is the relationship between man and woman, which results in the community of marriage and the family. The second is a multitude of relationships stemming from the necessity of working to live. . . . The third is the relation of people living together geographically, which results in the community of government at all levels. The fourth is the relation of the individual to all men (and of the individual nation to a family of nations). . . . The fifth is the relation of the individual to man in their leisure time activities."[36] Parish life was an area shared with the clergy, but in the other areas—family life, economic life, political life, international life, and cultural life, the laymen alone had to act. "Where are the great crises today?" Hillenbrand asked. "In economic life, in political life, in family life, in international life. The priest is subtracted from these fields. They are the layman's responsibility."[37] In Hillenbrand's analysis of the Church, the respective roles of clergy and laity were clearly defined. Each knew their spheres and their responsibilities. It was on the basis of this analysis that CFM developed its social inquiry program in the 1950s.

One final stamp that Hillenbrand placed on the movement was his insistence that CFM was not a "family movement" per se. The movement could not focus on the family as an isolated unit; rather, it had to address all the institutions affecting family life—parish, city, nation, world. The world had to be made into a place where it was easier to live a Christian family life. Moreover, the purpose of the movement was to create "full apostles, not just family apostles."[38] Limiting one's concern to one's own family was ultimately self-defeating.

Hillenbrand identified two problems as more critical than the family crisis—the economic crisis and the lack of lay participation in the Mass, with the latter being the more important. Hillenbrand's parish in Hubbard Woods was regarded as a "showplace for liturgical reform."[39] For Hillenbrand, real social reform began with the liturgy; put another way, the Mass was "the source and center of the lay apostolate."[40] The 1957–58 booklet reflected this outlook when it queried, "What impedes Christ more than any other simple thing? It is the fact that there is so little participation of lay people in Mass."[41] Good liturgy was crucial because "when the Mass bores the people . . . we are in trouble because Christ is defeated at the very center of our spiritual life."[42] Properly done, the Mass served to make participants more socially aware by making them realize their responsibility to the community of the Mystical Body and their responsibility as part of the Mystical Body.

Not everyone in CFM agreed with Hillenbrand. Veteran New York CFMer Martin Quigley complained, "If it is true that CFM's main goals are to spread the use of the sung Mass and carry out activities in the field of economic life, I have been stupid the last half dozen years. . . . Monsignor Hillenbrand notwithstanding, the main task of CFM lies in helping couples to live up to their faith in difficult times and to enable them to help their children in the even

FOUR

The 1950s
Becoming Citizens of the World

ACTIONS IN THE 1950S

Though Hillenbrand provided the intellectual underpinnings of CFM, the movement itself was defined by action. And while the movement developed a national structure, local groups continued to act in their local environments. A large percentage of group actions reported in *ACT* throughout the 1950s were similar to those of the late 1940s—CFMers set up baby-sitter and newcomer services; organized clothing and food drives for the needy; pursued actions to monitor the purity of literature, the movies, and television; created programs to assist the elderly; promoted various Catholic devotions such as perpetual adoration and the block rosary; supported Cana and Pre-Cana conferences, parish libraries, Scouts, youth groups. The continuing tilt toward simple responses to family, neighborhood, and parish needs reflect the fact that in this decade of rapid expansion, easily half or more CFMers were newcomers using the introductory booklet, *For Happier Families,* which retained its local focus through five revisions during the 1950s.

But what about the other half? With the introduction of a national program in 1950, more experienced groups undertook more significant actions. *ACT* reported that as a result of the unemployment inquiry one group established a vocational counseling service for the unemployed in their area.[1] As a result of the inquiries on the theme of politics, many groups began voter registration drives, while others pushed Catholics to run for public school board seats.[2]

57

A New York section attempted to set up medical services, which included low-cost obstetrical care. A Chicago section initiated the Hamilton Park Neighborhood Council to "reclaim the park," which had become "gang-infested."[3] Groups elsewhere became involved in neighborhood improvement associations of one sort or another. Many groups—South Bend and Pittsburgh were two—responded to the inquiries on facilities for youth recreation by developing or repairing neighborhood playgrounds, actions that drew members into coalitions with organizations far outside the cloistered Catholic orbit. In general, the annual programs encouraged greater civic involvement—CFMers attended city council meetings or invited civic leaders to speak at parish functions. Many CFM groups operated as grass-roots organizing committees getting people involved in local and civic activities, pushing them beyond their local, familial concerns.

As the movement matured, it was increasingly confronted with the problem of what to do with CFM veterans. Couples who had been in the movement several years outgrew the localized focus of the first year or two. Even the bigger actions inspired by the national program booklets did not seem enough. As early as 1952, concerns were expressed about what to do with "senior CFMers." Some argued that they should leave the movement—CFM was a training ground and, once trained, alumni should move into the community in their own special ministry. Others argued that senior CFMers had to be accommodated, their leadership and commitment were necessary to the ongoing success of the movement. The result was that during the 1950s the more seasoned elements of the movement increasingly tackled larger concerns. In this period countless CFMers ran for public office—school board, supervisor, judge, state representatives and senators.

In this context, many groups and individuals turned their focus to international concerns. CFMers were instructed that they were "citizens of the world," and as such they had to be concerned with the world's problems. "Too many Catholics are ostriches about world affairs," *ACT* declared.[4] The Church was an international church. For members of the Mystical Body, what happened in China was as important as what happened in their own neighborhood. This outlook was reinforced by the fact that in the 1950s Americans were experiencing the height of Cold War tensions. The prevailing view was that the world was in a cosmic battle between good and evil, between communist and free. While CFM clearly condemned communism (this was contested by some—see below), the movement saw that it was not enough to condemn communism. Positive actions had to be taken to create a world in which communism would have no appeal.

CFM firmly supported the United Nations and various UN policies, a stance that did not make them popular with many conservative Catholics. CFM repeatedly reiterated papal support of the UN. In one of the early national inquiries in 1952–53, CFM examined "Our Responsibility to the World Outside Our Community." In the inquiry, CFMers were asked to

A. Observe

1. "Do the couples [whom you surveyed] know what the United Nations stands for?"

2. "What do couples observed know about the United Nations?"

B. Judge

1. "Is a World Organization necessary?" "Is it working effectively?"

2. "Are we *citizens of the world* [emphasis mine], and as such do we have any responsibilities?"

The CFM answer, of course, was Yes, we are citizens of the world and we do have responsibilities. Such inquiries as "The Family and World Affairs" (1954–55), and "World Unity," (1955–56) reinforced the emphasis on the world community.

The international thrust of CFM culminated in 1960 with the yearly inquiry program focusing on international life and entitled "That All May Be One." A guest editorial in *ACT* entitled "A World to Win" reminded CFMers that there was "no room for comfortable Christianity" and counseled that we "must become missionary."[5] The international and missionary thrust that so epitomized CFM in the 1950s had three major manifestations: (1) CFM hosted thousands of international students; (2) CFM assisted thousands of refugees to come to the United States, and (3) CFM supported domestic and foreign missionaries. Out of these major concerns grew two new, enduring programs: the Foundation for International Cooperation and the Christian Mission Family Vacations.

INTERNATIONAL STUDENT AND VISITOR PROGRAM

One of CFM's most prominent characteristics during the 1950s was its openness to foreign visitors, particularly foreign students. The Chicago federation was particularly outstanding in this regard. By 1951, they had established an International Student Committee.[6] Patty Crowley recalls that the earliest gestures in this regard had begun many years earlier. "I remember the inquiry on foreign students. One of the actions was to have someone to dinner. The way we got it going—we had never heard of a foreign student—so we called the Chancery, and they didn't know any foreign students either. So then we called the "Y." We heard that they helped some. I don't know how we found out. We said we'd like to have a couple for dinner. So the first two students we had were two Philippine students. They had been here for two years and never met a Catholic family. That really hit us."[7] Other groups were pursuing the same inquiry, so hospitality for foreign students spread. Following World War II, families were sought to host foreign high school students. Through the efforts of John and Dorothy Drish, this became a popular action for CFM groups in Chicago. Students from Germany, Austria, Italy, and elsewhere lived with CFM families during the school year.

As a result of the Chicago federation's efforts, the student program caught on with CFM groups across the nation, testimony to the germinating force of the national conventions. By 1955, a special International Student Visitor subcommittee had been established by the national Coordinating Committee. In each subsequent annual inquiry program booklet, a special inquiry on foreign students was included.

CFM regarded the proper treatment of foreign students as an important element in the nation's foreign policy. Many students who came to the United States did not get a positive view of this nation. Ignorant and rude treatment was too often the rule. As a 1955 report to the Coordinating Committee warned, these students "are the cream of their nation's crop," who would one day assume "leadership positions." If they were mistreated, they would develop a negative attitude towards the U.S. that would cause future problems. As the report went on to state, the International Student Visitor Program would make a "positive contribution to the peace of the world."[8]

For Catholics, care of the student also had an evangelical component. Many Catholic students never encountered a Catholic family or were made to feel welcome in a Catholic Church. The result was the possible loss of faith. Again, it was of the utmost importance to keep "the cream of the crop" on good terms with the Church.

CFMers threw themselves wholeheartedly into offering hospitality to foreign students, and not just Catholic students—non-Catholic foreign students and visitors were just as welcome. Most federations sponsored annual gatherings/socials for foreign students. A Christmas party in Chicago in 1955 hosted 250 students from 40 different countries.[9] Each year a potluck picnic was held to greet the returning students. In 1955, 125 Chicago area families hosted 275 students from more than 40 different countries. Special attempts were made to ensure all students had a place to go for the holidays, especially Thanksgiving, Christmas, and Easter.

The student hospitality program was one of CFM's most widespread programs and one of the most popular. By 1959, more than 1,300 students were enjoying some form of hospitality from CFMers throughout the United States.[10] These efforts gained notice from other segments of the Church as well. Robert Murphy, director of the Foreign Visitor's Office of the National Catholic Welfare Conference, commended CFM for being "the most active Catholic organization" in welcoming "foreign students and visitors into their homes."[11] But the most important result of the program was the deep and lasting friendships established between foreign students and CFM families. Many students stayed in contact with their families long after they had returned to their native lands. As one Palestinian student put it before he returned to his country, in a statement repeated in similar terms by other students, "It is as hard for me to say good-bye to all these wonderful families I met through CFM as it was when I left home for here."[12] This was typical of the warm relationship that developed between CFMers and their student visitors.

REFUGEES

CFM's concern for the foreigner was not limited to students but was also manifested in its care of refugees. In at least three separate international crises, the CFM family responded to help victims: refugees from the Hungarian revolt and its brutal repression by the Soviet Union in 1956, the Dutch Indonesian crisis of 1959–60, and the 1960–62 Cuban revolution.

When the Bishop's Resettlement Committee of the NCWC called for resettlement help following the Hungarian revolution, CFM rose to the challenge. As usual, Chicago CFM led the way, assisting about forty-five refugees in the Chicago area. Most of the refugees were single men between the ages of seventeen and forty. Chicago CFM worked to find these men jobs and homes and helped them to learn English.[13] Several other CFM groups throughout the United States provided similar assistance.

CFMers became aware of the plight of the Dutch Indonesian refugees as a result of a social inquiry inspired by the fact that 1959 was World Refugee Year. In the mid-1950s, Indonesia achieved its independence from the Netherlands, with the result that Indonesians with Dutch citizenship were driven out. Internationally, the Catholic Church was working on their resettlement. U.S. Immigration would allow Dutch Indonesians special consideration, but each family had to have a U.S. sponsor. A letter asking for sponsors was sent to every diocesan Catholic Charities in the country. Surprisingly, it was a CFM group in St. Cecilia's parish in tiny Beaverton, Oregon, that was the first CFM group to become involved.[14] As Beaverton CFMer Charles Wilber recalls, "Our particular CFM group in Beaverton . . . decided to take one of these families as a pilot case for the diocese. The parish somehow donated a house, which we fixed up. We found a job for the man, raised money, and brought the family over. Then we went around speaking to other parishes. Eventually, about 60 families were brought in."[15] The effort spread to other locales. CFM families ultimately sponsored more than 250 Dutch Indonesian refugee families.

The most interesting program to assist refugees involved those from Castro's revolution in Cuba. What made this so interesting to CFMers was that in some cases CFMers were assisting Cuban CFM families. In the 1950s, CFM had been established in Cuba, where it was known as the Movimiento Familiar Cristiano (MFC). When Castro overthrew the corrupt Batista regime, the Cuban CFM leadership was not averse to the change. (Indeed, Castro himself had been a YCW leader.) In a letter to *ACT* in April 1959 from the Cuban CFM president couple, Gabriel and Beatriz Aurioles, and the secretary couple, Alberto and Esther Gutierrez, the Cuban leaders cautioned against "the false and unfair campaign started in the United States to discredit the course taken by Fidel Castro's revolution." Despite the methods employed by Castro, "it was worse under Batista," who presided over the "most cruel tyranny of our century." While acknowledging that the United States was a strong force against communism, they advised that the U.S. "must understand Castro represents Freedom and . . . Honesty."[16]

By the following year, their attitude had changed dramatically.

Both couples had fled Cuba—the Aurioles to Mexico and the Gutierrezes to the United States.[17] The hopeful prospect of 1959 had been disappointed, leading to a mass exodus out of Cuba. More than 30 percent of the refugees were from the professional class, and they endured many hardships to avoid the communist repression. One refugee lamented, "Really, it is not easy, when you don't speak the language very fluently, and when you are a lawyer, and have always been in the trading business, and you are not a technician, to find work; any kind of work that may permit us to live modestly is much better than to live in fear of a completely totalitarian country."[18]

Ultimately between 50,000 and 60,000 Cuban refugees came to the United States. The CFM response was magnificent. Sponsors for families were obtained, living space found, and jobs provided. Milwaukee CFM assisted 286 refugees; CFM in Canton, Ohio, more than 20 families. At one point, Catholic Relief Services, which played the lead role in the resettlement, needed to resettle thousands of children, most of them teenage boys sent by their parents to avoid the required youth indoctrination camps. The archdiocese of Chicago was asked to take care of 100 refugee children. At a meeting at the Crowleys' home, it was agreed that CFM families would take all 100. Omaha CFM sponsored more than 25 families, leading one Omaha priest to assert that "the resettling of refugees to Omaha is actually in the hands of CFM members."[19] As one community agency head in Canton observed, "The CFM couples were wonderful—they wanted to assume the entire financial load, although they all had growing families."[20] Overall, more than 20 CFM communities assisted in resettling the Cuban refugees.

In both the student and refugee programs CFMers showed that they had become citizens of the world. They opened their homes to the international stranger who was in need of assistance. Whether it was the lonely foreign student or the desperate refugee, CFMers showed they had learned the lessons of the Mystical Body well. Patty Crowley put it more simply: "I think the CFM people learned hospitality."[21] As with most CFM programs, it was not a theoretical knowledge, rather it was knowledge learned through action.

ORGANIZING THE MISSIONARY IMPULSE

CFMers were not content simply to host visitors in their homes. By 1960, CFM sections began to sponsor missionaries in the home and foreign missions. PAVLA (Papal Volunteers for Latin America), AID (Association for International Development), and other Catholic mission groups were supported by CFMers across the country. Beyond material and financial support, CFM inspired many to become missionaries themselves. The administrative assistant for PAVLA in the Chicago area observed in 1965, "My impression is the majority of them [Papal Volunteers] belonged to CFM prior to their PAVLA commitment."[22] The international missionary thrust of CFM parents bore rich fruit in the next generation. CFM children who had grown up with an openness to foreign visitors and an awareness of the world joined groups such as PAVLA, the Grail, Maryknoll, as well as secular groups such as the Peace Corps and, later, VISTA, in large numbers.

Several CFM families left their jobs and committed themselves to a year or more of mission work. More often than not, these CFM missionaries were supported by CFM groups that remained in the United States. Some worked in the home missions. In Oregon, Mr. and Mrs. Edwin P. Smith became full-time lay missionaries with the support of local CFM groups. The group obtained a home for the Smiths to live in rent-free. A small stipend for living expenses was also provided, so the Smiths could be "full-time lay apostles."[23] CFM groups throughout the United States experimented with different forms of home missions and different means of supporting them.

More typical was support of missionaries already stationed in other countries. Since its inception CFM had supported food and clothing drives to assist the foreign missions. Regular drives were also held to obtain medical supplies. As was the case with the home missions, by 1960 CFMers moved beyond simple support to becoming missionaries themselves. In Oregon alone the Beaverton CFM supported the Charles Wilber family's apostolate to Puerto Rico; Salem supplied the Reid Cerny family's mission to Latin America and Henry Woods' efforts in Morocco. These missions were merely an "extension of CFM. To help bring Christ to the underprivileged of the world."[24] St. Charles parish CFM in Albuquerque, New Mexico, supported Dr. Waldo Hanns, his wife, and their four children in their mission to a leper colony in Nigeria. Syosset, New York CFM supported Paul Deibels and the Latin American Mission Program (LAMP). Dallas CFM established "Operation Otomi" to work among the Otomi Indians in the Valle del Mezquital in Hidalgo, Mexico. St. Lawrence CFM in Redondo Beach, California, established a mission to nearby Mexicali (just across the Mexican border), operating "a peace-corps type project" there. They provided clothing, and medical and financial support. Through their efforts a school was constructed and staffed. Regular fundraising events were held in support of the mission. On one occasion, the group sponsored a fiesta to raise money to provide the mission with electricity. In essence, the Mexicali mission was adopted as an ongoing project of Redondo CFM.

Of CFM mission families the most famous was the Ed and Kay Faraday family, whose mission exploits were published periodically in *ACT*. In late 1966, the Faradays, six-year CFM veterans, with their six children, left Harrisburg, Pennsylvania, for the mission fields of Tanzania, East Africa, supported by CFM. Ed began teaching at the seminary while Kay worked as a nurse, ultimately hoping to set up a "training school." They reported being overwhelmed by the "poverty," "illiteracy," and "disease."[25] They set to work establishing a CFM group. They wrote a Swahili-language inquiry book that confronted problems such as polygamy and the young woman's need for a dowry to get married. In April 1968 Kay reported delivering her first baby serving as a midwife in the village. In late 1968 the Faradays' mission came to an abrupt end—their nine-year-old son had been seriously injured in a bicycle accident.

The Faradays returned home amidst an outpouring of support from CFMers across the nation.

Virtually every CFM group throughout the United States supported the home and foreign missions in some manner. As CFM repeatedly emphasized, CFMers could not limit their concerns merely to their own families.

Several things are striking about the CFM mission efforts. First, CFM supported missionaries *and* their families. Families with as many as six or seven children packed up and went to the missions. The solitary missionary was not the CFM model. Second, the mission impulse was stimulated by the simple observation that U.S. CFMers were in a privileged position. As beneficiaries of the affluence of the 1950s, their standard of living far surpassed that of the Third World, and justice demanded efforts to diminish the gap. Third, CFMers realized that the Catholic Church was an international Church. One could not limit one's concerns to one's parish; the Mystical Body demanded otherwise. Finally, in the heated atmosphere of the Cold War, CFMers perceived the efforts of missionaries as means of halting the advance of communism. By providing a positive Christian witness to the developing nations, as they were then called, the lure of communism would be thwarted. Simple condemnations of communism were not effective.

CHRISTIAN FAMILY MISSION VACATION

One of the more innovative and interesting offshoots of the mission impulse was the Christian Family Mission Vacation (CFMV). The CFMV was a "family-to-family" apostolate in which CFM families spent their vacations working in a mission parish under the direction of a mission pastor. In the early 1960s the CFMVers' tasks were many, including parish census work, home visits, teaching religious education classes, manning the trailer chapel, and running Bible camps. The families worked mostly in the poorer regions of Appalachia or the South in what was called "no priest country."[26]

The entire family participated—children and all. Parents were assisted by high school students known as Family Helpers, who babysat the younger children as the parents were out working.

The CFMV program began as an action of a CFM group in Rockford, Illinois. Led by their chaplain, Father William McMahon, four couples—Mark and Betty Conboy, Frank and Millie Zielinski, Dick and Beattie Muraski, and Red and Judi Farrell—spent two weeks working in Statesboro, Georgia, in 1961 with the Reverend John Loftus of the Glenmary Home Mission Society in the parish of St. Matthew. The couples visited some 557 homes for a parish census. This simple contact with many non-Catholics was essential to the mission. As one report observed, "Many citizens of Statesboro are meeting Catholics for the first time in their lives." The meetings were designed to be upbeat and nonconfrontational, to "dispel animosity and prejudice."[27] The prime purpose was not to convert the townspeople but simply to expose them to Catholicism. As a later CFMV handbook would acknowledge, "We are not to convert the world, we are out to give witness to Christ."[28] The emphasis on witness rather than conversion presaged the changes that would come to the Church at large with the Second Vatican Council, changes that were already operating within CFM programs.

Census aside, most of the other work of CFMV was designed simply to create a Catholic presence in an area where the Church was not very visible. One couple drove a trailer chapel to locales with Catholic populations too small to build a church, "just to give the people a chance to see a Catholic Church for the first time in their lives."[29] Barbara and Bernie Uttich with ten children and Jane and Jim Strenski with four children, worked in Claxton, Georgia, calling on fallen-away Catholics in surrounding mission towns. The results: "30 fallen-away Catholic families visited; a universally warm reception from all; and an intense interest and apparent appreciation of the fact that Catholic couples would travel 1,000 miles out of concern for 'fallen-aways.'"[30]

From CFMV's humble beginnings, a substantial program grew. In 1962, 13 families from 5 states participated in the program, increasing to 36 couples from 10 states and Canada in 1963. Nineteen sixty-four was a breakthrough year for CFMV. That year more than 100 couples participated in the program. In addition, Bishop Loras Lane of Rockford relieved Father McMahon of his parochial duties, thus freeing him to direct the movement full-time. The Farrells assumed the role of lay secretary couple. The Glenmary Home Mission Society, involved from the start, formally took over supervision of the program, providing guidance and operating funds.[31] Thus, by 1964 the CFMV was firmly established. It would later come under the auspices of the Foundation for International Cooperation (see below).

Whether or not the mission vacations were successful in bringing back any fallen-away Catholics into the fold, or in converting any of the non-Catholics, the CFMV made a profound impact on the many families which participated. As one CFMV parent observed, "Now the kids know what poverty is. They want to do all they can for these children."[32] Here again, the kids were learning by doing. Another couple observed of one of the homes they were called on to repair, "The place was just a shack, unbelievably filthy because even their few animals lived in the house. We put on windows and screens . . . and painted the place."[33] Yet another couple reflected on "the hopelessness of two girls crippled by polio, living in a lonely mountain cabin; the sorrow of families engulfed by poverty. [We returned home] physically tired out but spiritually enriched. . . . Our children learned that mountain children are no different than themselves, despite lack of material wealth. They learned little ways to give of themselves."[34]

Personal exposure to poverty pulled middle-class Catholic families out of their privileged world into the world of the less fortunate. The results were often dramatic, but even when they were not, no family was able to return to the isolated comfort of middle-class life. They had seen too much. As the 1960s progressed, the CFMV concerned itself less with creating a Catholic presence, through such activities as the parish census, and spent more effort on building schools and churches, repairing homes, and projects of that sort.

Though the CFMV was designed to be a vacation with a purpose it was meant to be part vacation. One report observed that "side benefits of the vacation were two weeks of family fun, including swimming, tennis, volley ball, badminton, picnics, trips to the ocean."[35] Besides such ordinary fun, there were the subtler joys. One couple recalled "the astonishment on an eleven-year-old's face seeing the first birthday cake of his life; the joy of fifty children having all the lemonade and hot dogs they could consume."[36]

Through the 1960s hundreds of CFM couples "vacationed" in various parts of Appalachia and the South, with some even venturing into Mexico.

FOUNDATION FOR INTERNATIONAL COOPERATION (FIC)

The international and mission thrust of CFM was further made manifest in the creation of the Foundation for International Cooperation (FIC), an organization initiated and supported by CFM. At the 1960 summer meeting of the national Coordinating Committee, Katherine and Martin Quigley, Jr., of New York and David O'Shea of Chicago proposed the creation of a "lay missionary foundation." The Coordinating Committee endorsed the following mission statement for the FIC: The goal of the FIC was to be "the collection and dissemination of information concerning all phases of lay missionary work and hospitality for overseas students and visitors," and "the provision of financial aid to selected projects of the international lay apostolate and the home missions."[37]

FIC was an independent organization that managed and funded itself, though it continued to be supported by CFM at the local level. In July 1960, the national Coordinating Committee approved sponsorship of FIC, and the following year, 1961, FIC was incorporated as a nonprofit organization in the state of Illinois and continued to receive wide exposure in *ACT* and at national conventions. The FIC was given office space at the CFM headquarters in Chicago.

Under the leadership of the Quigleys, the O'Sheas, and, later, Ann Marten, who served as executive secretary, the FIC spread quickly. By the beginning of 1963, the FIC had established branch offices in Buffalo, Portland, Oregon, and New York, and by the end of the following year it had twelve branches, including offices in Erie, Pennsylvania, Boston, Miami, and San Francisco. In locales without a branch office, the FIC asked each CFM federation to provide a contact person.

The FIC moved quickly to consolidate and provide support to two of CFM's most popular programs—the International Student and Visitor Program and the Christian Family Mission Vacation. The FIC's first significant action involved international students. Citing a *Wall Street Journal* article which said that of the 60,000 foreign students in the United States more than half would go home mad at the United States as a result of their experience, Chicago FIC created a summer job-placement program for international students that would give the students a more intimate knowledge of American life, as well as some income to allow them to live more comfortably. FIC members approached local businessmen to provide job opportunities. During summer 1962, the FIC found jobs for 110 students in Chicago with 65 different firms.[38] Similar programs were quickly set up in FIC's branch offices.

In 1961, the FIC also conducted a major study of African students at universities in the United States, a study funded by the National Catholic Conference for Interracial Justice. The study identified these major needs: better and more financial assistance in the form of scholarships, better U.S. advisors, better sources of information about the United States, and better relations and communication between African and U.S. students. FIC and national CFM encouraged local federations to "get practical" about these findings. One result of this call was the creation of the first African student organization for women, which held its first meeting in December 1961 at Trinity College in Washington, D.C.

FIC's efforts were not limited to college students. One of the FIC's most popular programs was a high school student-exchange program that grew out of the Buffalo branch of the FIC. Robert and Jo Noonan of Buffalo worked out an agreement with the CFM president in Quito, Ecuador, to begin a high school student-exchange program. The following year the program expanded to include Bogotá, Colombia. By 1964, CFM families were hosting 133 South American students from Ecuador and Colombia for a period of ten weeks. The same year 57 Buffalo students visited Ecuador and Colombia.[39] This openness to international visitors and to international travel and exchange was a trademark of CFM by the early 1960s.

The FIC also looked to support lay missionaries in foreign countries. Early on, they conducted a study to determine the needs of lay mission volunteers. The FIC supported Dr. Al Fonder, a dentist from Sterling, Illinois, who toured fourteen South American countries with a view to establishing a dental and medical family mission vacation. The program was begun shortly after he completed his study.[40]

As the 1960s progressed, the FIC increasingly became involved with the educational aspect of international relations. It sponsored foreign groups such as La Vie Nouvelle from France on tours throughout the United States. These tours typically housed visitors with CFM families, rather than in hotels. It also sponsored annual World Study Tours. For instance, in 1969, one tour visited India, Thailand, Hong Kong, the Philippines, and Japan. As with many of FIC's and CFM's efforts, the study tour was to expand the vision and experience of the participant. As the *FIC News Notes* observed, "It is through personal encounters that one's attitudes toward other countries are best formed. . . . [T]hese encounters are meaningful . . . [and] advance international understanding, an important step to world peace."[41] By the early 1970s the FIC focused primarily on student exchanges and study tours.

WORLD IMPORTS, INC.

Another offshoot of CFM that came under the umbrella of the FIC was World Imports, Inc., a small business designed to sell Third-

World workers' handmade goods. The idea was to generate enough income to pay the workers a living wage that would allow them to take care of their families. By thwarting the economic conditions that enabled communism to flourish, World Imports was to be another means of slowing the communist advance.

The program began in 1960, when the Reverend Varghese Chathaparampil of Kerala State, South India, came to Los Angeles looking for a distributor for the cocoa doormats made by the workers in his cooperative, the Institute of St. Joseph and Youth Center. In Los Angeles, he stayed with veteran CFMers Ned and Louise Taylor. After failing in his attempt to find a distributor, he persuaded the Taylors to take up the task. The initial arrangement was named India-California Imports. A warehouse was established, doormats obtained, and the business begun. After several years of mild growth, Taylor expanded the company to include handicrafts from Mexico and Haiti. By June 1964, the operation was incorporated as World Imports, with a board of directors that included Taylor as president, Patrick Crowley as vice-president, and Los Angeles CFM members Dan Lucey and Herb Springer serving as board members.[42] In the early days the business depended greatly on CFM volunteer help, a contribution that led to the company's success. By 1965 the company moved into its own warehouse in San Fernando. By the early 1970s, sales reached $187,000 per year.[43] The success of World Imports rests largely with the efforts of Ned Taylor. As Rose Lucey concluded, "His honest persuasion brought World Imports a bevy of faithful customers, many of whom appreciated his philosophy of helping people to help themselves."[44]

THE CAROTA FAMILY: CITIZENS OF THE WORLD

No family embodied the CFM notion of the family as citizens of the world better than that of Mario and Estelle Carota. Described by Rose Lucey as a "familiar and famous family"[45] and by another veteran CFM couple as "strange and wonderful," the Carotas presented a startling figure at the national conventions with their seventeen children (eleven adopted). Mario worked for the University of

California Radiation Laboratory until the nature of the work became incompatible with his conscience.

Mario and Estelle purchased a large apple farm in Aptos, California, which they dubbed Agnus Dei Farm, where they raised their children and entertained guests. They became good friends with a priest of the archdiocese of San Francisco named John Garcia. Garcia, known as a deeply spiritual man, had been working among the Mexican migrant workers in California since the early 1950s. At the 1958 Notre Dame Convention, Garcia called for a national project for CFM that would engage the "senior CFMers." The project would give CFM "unity and purpose."

The Carotas responded to Garcia's challenge by organizing a mission vacation (two years before CFMV), to Tacuba, near Mexico City. As the Carotas later remembered, "We felt CFM should send and support families to work in poorer countries." And as was typical of the Carotas, they decided to "do it first ourselves."[46] Contacting a Father Francis Marin, s.j., in Mexico, the Carotas planned a joint project with MFC (Mexican CFM) and California CFM. In July 1959 the Carotas packed up an old school bus and led a contingent of seven adults and nineteen children to the slums of Tacuba for a six-week "vacation." There, while being hosted by MFC families, they worked nine hours a day to build a training center for local workers. Reflecting on the effort, the Carotas explained, "the work of clergy and religious was good, but we felt better ways of helping people had to be developed. We had to begin to work with them in ways that we, the rich, did not predetermine, but, instead, in the ways that people wanted to be helped."[47] They were to "work, not preach."[48]

The trip was a CFM venture from start to finish—the Carotas left for Mexico following a regional meeting of CFM in California, and the trip finished with a journey to Notre Dame for the annual CFM convention in August. Again, the Carota project reflected CFMers' awareness of their responsibility as citizens of the world and of their privileged position residing in the richest nation in the world.

The Carotas became involved early on in the FIC, with Mario serving as a vice president. In 1961, under the auspices of the FIC, the Carotas planned another mission to Actipan, Mexico, this time with assistance from twenty students from Yale University. Again, the Carotas and their troupe were hosted by MFC families, and again they built a school and a "family life center."[49] The trip not only produced needed buildings for the Actipan community, it also gave the students a vital way of "learning through participation."[50] In keeping with the newly formed CFMV, the Carotas believed that "families are the best ministers."[51]

The following year, the Carotas sponsored a "reverse mission," in which students from Mexico traveled to Fowler, California, near Fresno, to help Mexican farmworkers build a church. For nine months the students worked, and "built the community as they built the church."[52]

In 1965, the Carotas began one of their more quixotic journeys, traveling to Rome during the Vatican Council in the hopes of establishing an international family life center. While there, they met with Pope Paul VI. Unfortunately, they ran out of money, and had no way of getting back to the United States. They were finally assisted by an American priest who "found" $2,000, which enabled the Carotas to return to the United States.[53]

The Carotas later moved to Canada during the Vietnam War to be with their sons, who opposed the war.

The Carotas continue their ministry to the present day. They recently published a book entitled *We Shall Raise Our Voice Again,* which is part memoir and part harangue against the Church's practice of usury. Typical of the Carota style, the book has stamped on the cover "FOR LAY PEOPLE ONLY." This is not the place for the Carota biography. Rather their story represents the best of the CFM missionary impulse. Refusing to accept a complacent, self-satisfied lifestyle they epitomized the risk-taking and trust in God that characterized so many CFM families. As Mario advised, "Go abroad without the aid of the government or corporations. God provides, despite sickness, hardships and differences in personalities. American

FIVE

The Movement
Goes International

From its earliest days CFM had stressed that Catholic really meant *catholic*, and that the doctrine of the Mystical Body, which underlay so much of CFM thinking, required Catholics to take an inclusive view of the world. In the previous chapter, we saw how CFMers as "citizens of the world" received foreign visitors and refugees and supported foreign mission work. It did not take long for CFM to "go international" in yet another way. By the early 1960s CFM had spread to all six continents, with particularly active groups in Canada, Latin America, and the Philippines. Canada became interested in family Catholic Action as early as 1946, when the Crowleys were invited to visit Saskatchewan, although the movement did not begin in earnest there until the early 1950s.

By 1964, CFM had groups operating in more than forty other countries: Hong Kong, Thailand, Japan, Formosa, Nigeria, Uganda, Korea, England, India, the Philippines, New Zealand, Poland, Ceylon, Denmark, Spain, France, Belgium, Germany, South Africa, Australia, Malta, Singapore, Ireland, the Bahamas, Haiti, Puerto Rico, Trinidad, the Virgin Islands, South Vietnam, Tanganyika, the Congo, and most of the Latin American countries—Mexico, Argentina, Uruguay, Ecuador, Chile, Venezuela, Peru, Bolivia, Colombia, Brazil, Paraguay, Honduras, Guatemala, Costa Rica, El Salvador, Nicaragua, and Panama.

CFM spread to all these countries in a variety of ways. Many students who had experienced CFM hospitality while studying in the United States returned home and began groups of their own.

Naturally, they contacted the national headquarters in Chicago for materials and assistance. Other groups began when an interested couple or priest wrote or visited the Crowleys. The Crowley dinner table was always an interesting place, with guests from all over the world discussing CFM, the Church, and the world. These couples, too, began groups when they returned to their countries. Priests who had experienced CFM while studying or on assignment in the U.S. often started groups when they went home. U.S. lay missionaries who wanted to use the CFM method began groups in the communities in which they worked. Some groups were begun by U.S. military personnel who were stationed overseas.

Most dramatic was the world travel of the Crowleys, CFM's ambassadors. Typical of their travel was the six-week trip they took at the beginning of 1956. Patty Crowley remembers, "I'll never forget the first trip. It was on a Pan Am prop plane, and I was scared to death. We had berths then. I did not sleep all night. It took us all night to get to Hawaii. We arrived and I was absolutely exhausted. And right away we had a meeting."[1] Their trip covered the Far East, India, and Europe. Included on their itinerary were Los Angeles, Hawaii, Tokyo, Osaka, Hong Kong, Manila, Saigon, Singapore, Ceylon, Bombay and southern India, Beirut, Damascus, Jordan, Jerusalem, Cairo, Libya, Malta, Rome, Zurich, Denmark, Belgium, Paris, and London.[2] Ten years later, in 1966, the Crowleys traveled around the world twice, went to Rome three times, and to South America once. Despite their exhausting schedule, everywhere they went—and they certainly went everywhere—the Crowleys encouraged groups that had already begun, and fostered new groups where there were none. As had been the case with the CFM in the United States, the Crowleys were the apostles of CFM's worldwide expansion.

CANADA

By far the most successful international branch of CFM was Canada. Indeed, Canada was not treated as a separate entity the way other foreign nations were; rather, it was incorporated into the structure of U.S. CFM. Canada was represented on the national Coordinating Committee, and after 1958 it always had at least one couple on the national Program Committee. By 1964, Canada was divided into four areas equal in status to the fifteen U.S. areas: (1) British Columbia and Alberta, (2) Saskatchewan and Manitoba, (3) Quebec and Ontario, and (4) the Maritime Provinces. Thus, Canadian couples played an integral role in the development of U.S. CFM, or what might be more appropriately called North American CFM. In 1967, Canadian CFM would break off and establish its own national structure, but it continued to use the U.S. CFM program materials. At its height, Canadian CFM counted more than 3,000 couples.

Origins in Canada

CFM came to Canada through the efforts of Al and Lettie Morse of Aylmer. In 1951, the Morses were introduced to CFM through reading an article in a popular Catholic magazine. They had just moved from Winnipeg with their six children, and CFM seemed to them an ideal organization to start in Canada. Not knowing how to proceed, they wrote to the Crowleys in Chicago, who sent them copies of *For Happier Families* and other materials. The Morses then approached several other young couples in similar circumstances, and Canadian CFM was born. They were encouraged by their pastor, a French Canadian, who was enthusiastic about Catholic Action. Their first chaplain was Father Bisson.

The Morses kept the Crowleys informed of their progress, and in 1952 Al became the first person outside the United States to attend a Coordinating Committee meeting, leading Pat Crowley to comment that the movement was "now truly international."[3]

As was the case with U.S. CFM, the early expansion of CFM in Canada is a bit hazy. By the end of 1951, groups had sprung up in Regina, Saskatchewan, begun by Dave and Mary O'Connor, and in Windsor and Chatham, Ontario. In 1952, the Crowleys made a trip to Canada, speaking at various locations including Toronto and Combermere, Ontario.[4] More groups began.

About this time, the Morses heard from a couple from Toronto,

Charles and Kathy Connolly. The Connollys had also read about the movement, and had also written to the Crowleys. At the Crowleys' urging they went to Aylmer to meet the Morses. Excited by what they observed, the Connollys returned to Toronto and with the assistance of their mentor, Basilian Father John Ruth, began one of the first groups there.

While the Morses brought CFM to Canada, it was the Connollys who were most responsible for its spread throughout Canada. The Connollys, much like the Crowleys, used personal contact as the chief means of expanding the movement. Like Pat Crowley, Charlie worked for his family's company, which gave him a good deal of freedom to travel about Canada pushing CFM. Also like the Crowleys, the Connolly dinner table always featured several guests in addition to family members. In contrast to the Crowleys, the Connollys had a "low-key, soft-spoken style."[5] Nonetheless, their seemingly endless energy and their example were highly effective. One former CFMer noted that she had "never seen a couple more active" than the Connollys.[6] The Connollys also had the gift of making the person or group they were with feel as if they were the most important thing in the world. Kathy Connolly's simple dictum was, "Nothing matters except the person you bring into your home."[7] Other concerns would have to wait. The Connollys rightfully are referred to as "Mr. and Mrs. CFM" of Canada. In 1967, they would become the first Executive Secretary Couple for Canada.

The founder of CFM in Montreal was not even married. Following World War II, English-born Tony Walsh had traveled to British Columbia to work with Native American groups. He then journeyed to Montreal, where he began working in the less desirable parts of the city. He established Benedict Labre House, which, like Dorothy Day's Catholic Worker houses provided shelter for homeless persons, and ran a soup kitchen. Walsh, who became noted for his great personal holiness, wanted to assist senior men who were finding it difficult to live on their meager pensions.

He also came into contact with many young couples who provided food or served at his soup kitchen. Sometime in the early

1950s, he called a group of them together and urged them to begin a CFM section. The group met several times, then each couple went off to start an action group, and thus was Montreal CFM born. By 1953, a federation had been established.[8]

By 1958, CFM in Canada was flourishing. Groups were operating in London, Ontario, Ottawa, Toronto, Sarnia, Charlottetown, Moose Jaw, Saskatoon, Regina, Windsor, Tecumseh, Belle River, Montreal, Vancouver, Halifax, Calgary, Winnipeg, St. John, and Aylmer. Groups were springing up throughout Canada.

A Canadian National Structure

Canadian CFM prospered as part of U.S. CFM through the early 1960s, but as it continued to expand, the notion of a Canadian national structure began to be explored. Not everyone wanted to change; many Canadians thought things were just fine as they were. The prochange advocates, who ultimately prevailed, put forth two main arguments: Change was needed to promote and sustain the enormous growth of the early 1960s; CFM could make a greater impact in Canada with a national organization. The notion was first officially discussed in August 1964 at a semiannual national Coordinating Committee meeting in Poughkeepsie, New York. No consensus was reached.[9] The same year, Montreal hosted the first Canadian area convention (Quebec and Ontario), at Loyola College of Montreal. More than 200 couples and 125 children attended. Featured speaker was Paul-Emile Cardinal Léger. The convention was organized by Ted and Pat Radigan and Mike and Muriel Dumaresq.

The move for a Canadian structure grew when the Coordinating Committee met in June 1966 in Toronto, the first time they had convened on Canadian soil. Several "Canadian-only" meetings were held, and a sense of "Canadian CFM" grew. Notes from the meeting record, "No decisions, but a lot of good discussion on structure, programming, and Area problems."[10]

According to Isabelle and Rolly Leroux, national sentiment

increased in 1967, when Montreal hosted the World's Fair known as "Expo '67." "[T]his event was a truly national event, since it was Canada's centennial year."[11] In June 1967, Canadian Area leaders and chaplains met in Winnipeg. At this meeting, a national structure was organized. Kathleen and Charles Connolly were selected Canadian executive secretary couple, with Mike and Muriel Dumaresq of Montreal serving as the first national secretary-treasurer. Toronto was to be headquarters. Jim and Margaret Beaubien from Victoria, Larry and Loraine Henerling of Winnipeg, and Cletus and Edna Murphy of Charlottetown completed the Executive Committee. The arrangement was ratified at the 1967 Notre Dame Convention. Father John Ruth was named the first national chaplain. Canadian CFM also became one of the charter members of the ICCFM, of which more will be said later.

The entire structure was ratified in 1968 at a meeting in Ottawa. Canada was divided into 7 areas: (1) British Columbia, (2) Alberta, (3) Saskatchewan, (4) Manitoba, (5) Ontario, (6) Quebec, (7) Maritime Provinces. Each area was to elect an area couple to be on the Canadian Executive Committee and an area chaplain. Canadian CFM remained affiliated with U.S. CFM and continued to use U.S. programming materials. No Canadian Program Committee was ever established.

Canadians continued to be part of the U.S. national Program Committee—Al and Lettie Morse were the first, followed by Vivian and Grant Maxwell, Bernard and Mae Daly, and finally Monsignor Dennis Murphy in the early 1970s. Canadians also participated actively at the national conventions at the University of Notre Dame. Indeed, the Notre Dame convention provided the one time many Canadian CFMers got to meet with one another. According to the Lerouxes, "most communication between Canadian areas occurred at Notre Dame conventions."[12]

The Connollys served as executive secretary until 1970. By that time Kathy was quite sick, so the Connollys turned the reins over to Mike and Muriel Dumaresq, who served only one year. In 1971, they were replaced by Rolly and Isabelle Leroux. In 1973, the

Lerouxes became Canadian representatives to ICCFM, and so Malcolm and Fran Peake became executive secretary couple. Father Ruth was replaced as national chaplain by John Carley in 1970. In 1973, Father Gerald Reilly replaced Carley.

Ironically, the Canadian national structure was in place just as CFM in Canada was undergoing serious decline. By 1972, when Canada held its first national convention at Regina, Saskatchewan, national membership had declined to 600 couples. National conventions were held biennially, at Toronto in 1974, at Montreal in 1976, and in London, Ontario, in 1978. By 1980, membership would hover around 100 couples, and the movement in Canada was all but finished.

Canadian Actions

Canadian CFMers were reputed to be more "with it" than their U.S. counterparts when it came to social action. The social progressivism of Canada contrasted sharply with the rugged individualism of the United States. However, most CFM actions in Canada were not greatly different from actions by CFMers in the United States and, as one CFMer put it, "were hardly world shaking at all."[13] Baby-sitter services were begun, Cana Conferences sponsored, international students invited home for dinners, and so on. In Montreal, one group organized to eliminate the "foul language" of some of the older boys at a local skating rink. CFMers became more active in civic and social affairs. Many ran for school boards or other elective offices. In 1967, *ACT* published a list of activities undertaken by Canadian groups that year. Actions ranged from inviting foreign visitors to their homes in Antigonish to improving relations with local Indians in Truro, to visiting a mental hospital and assisting in patient outings in Ajax, to assisting at Charity House, a "citywide home for the down-and-out," in London, to working for better housing for the poor in Lazare.[14]

Several actions took a particularly Canadian cast. Many Canadian groups were disaffected by the yearly inquiries that focused on race

(1957–58 and 1964–65). They complained that the inquiries dealt too much with black-white relations, which did not apply to the Canadian situation. After some reflection, the Canadian groups adapted the inquiry to the relationship with the Native Peoples of Canada. Many CFMers made personal contact with Indians for the first time. The focus became increasingly important as many Indians began to move into urban areas during the 1960s. Other CFM groups addressed the problems of other people of color, namely, Asian and Caribbean immigrants, who were being met with increasing hostility. As in the U.S., Canadian CFMers worked to improve the conditions and treatment of these minorities.

One long-standing tension was between English-speaking and French-speaking in Quebec. The Morses' CFM members in Aylmer worked at promoting better understanding between the two groups. One of their most striking actions was to send their children to the French-speaking grade schools. The result: bilingual children and a better understanding between French- and English-speaking.

One of the most enduring actions undertaken by Canadian CFM was that of a Toronto group, which purchased 75 acres just south of Owens Sound in Ontario in 1969. There they established Camp Kumontome, literally "Christian Family Holiday." The camp consisted of five cabins, a chapel, an arts and crafts cabin, several other communal buildings, a small lake, and plenty of woods. A chaplain was always in residence. The camp gave families an inexpensive vacation, mixing wholesome recreation with religious reflection. The camp was an enormous success and continues to operate as of 1997.[15]

This brief outline in no way does full credit to the energy and importance of Canadian CFM. Much of the Canadian contribution to CFM was not as "Canadian CFM"; rather, it was part of the larger movement headquartered in Chicago. Canadian CFMers held important positions in the Executive, Coordinating, and Program Committees, and thus made a major impact. Their story is incorporated in the basic story of CFM.

LATIN AMERICA—
MOVIMIENTO FAMILIAR CRISTIANO

One of the most striking CFM foundations was in Latin America.[16] Though the first Latin American group began in Buenos Aires, Argentina, in 1948, the real beginning of CFM in Latin America is dated from 1952 in Montevideo, Uruguay. The designation of "founder" is often given to Father Pedro Richards, who hosted a retreat out of which MFC grew. Here, too, the hand of the Crowleys can be seen.[17] It was they who had introduced Father Richards to CFM, when Father Pedro had found his way to Pat's law office in Chicago (it was, after all, the official address of the movement at the time) during a trip to the United States. Predictably, he was invited to the Crowley home for dinner. Again, predictably, he began the Movimiento Familiar Cristiano (MFC), as Latin American CFM was known, upon his return to Uruguay.

From that point on, Montevideo provided the leadership and the drive for MFC's expansion.[18] Uruguay held its first national convention in 1954. By 1957, more than 1,000 copies of the Spanish translation of *For Happier Families (Por una Familia Mas Feliz)* had been distributed in South America.[19]

By 1957, MFC had expanded to such a degree that the first "Inter-American" meeting of MFC was held in Montevideo in late June. Uruguay, Argentina, Chile, Peru, Spain, Venezuela, Bolivia, Colombia, Mexico, Paraguay, and Puerto Rico were all represented at the assembly. The Crowleys were also present, representing the U.S. The MFC, like its counterpart in the United States, was on the cutting edge of the liturgical movement. Each day at the convention the dialogue Mass was offered with the altar and celebrant facing the people. MFC, as reported at the assembly, existed in many varieties, not all of which placed significant emphasis on social action. The most common action reported was the sponsoring of a couples' retreat.[20] Nonetheless, the inter-American meeting created a spirit of cooperation and support among the many Latin American CFM groups.

Another inter-American meeting was planned for 1960, setting in motion a three-year cycle, with additional meetings in 1963, 1966, and 1970. The 1963 "Latin American Assembly of CFM" was held in Rio de Janeiro with more than 800 couples, 350 priests, and 15 bishops attending. Mario Carota was there as an observer for U.S. CFM. The Assembly reflected the blend of moral conservatism and social progressivism that marked the early days of U.S. CFM. It published a manifesto to halt the "Avalanche of Immorality," while at the same convention the revered archbishop Dom Helder Camara stressed the Christian social obligations to the poor.[21]

MFC had truly come of age by 1963, with an estimated 30,000 couples, with the leading nations being Argentina (8,000 couples), Mexico (6,000 couples), Brazil (5,000 couples), Chile (2,000 couples), Uruguay (2,000 couples), and Venezuela (1,000 couples).[22] Father Richards remained the moderator for Latin American CFM. Two significant pairs of lay leaders emerged. Federico and Hortensia Soneira continued Uruguay's important role in the inter-American movement, and Jose "Pepe" and Luzma Alvarez Icaza rose to the leadership of MFC in Mexico. Mexican CFM was one of the fastest-growing federations in the Americas. It was the Alvarez Icazas who laid the groundwork for a world merger of all CFM groups. More will be said later of their brainchild, the International Confederation of Christian Family Movements (ICCFM).

In 1966, Latin American CFM hosted its fourth inter-American congress in Caracas, Venezuela. Members from twenty-one nations attended. Several significant events occurred. At this congress a split surfaced. The secretary of Latin American CFM and president of Mexican CFM, Jose Alvarez Icaza, called for CFM to reach out to the marginalized in society, to the social outcasts. "We have to reform our attitudes regarding situations considered dangerous, contaminating. Let us all become contaminated. Let us all have the Christian boldness to stretch out our hand to the divorcees, social outcasts, so as to bring Christian love to them all."[23] Mexican CFM advocated "direct involvement in the problems of the community." In opposition to this emphasis was the founder of Latin American

CFM, Father Richards. He stressed that the movement should focus on the "development of family spirituality."[24] A similar conflict had erupted at the U.S. CFM national convention at Notre Dame in 1961. The split was a creative tension that always confronted the movement.

Ralph and Reggie Weissert of South Bend, U.S. CFM observers at the 1966 congress, believed the "family spirituality" faction had the upper hand. They observed, "Latin American CFM is a different brand than that existing in the United States. Their concentration is more on family life and there is practically no involvement in social action."[25] One group with whom the Weisserts spoke believed that the Scripture-Liturgy inquiries were the most important part of the meeting. The Weisserts wrote, "We tried to convince them otherwise." Given the political situation of most Latin American countries—twelve of the eighteen nations were ruled by military juntas or leaders propped up by the military—significant social action was not just difficult, it could be downright dangerous.

Beyond the conflict, the conference did highlight some significant contributions of Latin American CFM. First, it was noted that the MFC has "raised the social consciousness" of many members of the middle class in Latin America. Second, CFM had contributed to the "equalizing" of the wife within the family.[26] This was particularly important in a culture where one of the main challenges to family life is machismo.

Finally, the Caracas congress was the site of the first official merger of Latin American CFM and U.S. CFM, resulting in MFC-CFM, which would grow to be ICCFM.

THE PHILIPPINES

CFM also spread across the Pacific to the Philippines, though growth was slow during the 1950s. The founders of Philippine CFM were Tony and Teresa Nieva of Forbes Park, Manila. Sometime in the mid-1950s the Nievas came to the United States. There, Cana founder Father John Delaney sent them to meet the Crowleys.

The Nievas were completely taken with the Crowleys' description of CFM. In 1956, during the Crowleys' world tour, they spent three days with the Nievas in Manila. Together, they met with the archbishop of Manila, Rufino J. Santos, who gave his permission for the establishment of CFM in the Philippines. Shortly after the meeting, the Nievas met with seven other couples in their home, and Filipino CFM was born.

CFM spread slowly, but after one year a national federation was formed and national officers elected. The U.S. introductory text, *For Happier Families* was adapted for use. From 1960 to 1966, a Philippine program committee simply revised the annual U.S. program book published out of Chicago to fit the local needs. By 1966, the Philippine program committee was ready to write its first original program. The program's focus was "four centuries of Christianization in the Philippines," and it asked the question, "To what extent had Christianity actually taken hold in the Philippines?" The themes for the next three years were education, family, and politics. Most significantly, the 1970 program took a close look at the proposed constitutional convention to be held in the Philippines that year.

At the end of 1970, Philippine CFM issued a bold "Manifesto" entitled "We Can No Longer Sit and Watch and Wait." The manifesto warned that the nation faced a violent revolution unless dramatic change and reform occurred soon. "We believe that if purposive Christian action is not undertaken NOW, our country may be engulfed in a violent revolution. . . . We, therefore, take a stand and manifest these our firm convictions: We join the youth in their legitimate demands to correct the social, political, economic and religious ills in our country. In particular:—We demand a nonpartisan Constitutional Convention and the adoption of a truly Filipino Constitution."[27] The manifesto then called for a more equitable distribution of wealth in the country and an end to graft and corruption in the Filipino government. In 1971, CFM discussed these issues "at great length with Mrs. Imelda Marcos," but its call for significant reform would not bear fruit until more than a decade and a half later.

By 1968, when the Philippines joined the ICCFM, the movement's membership peaked with slightly more than 4,000 couples. By 1973, that number had declined to about 3,000 couples. Like CFM in other countries the Philippine CFM struggled with the family versus social-action debate. And in a nation where class divisions were deep, many questioned the elite character of CFM, the majority of whose members were middle or upper class and mostly college-educated. How was CFM to become a mass movement?[28]

JAPAN

Peter and Emko Sawada founded CFM in Japan. Peter had encountered CFM while pursuing graduate study at the University of Purdue in Indiana. Upon his return to Japan, he began a group in August 1952 in Tokyo. The first group was quite elite. Peter reported in 1953 that their section meeting was held at the "Palace of Our Crown Prince." The group included one of the prince's chamberlains, the niece of the emperor, and the daughter of the prime minister.

CFM spread slowly, using mimeographed translations of *For Happier Families*. The Sawadas were joined by John and Mary Nakamura as leaders in Tokyo CFM. Japan CFM confronted some basic cultural issues. One problem was mixed marriages. In the United States a mixed marriage generally meant two Christian denominations; in Japan it usually meant a Catholic with a partner who was Shinto or Buddhist. Religion aside, CFM called upon members to break with powerful traditions. A CFM meeting might be the only place where husband and wife sat together. As Sawada reported, "This system of CFM is entirely new to us."[29] Nonetheless, CFM husbands were committed "to share with their wives despite the strong tradition against this."[30] He concluded, "Now our wives walk alongside us, instead of behind us husbands, which surprises many people."[31] He also reported that CFM increased communication between couples in the parish.

Despite its successes, CFM was never a major movement in Japan, in part because Japan has so few Catholics. By 1970, CFM was present in fifteen parishes in Japan, with about eighty couples participating.

INDIA

CFM came to India in 1956. According to one report, it was introduced to India after a Father Dalmeida visited the Crowleys while studying at Notre Dame. Then, during their trip around the world, the Crowleys met Father Angelo Fernandes in Bombay, who worked to establish the movement there. Fernandes later became the archbishop of New Delhi. CFM spread slowly. One of the early problems reported was that the homes of CFMers could not begin to hold the entire group.[32] Typical of CFM, one of the earliest actions of the initial CFM group was to take in an orphan over the Christmas holidays.

By 1968, only eleven CFM units survived, but by 1971 the movement had grown to 250 couples, and *FHF* had been translated into Hindi. Leadership of Indian CFM fell to Joe and Margaret D'Silva.

AFRICA

CFM also spread to Africa. By 1956, groups had been established in Tanganyika (begun during Advent, 1955), Transvaal, South Rhodesia, and Uganda.[33] CFM had been introduced to Uganda by Father Joseph Kalibeala, who transformed an existing family group into CFM by translating *FHF* into the native language.[34] One obstacle to growth there lay in the fact that the Catholic Church was regarded as a "foreign object" and so was often discarded by socially mobile Ugandans. CFM was introduced into Nigeria in 1958 by Edward and Bessie Taiwo. They had first encountered CFM while in the United States at one of the Crowleys' famous dinner parties. When they returned to Nigeria they began a group.[35]

As in other nations, CFM spread gradually. In Africa, however,

CFM faced perhaps its biggest problem in adapting the program to the local scene. The deeply rooted tribal and extended family traditions were in direct conflict with the modern, democratic family encouraged by CFM. One CFM missionary chaplain in Malawi complained of the "pagan atmosphere of their family life, with their taboos, fears, initiation rites, etc."[36] The problem of the woman's dowry was a major concern, but CFM found it could do little to affect this local custom because it was woven into the fabric of family and tribal economies. Equally as troubling was the second-class status of women. One of the early actions of one African CFM group was "man and wife do activities together . . . husbands must help their wives in a certain number of household duties, without consideration for human respect."[37] CFM's adaptation to Africa would have to take into account the much different family structure and customs of the African family.

NEW ZEALAND

CFM came to New Zealand in 1955. By 1961, New Zealand CFM had 900 couples and held its first national convention. More than 300 couples attended. By 1965, CFM had grown to 1,300 couples in 78 parishes.

WORLD CFM

By 1966, CFM had spread to almost all the corners of the world, and was present in more than fifty nations. The driving force behind this expansion was, once again, the Crowleys, who envisioned a world movement that would work to make it easier for families to flourish throughout the world. In a message to an MFC meeting in Bogotá in 1968, the Crowleys wrote, "It is in the family we must begin. Today's family contains within it the possibility of Christian revolution. It is for all of us, the families of the world, to make that revolution a reality."[38] The Crowleys were sensitive to the many pressures placed on families in "developing nations," in nations torn by war or subjected to authoritarian rule, communist or otherwise. Still, they stressed certain similarities between all families in the world. "We have found that almost all couples share similar aspirations. They yearn for better communications with one another. They are anxious for better communications with their children and with their neighbors. The desirability of dialogue was recognized wherever we went."[39] To solve the problems that confronted the families of the world, the Crowleys offered CFM.

One criticism leveled at the Crowleys was they did not understand the complexities of family life throughout the world. Many felt they were overly optimistic about the similarities of families in other nations. More seriously, some complained that the Crowleys were bound by a Western, middle-class concept of family life that they sought to superimpose on the rest of the world. They particularly underestimated the problem of the status of women in many countries. While women in the United States might bemoan their lack of equality with men, women in many other nations were still fighting for simple human respect.

CFM did make some breakthroughs in this area, as already suggested, in Japan and Africa. Father Richards reported a similar success in Guatemala. "We had tried everything to change the centuries-old ways of the Indian home where the woman is practically a slave. Now that we have a few hundred Indian families in CFM, the husband has not only stopped beating his wife, but he lets her talk and even listens to her advice."[40] Despite such modest triumphs, the status of women would be a major problem for world CFM. It was to be a major topic of the meeting of world CFM, "Familia '74" held in Tanzania (see below).

Nonetheless, the Crowleys' dynamism spread the gospel of CFM far and wide. The movement and its methods did appeal to people throughout the world. By 1966, it had spread around the globe. In that year, a merger was effected between the Latin American MFC and U.S. CFM, creating the basis for what would become the International Confederation of Christian Family Movements (ICCFM).

SIX

The Movement Matures: Self-Criticism and Critics

As CFM entered the 1960s, the movement was flourishing. Membership had reached more than forty thousand couples, with thousands more in the ranks of the alumni. CFM had penetrated nearly every major diocese in the United States. It was time for the movement to pause and to reflect on where it was headed and where it should be headed.

In early 1960, Don Thorman, the editor of *ACT* (and future editor of the *National Catholic Reporter*), at the urging of the national Coordinating Committee, invited CFMers to assess the movement. It was believed that "self-criticism" was "healthy" and a "sign of maturity."[1] Indeed, chaplain Dennis Geaney saw "the relentless spirit of self-criticism" as "a most hopeful omen."[2] Without self-criticism, the movement might grow complacent. One thing CFMers were never complacent about was offering their opinions, nor were they shy about critiquing of the state of the movement. Thorman asked "Have we accomplished our purpose," and, more fundamentally, "What is our purpose?" It was an opportunity to revisit persisting tensions, especially that between those who saw CFM as primarily a family movement and those who perceived it to be a social action movement. This tension would erupt at the 1961 National Convention. However, this was not the only conflict that beset CFM.

Several problems repeatedly appeared over the first fifteen years of the movement's history. The basic group meeting, which was held every other week, was regularly analyzed and criticized. Too often the meeting was ineffective, it was charged, because members came ill-prepared, had not made good observations, or had not carried out their action. Some apparently were interested only in the social (not social action) aspects of the meetings. Their most important concern was what was for dessert. Some groups had individuals who dominated the meeting, others had spouses who could barely feign interest. Some chaplains came unprepared or, worse yet, spoke too much and inhibited open discussion among the lay members. Often too much time was spent on the Gospel inquiry. Some groups devolved into simple discussion groups. Other groups lost focus. The pages of *ACT* and the correspondence received by the national office were filled with problems of group dynamics.

As a result, a good deal of effort was spent in developing more effective mechanics for meetings. The annual inquiry book began scheduling a meeting to evaluate each group's progress, and the 1960–61 inquiry booklet devoted an entire evening to the topic "Toward a Better Meeting." Considered essential to an effective meeting was a good leader. As a result, CFM leadership spent countless hours discussing how best to create leaders. Leadership training seminars were constantly offered at the annual national and regional conventions. A special leadership training manual was published, then revised. The need for effective leaders who could move the weekly meetings along, keep them focused, keep all members involved, and direct the meeting to a specific action was a continual concern.

Responses to Thorman's request also revealed a series of other concerns. Of particular concern was the nature of the actions that resulted from the inquiries. Many felt that many of the actions were inconsequential and meaningless. The actions seemed to have no effect on the bigger social problems. The 1960–61 inquiry book reminded, "Many times our cross is not to see the result of our work."[3] Many called for continuing actions so a direct effect could be observed. A cartoon in the 1960–61 booklet showed a beggar appealing to a CFMer, with the CFMer's response, "Too bad you didn't come last week when we were on beggars. Now we're on to

International Law." But as Hillenbrand constantly reminded, the result of any particular action was not as important as the effect of the action on the CFMer. Acts were formative; that is, "formation came through action." Well-trained, informed lay people would transform the world. Despite this definition, CFM also sought to transform the environment, not just its members. For the experienced and committed, an endless stream of unconnected two-week actions did not suffice. Simple acts of goodness were no longer enough.

Veteran CFMer Burnie Bauer also joined in the controversy. Bauer claimed that CFM actions, to be efficacious and to sustain the group, should benefit the group performing the action, or at least should benefit one member of the group. "The impact CFM will make upon the institutions of this country will be more genuine if the social inquiries result in actions that are a genuine benefit to the members of the group making that inquiry. By helping themselves, CFM groups will be best helping others in the community and from this will result solid leadership in reconstructing our social institutions."[4] Not everyone agreed with Bauer. Several letters in *ACT* claimed his approach was too selfish. Reverend John Morgan wrote that CFM, to be authentic specialized Catholic Action, "can't concentrate on our own needs . . . can't simply ask 'what can I get out of it.' " He went on to label Bauer's approach "dangerous and destructive."[5] Despite the stinging critique, Bauer's "enlightened self-interest" approach had its backers. The nature of the ideal CFM action remained problematic.

Other critics suggested that CFM needed to deepen the spiritual life of its members. This had long been a source of debate, but in fact this debate was over means, not ends. Hillenbrand would have been the first to assert that this was a primary goal. But he repeatedly stressed that the spiritual life of lay people was not to be a pale imitation of the spiritual life of religious. Living in the world, one could not be expected to maintain a monastic schedule for prayer. The spiritual life of the lay person was based not merely on reflection but on action. Their actions were a form of prayer—the lay person grew through action. Nonetheless, CFM did begin to pay greater attention to the more traditional forms of spiritual formation. An evening of reflection was scheduled in each inquiry booklet, and various other devotions were encouraged, particularly at the federation level. One of the chief tasks assigned to the group chaplain was to guide the spiritual life of the lay members. The tension between traditional notions of spirituality and the newly evolving spirituality of action remained within the movement.

As usual, the most significant critique of the movement was provided by Hillenbrand. Hillenbrand highlighted what he considered to be the three most glaring "difficulties" in CFM in 1961. First, formation had not been thorough enough. Hillenbrand charged that often there was "no change of mentality" and that the CFMer still suffered a "double conscience," especially in the field of social doctrine. Second, he claimed that often the action which grew out of the social inquiry was "negligible," particularly in the "lay areas." Groups, apparently unable to understand the program, seemed content to select the "weakest, most anemic" of potential actions, and expected CFM to be "heady, novel and easy." Many continued to see CFM as a "family and neighborhood improvement movement." Finally, Hillenbrand contended that there had been inadequate spiritual advance, particularly as regards attendance at and participation in the Mass.[6] Here, he affirmed, was the premier formation tool, from which all other goods would flow.

The national Program Committee reiterated Hillenbrand's assessment. According to one member of the Program Committee, the major problems confronting the movement were (1) the education of members, (2) the Catholic education of members, (3) the motivation of members, social versus apostolic, (4) the priest's guidance, and (5) the spiritual life. The Program Committee called for a renewed commitment to the doctrine of the Mystical Body of Christ. A proper understanding of the Mystical Body was essential if the movement were to stay on course. Again, CFMers were reminded that they were the "hands of Christ." Finally, CFMers had to be reminded that such broad topics as international life, politics, economics, social problems, etc. were "not remote from family life, and that it is through Christ-like action in such areas that lay spirituality should be developed."[7]

As the movement struggled in its ongoing attempts to define itself, three issues surfaced in the late fifties and early sixties that took on special import—the problem of minority and working-class groups, the communist peril, and the conflict between family and lay apostles.

MINORITY AND WORKING-CLASS CFM

Since the first national meeting, CFM had been plagued by the fact of its upper-middle-class, white, professional membership. Repeated efforts had been made to attract working-class and minority members. One basic problem that tended to bar working-class involvement was lack of leisure time. The backbone of CFM was the wives, most of whom did not have to work outside the home. They planned and prepared for meetings as their husbands went off to work. The working class did not have this luxury—most wives worked. Add to that irregular hours and shift work, and the barriers to participation were high.

Nonetheless, year after year, CFM lamented its lack of appeal to the working class. Typical of comments was that of Fred and Norma Moore of Niagara Falls, New York, who concluded in 1958, "CFM will never accomplish its purpose, however sublime, unless the ordinary working class becomes part of its apostolate."[8] The issue was highlighted at the 1958 national convention in a speech by Father John Garcia of the archdiocese of San Francisco. Garcia challenged CFM to become "more inclusive," calling for more minority groups and more from the lower economic classes. The speech caused a stir at the convention but did not generate much change. Throughout the 1960s the movement struggled with this issue.

Father Garcia was the right person to challenge the conscience of CFM. Of Portuguese heritage, he had been part of a special band of priests working with the migrant farmworkers in California's fields in the rural areas outside of Oakland. He was famous for his tremendous rapport with and understanding of his people. Perhaps more than any other CFM chaplain, he was able to begin CFM groups among Mexican workers and get them involved in leadership at the federation level in San Francisco. Garcia's success in an area that perennially pricked CFM's conscience made him a respected figure in the movement. As late as 1966 Garcia repeated his charge, "Why is it that we have so few of the poor, especially the poor Mexican, the poor Negro in our CFM sections?"[9]

Beyond not being able to attract the working class, the suburban middle-class makeup of CFM had other important implications. Chaplain and conscience of the movement, Dennis Geaney, warned of the danger of the Church becoming "bourgeoisied." He posed the question, "Is CFM transforming the suburbs or is CFM being transformed by the suburbs?"[10] Similar concerns were voiced by friends of CFM—John Cogley, editor of *Commonweal* magazine, and Monsignor George Higgins, director of the NCWC Social Action Department. Cogley criticized, "The intense young Catholics of today hold their meetings not in slum buildings but in ranch type suburban homes. The emphasis has shifted from the workers' apostolate to the family movement. The good talk in the suburbs may still be about Simone Weil or Pere de Foucauld but the accents are at least faintly those of Norman Vincent Peale."[11] Higgins suggested that CFM was "potentially dangerous . . . it could become a sort of bourgeois type of movement which gives people the feeling that they are doing something very important because they are welding little families together and solving problems on the local level but which are not interested in the broader social problems."[12] The movement was in danger not only of subverting its own goals of social involvement but the entire social apostolate as well.

These reflections were echoed in many of the CFM publications and provided much food for thought throughout the 1960s.

INTERNATIONAL LIFE AND THE RED SCARE

As noted previously, CFM ended the 1950s by focusing on international life. The 1950s had been defined by the Cold War between the United States and the Soviet Union. The decade had begun with the anticommunist hysteria of the McCarthy era. Catholics were particularly susceptible to the cause of anticommunism (but then again, so were most other Americans). For more than a century, the loyalty of American Catholics had been questioned. Now Catholics had an issue in which their position could not be questioned. No one was as anticommunist as the Catholic Church.

Despite the clear stand of Catholicism against communism, groups such as the CFM were considered somewhat suspect by conservative Catholics and others. CFM, while condemning communism, believed that condemnations were not enough, nor were they effective. To combat communism, Catholics had to be just as committed to their faith and the task of building the City of God on earth as the communists were to their faith and the construction of their worldly kingdom of man. As the 1960–61 inquiry book asked, "Do you feel that our love and zeal for democracy equals that of Communists for communism?"[13] CFMers, and indeed all Americans, needed to build a world in which communism would have no appeal.

CFM's liberal social agenda made it suspect. While not all CFMers were political liberals, the inquiry programs tended to support a liberal social agenda. CFM, through its yearly programs, tended to endorse the progressive social legislative agenda as articulated by the great Catholic social theorist Monsignor John A. Ryan. So, even though CFM never officially took a national stand on any legislative issue, the tone of the annual programs was liberal— against discrimination toward minorities, for labor unions, for the right of the state to intervene in the economy for the common good, and so forth. When asked about the liberal slant of CFM, Hillenbrand remarked that CFM was liberal because the Gospels and the papal encyclicals were liberal.

In reality, CFM reflected the papal and episcopal programs in being both liberal and conservative. The conservative bent showed up most clearly on issues of sexual morality—television needed to be controlled, birth control discouraged, good reading made available, and pornography banned. But that was not good enough for "real" conservatives.

And the 1960–61 program on international life was one step too far, for a great many conservative Catholics. Program Committee chairman Jim Cockrell knew from the start that the topic of international life would be a tough sell to many CFM families. "The subject sounds imposing and sounds as if it's so far removed from family living that 'why is CFM bothering itself with the world?' . . . Everybody wanted a book on family life and this is really family life."[14] CFMers were reminded that as members of the Mystical Body the entire world was their concern, and international life *was* one of the areas of lay responsibility.

The inquiry booklet dealt with many topics with which CFMers were already familiar: international guests, world missions, world hunger. It also dealt with such topics as world awareness, world law, the population explosion, the United Nations, foreign aid, foreign trade, migration, self-development, and of course, communism. CFM's disdain for communism is clear. Included in one inquiry was a quote from J. Edgar Hoover's anticommunist classic, *Masters of Deceit.*

Despite the condemnation of communism, the annual inquiry set off a firestorm of criticism, especially from southern California, where more than one hundred couples left the movement as a result of the booklet. Hundreds of letters to the national CFM office in Chicago accused the Program Committee of being "Communist dupes."[15] Several crucial issues stood out in the letters. First to be attacked was CFM's clear support of the United Nations. Under Hillenbrand's direction, the program treated the UN as a key institution in achieving world peace. To several of the letter writers, the UN was part of the "Communist conspiracy." Their view was encouraged by the rabidly anticommunist cardinal archbishop of Los

Angeles, James Francis McIntyre. Second, the inquiry booklet had also listed a number of international agencies or organizations that could provide information on international affairs. One such was the Foreign Policy Association, which, several letters claimed, had been declared "subversive" by the American Legion. Several other agencies were suspect. Finally, the letters contended that not enough mention had been made of the archconservative Cardinal Mindzenty Foundation. Actually, the CFM inquiry booklet had recommended the foundation's ten-meeting program and given a contact address. This was not enough. A letter of protest was received from the director of the foundation, Eleanor Schlafly.

The winter meeting of the national Coordinating Committee at Notre Dame in January 1961 discussed the violent reactions expressed by a small minority of the groups. Clearly, the passionate opposition to communism was better understood by the Program Committee, which urged avoiding conflicts with "extremist groups" in the future. Nonetheless, when Pope John XXIII proclaimed his encyclical *Mater et Magistra,* an editorial in *ACT* asserted that it was a "vindication for the program on international life." The papal encyclical affirmed what Hillenbrand had contended all along— CFM was merely articulating the papal vision. (Not everyone was equally enthusiastic about the encyclical. Proclaimed William Buckley and the *National Review,* "Mater, Sí, Magistra, No.") The *ACT* editorial went on to proclaim that the encyclical should be considered the "Magna Carta for CFM."[16] In it, Pope John endorsed the Observe-Judge-Act formula of Catholic Action. CFM's international program was further vindicated in 1963 with Pope John's encyclical on international life, *Pacem in Terris.*

FAMILY APOSTOLATE?

One of CFM's central debates throughout the years was over the place of the family within the movement. Many had criticized the program on international life as being too remote from family life. What did discussions of the United Nations have to do with the family? In the process of becoming a mass movement, CFM attracted many couples who were drawn to it with the hope of improving their own families but who did not properly understand the real thrust of CFM. While CFM wanted to improve family life, it did not believe that it could be improved by focusing solely on matters internal to the family. For families to lead better lives, the environment in which the family was located had to be changed. As an early article on the movement observed, "By gradually removing the obstacles to Christian living, the Family movement hopes to metamorphose society. It hopes to help build a society in which the ordinary husband and wife, the ordinary family, can attain sanctity."[17] In other words, CFM would help build a world in which it was easier for families to be good families—not just easier for CFM families, but for all families in the community.

CFM differentiated its purpose from those of Cana and the Family Life Bureau on exactly these grounds. Cana focused on internal family matters, while the Family Life Bureau focused on education. Though CFM saw the need for those elements, they were not CFM's primary aim. CFMers were to reform the social order and, in so doing, to offer their own families opportunities to grow—to grow close to one another by sharing their efforts.

The presence of so many couples who failed to grasp the outward thrust of CFM forced the movement to accommodate their viewpoint. An editorial in *ACT* in 1958 acknowledged that the movement had to have a "two-pronged approach," which stressed both internal family improvements— "Individual families must become more Christ-like"—and reform of the society in which families had to function.[18] The accommodation was reflected in plans for the 1959–1960 annual inquiry program. Program chair Jim Cockrell pointed out the difficulty of "bringing the areas of concentration down to the family," narrowly perceived. The national Coordinating Committee dictated that the upcoming program would focus on one area "outside of family life" and "one aspect of family life,"[19] a choice of words that conceded a great deal to the critics of the 1958 program. By the following year the Program Committee once again found it necessary to reiterate the primary thrust of CFM. No electives were to be offered, as too many groups were avoiding the topics that addressed issues outside the family. The committee reminded members that we "must not confine our efforts to perfecting our own family. We must change our society so that Christian life may flourish."[20]

In 1959, *ACT* clearly stated the movement's "objective": "The Movement is primarily concerned with the social environment itself to make it easier for individuals to save their souls. By making the parish, the neighborhood, the nation, and even the world a better place in which to live . . . CFM is contributing to the salvation of souls. But the first objective of CFM remains to work for changes in the environment, in the society."[21] However, by the following year, when the national Coordinating Committee rearticulated the goal of CFM, it had returned to the "two-pronged approach," though the emphasis was clearly on social action. "The goal of CFM is to form members of Christian families, through spiritual direction and action on temporal problems, to assume their place in the lay apostolate so they can competently bear witness for Christ in the particular fields of endeavor or circumstance of life in which they find themselves."[22]

The debate over the place of "family" in the Christian Family Movement reached a crescendo at the 1961 annual convention at Notre Dame. The convention was abuzz over the attempt of Monsignor George Kelly, family life director of the archdiocese of New York to redefine the nature of CFM. Kelly had come to the movement in the mid-1950s and had hailed it as a most promising development. In a regional convention in New York, he had told the gathering that the purpose of CFM was "to change the environment through the actions and services performed by couples in a lay-administered movement." He went on to predict that CFM would have an impact "to be felt down through the centuries."[23]

By 1961, Kelly had grown disillusioned with the social action thrust of the movement. He believed that "the family mindedness of CFM was not getting a proper hearing,"[24] and that CFM "was not meeting the basic needs of married couples."[25] In an address to the clergy at the 1961 convention, Kelly joined the call for self-criticism, in his talk entitled "Is CFM Truly a Family Movement?" "The time has come for CFM to decide where it wants to go and what it wants to be." He attacked what he perceived as the growing "anti-family bias" among CFM leaders. "Some theorists have down-graded CFM as a family organization and have sought to make married couples primarily responsible for the reconstruction of society." The annual programs, he claimed, reflected this bias, a bias that was contrary to the wishes of the majority of CFMers. In the recent program, Kelly complained, he had searched page after page in vain to even see the word "family" in any context. Kelly urged, "The time has come . . . for CFM to make social reform a secondary, indirect, and long-range objective, rather than a primary, direct, and immediate concern. The time has come to give CFM back to the families and the family-minded people who make up its mass." Greater attempts were necessary to support the family as family, and actions were needed to assist the family directly. Kelly concluded that CFM actions should be (1) "directly related to family life" and (2) "social actions which have meaning for the family and which can readily be done by family groups."[26] In essence, CFM was a family movement, not an apostolic movement.

Kelly's speech was the talk of the convention. In small-group discussions and in informal gatherings the issues he raised were debated by CFMers. One observer reported that "the fascinating discussion . . . went on for four days over the goals of CFM." As might be expected, Monsignor Hillenbrand had no use for Kelly's talk. He later observed that the "priests at Notre Dame did not take him [Kelly] seriously."[27] The public rebuttal of Kelly was left to the Reverend Louis Putz.

In an address entitled "Social Leadership Through CFM," Putz systematically rebutted Kelly's address. Putz began by acknowledging "the lively controversy stirred up during this convention" and observed that "controversy and discussion is always to be welcomed." Putz addressed the question, "Is CFM primarily a family movement or a social apostolate?" He answered, "Of course, it is both." Putz stressed that the family was a social institution that was dramatically affected by other social institutions. In the complexity of modern life, all institutions were "interlinked" in some fashion. Thus, the family could not be treated as an isolated unit. Betterment of family life could not occur in isolation from the rest of society. Putz returned to the earlier definition of CFM that had derived from the other, and earlier, specialized Catholic Action movements. CFM was "to represent," "to serve," and "to educate" families. Thus, the movement had to be involved with the world outside "the walls of our kitchen and living room."

Putz concluded his talk with a postscript that directly challenged Kelly's understanding of the movement. "If Monsignor Kelly . . . had put Cana and Cana Movement where he speaks of CFM, then he would be almost 100 percent correct. When he talks CFM, he is really thinking of Cana. . . . I would say that Monsignor Kelly does not only not understand CFM, but he also has a very restricted notion of the lay apostolate. For him the lay apostolate is the laity helping the priest. But this is a very small aspect of the lay apostolate. The greater function of the laity is to be responsible in the temporal order and there the priest must help the laity."[28]

Kelly left the convention and prepared a series of inquiries that focused more directly on the family. He submitted them to the Program Committee as "supplemental programming." His proposals were not well received. The criticism: the inquiries involved too much discussion and not enough action; if they were followed, CFM might become just another "Cana Club." Chaplain Laurence Kelly of Chicago and the Program Committee wrote Kelly, "Where CFM has really worked, it has produced people with a social consciousness, people who saw the 'big picture' in race relations, labor, world unity, liturgy, etc. Their formation was qualitatively different from the layman oriented strictly toward marriage and the family. We should not lose this."[29]

Despite the rejection of Kelly's proposal, the topic remained a source of discussion among CFMers for years to come. Laurence Kelly clearly stated the problem, "Is there room and especially program machinery for an action movement which will address itself to the problems immediately impinging upon the American Catholic family and at the same time open this family up to the broader social challenges facing the Church today?"[30]

Though Monsignor Kelly drifted away from CFM, in 1979 he returned to the fray. In his *The Battle for the American Church*, he lamented that the tremendous good that CFM could have done was lost as a result of the control exercised by the Chicago leadership, which would brook no dissent. Kelly claimed that what CFM did was to encourage an "anti-authoritarian" mentality that infected members of the movement and resulted in the many problems of the 1960s. In this book, Kelly shows no better understanding of the movement than he had in 1961. He was not pleased with the direction CFM took in the 1960s.

Kelly's family-based critique of CFM surfaced repeatedly during the 1960s. For instance, in 1966, Terri Mudd of Lewiston, New York, wrote an article in *ACT* "Is CFM a Family Apostolate?" that basically reiterated Kelly's views.[31] Ironically, Kelly's view ultimately won out. In the early 1970s, CFM leadership decided that the movement had to place greater emphasis on family in its programming. This will be explored in a later chapter.

SEVEN

The Council and the 1960s

CFM prospered mightily in the early sixties despite the flare-ups over the role of the family in the social apostolate. The movement as a whole throve on the unprecedented challenges presented by the nation's nonstop social dislocations and traumas. And the Second Vatican Council (convened in Rome in 1962) seemed heaven-sent, a signal that the Church was ready to alter its age-encrusted view of lay people. Race; war; poverty; sexuality and gender; authority within the Church and within society; Church renewal; ecumenism; the Third World: each issue called out for redoubled efforts. But the turmoil of these heady times also took their toll, as the decade wore on. Race riots, student protests, antiwar protests, and the emergence of a counterculture all gave a violent edge to life in the 1960s.

From the student sit-ins of 1960 to the resignation of President Richard M. Nixon as a result of the Watergate scandal, America was a topsy-turvy world, in which each day seemed to hold a new surprise or shock. To many, the disciplined, incremental approach of CFM seemed too slow; change had to be effected *now*. For others, the constant turmoil of the 1960s produced a backlash, a turning away from social action to inner reflection. CFM was profoundly affected by these currents within the Church and within society.

IMPLEMENTING VATICAN II

The Christian Family Movement and its membership greeted the opening of the Second Vatican Council with enormous enthusiasm.

Few groups were better prepared than CFM to accept the changes initiated by the council. Few groups were better suited to implement the council's call for renewal. The council's new definition of Church as the People of God came as nothing new to CFMers, who had been steeped in the theology of the Mystical Body and who had been told for close to two decades that they were the Church. An editorial in *ACT* declared, "The year 1964 may well be remembered as the year that renewal really started to take hold. . . . These are days of hope and opportunity. . . . We are the Church—you and I."[1]

The council called for greater lay responsibility and involvement. CFM was ready. The council sought to reform the liturgy and to encourage greater lay participation. CFM was ready. The council told Catholics to engage the world and its problems. CFM was ready. The council called for greater openness on the part of the Church. CFM was ready. Not only was CFM ready, it had been espousing and pursuing just these goals since its inception. The council seemed to be a clear vindication of CFM's vision and method. As one CFM leader observed, "The relevance of CFM has never been greater than in the period after the Second Vatican Council."[2]

CFMers were particularly excited by the documents on the liturgy, on the laity, and on the Church. However, while excited by the general thrust of the documents, Pat Crowley was not alone in his disappointment that the document on the laity neglected the wisdom of the family apostolate. As progressive as council documents were, they had still not caught up to CFM. In a prepared statement, which provides a good summary of Pat's vision of the movement, he observed:

> Those engaged in the family apostolates must be pleased that their work has been mentioned in a chapter of the schema devoted to the laity, even though many of the ideas articulated are a reformulation of the tried-and-true.
>
> We wondered about the emphasis that the family is especially important in places where the seeds of the gospel are being sown. We think the family is important everywhere. Perhaps we expected

too much or perhaps we are looking at the schema from the point-of-view of those who have for many years worked in the family apostolate. To others, in different countries, these old ideas may be new.

What is surprising is that even some of the familiar ideas, the ideas that the Christian Family Movement has been talking about and acting upon for many years, were absent in the discussion of family. A brief listing may illustrate this point.

The importance of happiness in marriage; the mystery of conjugal life and the value of conjugal love; the family as a training ground for developing an interest in and understanding of the world; the family as the ideal and ultimately the most important place for its members to learn to love God and the world; the breathtaking challenge and responsibility of parents—these have been talked about so often and at such great length in family apostolates as to have become platitudes.

If parents love one another and learn to love God and love the world, charity will become a valuable reality. If parents are humble, open-minded, meek, and patient as well as courageous, they will help solve the problems of today and tomorrow.

Only those who are extraordinarily blessed will achieve these virtues quickly. For most of us, reaching them is a life-long objective. We must work; we must train ourselves. To learn, one must study; to act with conviction and purpose and understanding, one must train one's self. Systematic study and discussion that lead to quiet action within the world are characteristic of the approach that has produced positive value in the married apostolate. What's more, systematic training, properly considered, will produce virtues and values within marriage and outside of it. They will help members of the family to reach out into the world and do what they can to change it.

We rejoice that the family apostolate is mentioned, but are sad that so little of what has been learned during the past 20 years found its way into the document.[3]

More satisfying to CFMers was the ensuing council document, *The Pastoral Constitution on the Church in the Modern World*. Here was a clear endorsement of CFM and its program; it incorporated much of what Crowley lamented had been neglected in the schema on the laity.

Significantly, Canadian CFM played an important role in the different tone of the document as regards conjugal love. At the prodding of CFM couples in Canada, former CFM chaplain Bishop Remi De Roo of Victoria, Canada, made an intervention at the Council in "the name of 33 bishops and many married couples in Canada."[4] De Roo argued [as paraphrased by Xavier Rynne] that "The laity should be encouraged to progress toward a fuller, more ecclesial married life. Therefore the bishops should set aside pre-occupations with the pitfalls of married life and insist rather on the positive vision of the riches of human love and the height it could reach through grace."[5] De Roo continued, "Married couples must never abstain from the daily practice and development of authentic conjugal love. The Council will promote the redemption of all humanity by exalting the positive values of conjugal love."[6] The final document endorsed De Roo's emphasis; as one commentator noted, "This stress on conjugal love and the strongly personalist tone of the entire section on marriage carries us far beyond legalisms and philosophical abstractions indeed."[7] Such had always been the intent of CFM and the Cardijn technique.

CFMers were so excited about this document that the program committee published a new edition of *For Happier Families* in 1966, only a year after the preceding edition (which was now "out-of-date"),[8] in order to include large sections of the document. Indeed, on its back cover is a quote from the pastoral constitution that could have been lifted from previous CFM literature. Alongside the quote is a list of annual inquiry topics investigated by CFM since 1954. The intended implication is clear, the constitution is endorsing CFM's program: "Of the many subjects arousing universal concern today, it may be helpful to concentrate on these: marriage and family, human culture, life in its economic, social, and political dimensions, the bonds between the families of nations, and peace. On each of these may there shine the radiant ideals proclaimed by Christ. By these ideals may Christians be led, and all mankind enlightened, as they search for answers to questions of such complexity" (*The Church in the Modern World*, Article 46). Here was the Council endorsing the seven areas around which CFM had centered its programming. Here was an implied endorsement of the Cardijn method.

Again in 1966, the annual program booklet, *The Family in a Time of Change: 1966–67 Inquiry Program,* focused on the *Dogmatic Constitution on the Church (Lumen Gentium)* for the Scripture-Liturgy inquiries. CFM leaders believed that an understanding of this council document was essential to the rounded development of lay people—a restatement of their place in the Church as *Pacem in Terris* was a restatement of their work in society.

Both the program book and the new *FHF* reflected the full span of the council's work from 1962 to 1965. They also reflected CFM's five-year effort to digest that work and to determine how best to translate it into real life through the CFM program. In 1964, the Coordinating Committee and the Program Committee discussed how best to implement the document on the Sacred Liturgy. The 1964–65 annual book included a study night on the reform of the liturgy. By and large, CFMers embraced the liturgical changes. For years, CFM had advocated greater lay participation in the liturgy. Now it was a reality.

As the council progressed, so did CFM discussions. In 1966, much of the winter meeting of the Executive Committee was spent discussing the council and its implications. Bill Morhard of Falls Church, Virginia, put his finger on a key point, "[I]f CFM wants to be visionary and implement Council documents, we must lift ourselves from our ghetto mentality."[9] Since the mid-50s CFM had attempted to push Catholics beyond the Catholic ghetto; now implementation of the council seemed to require it.

The Executive Committee focused on two related ideas: "1) study, discussion, and implementation of renewal, and 2) actually implementing renewal while studying and discussing." As always, CFM put its stress on action, to prevent discussion from devolving into a glorified study club. "The IDEA is to study and discuss and at the same time to live some of the main Council ideas."[10] Or, as the 1966–67 inquiry booklet put it, the "program must help the Council to bear good fruit." By your fruits you shall know them.

Implementation did not come easily. Ironically, CFM's very success, with the council's seeming endorsement of it, raised questions of purpose. An article in *ACT* reporting on the summer meeting of the Coordinating Committee reflected, "CFM finds itself at a turning point." For years CFM had regarded itself as the "advance guard of the Church"; now, "after Vatican II, it finds that much of what it worked for is part of our present. What is next?"[11] One chaplain, William Nerin, went so far as to suggest that CFM should disband. It had served its purpose, and now its members should move on to other concerns. More will be said of this proposal later. Though Nerin did not find many willing to dismantle the movement, it is a fact that from this point forward, CFM suffered a steady decline in membership.

The reasons are not far to seek. The council had expanded the areas for lay involvement and responsibility, and many pastors were quick to avail themselves of a ready-made workforce of educated, committed lay people. This development drew many CFMers more deeply into parish and diocesan life even as others were embracing emphatically the call of the wider world for help and leadership. CFMers were active in newly formed parish councils, or on parish finance councils. Quite often CFMers were the people who pressed less than enthusiastic pastors for postcouncil changes. When a diocese undertook a program designed to inform the laity about the council, CFMers were the natural leaders. One such program in St. Louis, Operation Renewal, relied heavily on CFMers for leadership. The result: "CFM . . . in a holding pattern"—then the collapse of many groups.[12] The experience of St. Louis was repeated in a number of different locales. In a sense, CFM had done its job too well. As the need for qualified lay leaders increased, CFM membership rolls suffered.

The council also brought division to the Church. The speed and magnitude of the change wrought by the council caught many Catholics off guard, even many CFMers. While most CFMers were prepared for the change, some were not. Therein lay one source of friction. Involved lay people also encountered tremendous resistance from priests and bishops, unwilling to share their authority with lay people. The twin pressures—from those chafing for rapid change and those blocking any change—placed veteran CFMers like Bill and Laura Caldwell under extreme stress. They reflected on the difficulty: "[O]ne of our chief tasks time-wise is trying to chart the course between those (priests, nuns, laymen) so impatient with the pace of renewal that they are ready to leave the Church—we keep them in and try to give them hope—while at the same time, we expend huge amounts of time and energy trying to educate others in Vatican II, and to push the institutional church to action. It is a painful and thankless (in human terms) task, but one we see as our vocation at present."[13]

The division between traditionalists and reformers widened as the 1960s progressed. These divisions were further exacerbated by ongoing divisions within American society over issues such as race, poverty, war, sexuality, and gender. CFMers strove to build bridges between groups but were not afraid of confrontation or conflict as the occasion demanded. Many pastors believed CFMers were more inclined to conflict than to its resolution.

A NEW CLERGY, A NEW LAITY

One major area affected by the reforms of Vatican II was the role of the priest in the movement. Before the council, the role of the chaplain was clearly defined, and though CFM was a lay-directed movement, the chaplain played a major role. Each CFM group was to have a chaplain, but the chaplain was to speak only two times during the meeting, at the end of the Scripture-Liturgy Inquiry, and at the end of the meeting, following the Social Inquiry. The chaplain was responsible for meeting with the group's leaders to prepare the meeting. He was also responsible for the spiritual development of the group. Besides offering individual and group counseling, the chaplain was to provide evenings and/or days of reflection. He prepared the lay person to work in the world and thereby transform society. The priest was not to impinge on lay areas. As the Executive Committee asserted in 1964, "Laymen are formed by the priest to transform the world. . . . Everything is done by the laity, but nothing without the priest."[14]

Even though the roles of clergy and laity were clearly defined, CFM brought the two into a new relationship—priest and people were equals. This was a breakthrough. The old Baltimore Catechism contained a picture of a priest being ordained and a couple being married. Under the latter it read, "This is good," and under the former, "This is better." CFM chaplain Forrest Macken disagreed, "Laymen are not second class members of the Body of Christ. . . . In literal truth you as a layman are no less a member of the Church than Pope Pius XII."[15]

If this were true, the old relationship of priest and people had to change. Laity had to be treated as adults, not children. Eminent scholar Gustave Weigel, S.J., speaking to the Coordinating Committee, derided priests who expressed "insensitivity . . . to what laymen feel," who acted with "domineering arbitrariness," and "secretiveness," the attitude that the priest was not to be questioned.[16] And another well-known scholar, Joseph Fichter, S.J., told a convention crowd, "Lay people are willing to work in their parishes, but they want to do meaningful work, and they don't want to be pushed around."[17] In sum, the clergy had to respect their lay brothers and sisters and allow them to perform vital services for the parish and the clergy. Many pastors did not share their authority well—good CFM chaplains did.

For chaplains who adapted to their new role, CFM could be a life-changing experience. Dennis Geaney, author of *CFM and the Priest*, observed, "The priest today knows that the pastoral techniques of another century are not geared to his problems. CFM . . . gets to the heart of priestly ministry." For many chaplains, CFM became their most exciting and meaningful work. CFM brought them into intimate contact with couples and families that broke through traditional clerical isolation. One chaplain observed, "It has been my experience that [the chaplain] falls in love with the couples, he falls in love with the movement. . . . The heart is put back into him by CFM."[18] Chaplain after chaplain acknowledged the importance of CFM in their lives. Father John Coffield noted that the annual convention "was so much more inspiring and renewing of my priesthood than my annual priests' retreat."[19] While CFM revitalized some ministries, many priests became so comfortable with family life that they left the priesthood to get married. This became increasingly true during the 1960s.

While pre-Vatican II CFM forged a new relationship of priest and laity, there still existed a clear definition of the chaplain's role and of the priest's proper sphere of activity. This clarity began to disintegrate following the council, as did the clear distinction between lay areas and clerical areas. As Father Laurence Kelly told the Executive Committee, "[N]ew priests are almost obliterating the distinction between lay and priest."[20] Even before the council ended, trouble was afoot. In 1964, CFM chaplain James Halpine, the assistant national chaplain, stressed in a speech the time-tested notion that the lay person should become involved with the "welfare of the community." Halpine was surprised by the "negative reaction" of the CFMers there. He observed that they were "suspicious that priests were doing this to distract the layman from his attempts to become more involved in Church responsibilities." Halpine went on to assert that the central need of the Church was "the layman's commitment to the lay life."[21] The following year at the annual convention at Notre Dame, speaker Father François Houtart, warned that "Their [lay people's] first responsibility is their relationship with the world and not fruitless action within the Church."[22] As the sixties progressed, the two worlds continued to blur, and the laity did become, at times, preoccupied with fruitless action within the Church.

As lay people stepped up their demand for full participation within the Church, there were also attempts to declericalize the Church. In an address to the Coordinating Committee in June 1966, Father William Thompson of Joliet told the committee that "every one of us has a priestly vocation." Over the centuries the Church had become too clerical, for a variety of reasons. Vatican II was now trying to reverse that and balance the scales between laity and clergy. Thompson claimed that the new relationship of priest to lay person should be "brother to brother," and that laity and clergy should strive for greater unity.[23] These ideas had a familiar ring to CFMers.

The new vision of clergy and laity directly affected local CFM groups. Initially, the possibility of having women religious and seminarians serve as chaplains was explored. By 1968, the chaplain's special status had been removed; he was now just an equal member of the group. The result, according to Chicago CFM, was the "total loss of role for the chaplain."[24] The chaplain's new status (or lack of status), indicated a clear break with the 1950s. The collapse of clerical identity was reflected in the larger Church culture by the exodus of many from the clerical to the lay state, and the loss of vocations. This created another problem for CFM. It had always been difficult to obtain enough chaplains for all the groups; now, with the growing priest shortage, it became even more difficult. No matter. By 1968, the chaplain's special role was a thing of the past.

LITURGY

The liturgical changes mandated by Vatican II were readily received by CFMers. In a 1963–64 inquiry, CFM groups were asked what liturgical reforms they would like to see. The survey results reported CFMers wanted more vernacular, Mass with the priest facing the people, simplified liturgies, greater stress on community worship and better understanding of the liturgy.[25] And so Vatican II ordained. But it did more: It changed our basic understanding of liturgy: Greater emphasis was placed on the community. As one priest told the Coordinating Committee in 1966, "To be holy means to be like God. The essence of God is love. The new liturgy is to make the people one. It helps us experience togetherness. You never know love until you experience it. The essence of worship is the community coming together and experiencing each other."[26] A later observer stressed in 1972 that the creation of community had to precede the Mass. "Indeed, it is difficult for community to be formed at all at the Eucharist itself, for the Eucharist merely reflects and intensifies the understanding and togetherness already present in the congregation."[27] The priest, then, was not only the presider at the Eucharist, the priest also had to work at creating community if the Mass were to mean anything.

CFMers threw themselves wholeheartedly into support of the new liturgy. Besides supporting parish liturgies, CFMers frequently hosted home Masses or other more intimate liturgies. Many CFMers grew frustrated with the liturgies in their parish and established their own small experimental communities that provided innovative, meaningful liturgies. Even after Vatican II, CFM remained in the forefront of liturgical reform.

ECUMENISM

Another element of the council that directly affected CFM was the opening toward non-Catholic churches, "our separated brethren," as Protestants used to be called. CFM took seriously the call to be ecumenical. This was yet another sphere in which it had been well ahead of mainstream Catholicism. Since its inception, CFM, though distinctly Catholic, had been open to all Christian denominations. In fact, it was for this reason the movement had used the term "Christian" rather than "Catholic." By the late 1960s, an Episcopalian couple and a Methodist couple had served consecutively on the Program Committee. In 1969, the committee published the first ecumenical inquiry booklet that was intended for all CFM groups. This commitment to ecumenism caused some problems among the rank and file. The movement's clarity of the 1950s, its heavy reliance on papal and episcopal statements, was clouded. More will be said of this later, but the shift to ecumenism created severe questions of identity and purpose.

And this was not the only post–Vatican II crisis for CFM. Paradoxically, both successes and failures took their toll. Some of the movement's most active members were sucked back into what might be described as a neo-Catholic ghetto—they labored on parish councils, led liturgical committees, worked to transform parish education, and generally committed themselves to the vision of the perfect parish. Others became disaffected when their parishes refused to go along with the council. And those who did go out to shape the world gradually found the time demanded by CFM losing out on their agendas. This is not even to mention the impact of the social struggles of the 1960s. It is worth a closer look at the specifics. How could a movement that crested during 1963–64 be struggling to stay afloat by 1974? What happened?

EIGHT

CFM *and* Race

CFM came of age during one of the most intense periods of racial change in U.S. history. The year 1954 is often regarded as the starting point of the modern civil rights movement. That was the year in which the U.S. Supreme Court delivered its stunning *Brown v. Topeka Board of Education* decision, which overturned legalized school segregation in the South. In reality, the struggle for equality had already been engaged during World War II and immediately after. The African American soldiers who fought against Hitler and his racist ideology were not about to return to second-class status at home. Modest victories already could be tallied: President Franklin Roosevelt had ended job discrimination in the war industries, and President Harry Truman brought an end to segregated fighting units in the U.S. armed forces.

Changes that required more than a presidential fiat were not to come as readily. In 1948, Senator Hubert Humphrey pushed through a civil rights plank in the Democratic party's national platform. A major schism ensued. Southern Democrats created a third party, the States Rights Democrats, or Dixiecrats, as they were called. The breach in party alliance indicated the depth of the problem.

The *Brown* decision buoyed civil rights workers. In 1955, the Montgomery bus boycott gained national attention and signaled the emergence of the extraordinary Dr. Martin Luther King, Jr. For the next several decades racial concerns would weigh upon the American heart and conscience.

The civil rights movement confronted Catholics with difficult

119

decisions. Despite clear papal statements to the contrary, most U.S. Catholics tolerated segregation and discrimination with easy consciences. In his brilliant study, *Parish Boundaries,* John McGreevy suggested the difficulties Catholic civil rights activists faced in the north.[1] Catholics in the urban North equated neighborhood with parish, and more often than not they also equated the two with nationality or "race." It was not an outlook that would naturally favor, or even understand, integration. Bishops could, and eventually did, proclaim for racial equality and justice; urban Catholics regarded the issue more viscerally. The coming of even a single African American into their neighborhoods was regarded as an "invasion" that threatened the fabric of the closely knit ethnic neighborhood and parish. Catholic liberals might refer to segregation as a "sin," but to white homeowners the coming integration threatened property values and the survival of the parish. Those Catholics who sought integration in these neighborhoods were seen as interlopers, naive at best, and possibly evil. Out of—and into—this milieu CFM emerged.

From its inception, CFM was committed to integration and to uprooting the racism which Hillenbrand called "our national sin." A case in point: The precursor of South Bend CFM, the Catholic Action Apostles at the University of Notre Dame, brought the first African American student to the university, despite the complaints of some Southern white students. Early actions in South Bend CFM saw some workers attempting to socially integrate their workplace by eating lunch with their black coworkers.

In Chicago, the Crowleys and Hillenbrand became deeply committed to the struggle for black equality long before it was fashionable. Pat was introduced to and became friends with the Baroness Catherine de Hueck. The Baroness, a Russian immigrant, had established Friendship House in Harlem in 1938 to address problems of race in the inner city. She established another house in Chicago in 1943, on the city's South Side. When Friendship House was threatened with eviction, Pat persuaded Rosary College to make a loan to it, thus solving their short-term problem. He then worked at getting a new building, which became the permanent home of Friendship House in Chicago. Pat also obtained the release of a Friendship House volunteer who had been unjustly imprisoned, while serving in the Army, for "displeasing a Southern white officer."[2]

From this early contact with Friendship House, the Crowleys and other members of the early Catholic Action groups saw the bleak results of racism and segregation. Pat and the businessmen's group, and Patty and the married women's group, began traveling to Chicago's South Side to attend lectures at Friendship House. In September of 1946, Pat was featured as one of the lecturers.[3] The Crowleys soon made friends of their new associates and decided to have them come to a party in suburban Wilmette. African Americans in the suburbs of Chicago was unheard of at that time. Patty Crowley recalls, "We had a lovely party, and you know, to see black people coming into our house in Wilmette that weren't maids! I guess we were talked about in Wilmette quite a bit."[4] The "scandal" was not limited to Wilmette—Patty's mother was appalled by the idea of her daughter mixing with black folk and told Patty she was committing a "mortal sin."[5] Racial antagonisms were not to be overcome easily.

CFM pioneers' early encounters with African Americans ("Negroes" in those days) set the tone for future CFM efforts on behalf of the civil rights movement. The Crowleys and their friends engaged African Americans on a personal level. Civil rights was not some abstract concept. The genius of CFM was to embrace the particular, the observed, the real, and to eschew abstractions. In the CFM inquiries dealing with civil rights, chaplains reported seeing couples struggle with their own prejudices. They observed the situation, saw it in light of the Church's teaching, then struggled with their own inadequacies. CFM's greatest impact on the racial issue may have been its transformation of many individual hearts. With the Cardijn technique, couples were not allowed to remain comfortable with their prejudices. Many couples who did not, for whatever reasons, follow through with any substantive action were nonetheless changed on a personal level.

Pat Crowley's reputation spread beyond Chicago. In 1946, Reverend Henry V. Sattler, C.SS.R., wrote Pat asking him to help a young black woman, Grace Rowe, who was coming to Chicago to practice law. Sattler was "anxious that she meet the right Catholic people," so he sent her to Pat, because "Father Sheedy has told me of your little social methods of breaking down racial prejudice."[6] The "little social methods" was, of course, the Cardijn method.

The early national programs reflect these pre-CFMers' pioneering attitudes on race. In the two earliest national programs, a Social Inquiry was devoted to "prejudice." One 1950 inquiry read, "The purpose of this inquiry is to examine the problem in your neighborhood of the most prominent (and common) types of prejudice; those pertaining to race, religion, and color." The participants were asked to observe any "critical" remarks directed at "Catholics, Jews, Negroes or any other social or religious group." Another Observe: "Is anything being done in the community to combat prejudice?" During the Judge segment, participants were asked, "Against what commandment is prejudice?" and "What is the Church's teaching on racial prejudice? What did the Congregation of the Propaganda say about it in a recent letter?" And the couples were then led to act: "If you find prejudices you think bad, figure out what can be done to counteract it in particular or in general."[7]

The following year, the issue was thought to be so important that the same inquiry was reinserted in the annual inquiry booklet under the title "Prejudice in Children." The overall theme of the booklet was "Social Pressures As They Affect the Parent-Child Relationship." The questions from the previous booklet were repeated, but the new book's theme was underlined with the question, "Did parents make any of these [prejudiced] remarks in front of their children?" And in the Judge section: "Where do children acquire prejudices? Give specific examples."[8] The Cardijn method forced couples to observe prejudice as it existed in their neighborhood, and perhaps even in their own families.

In each of the following years, inquiries addressed the issues surrounding prejudice, such as "Minority Groups" (1953–54) and

"Equality in the Community" (1954–55). These inquiries called for specific actions, and that is what they produced. In San Antonio, Texas, in 1953, the CFM group worked toward integrating the Catholic school there. In Joliet, CFM worked to integrate the public schools. Many CFMers became involved in their local Catholic Interracial Councils. In other communities, CFM organized neighbors to try to prevent "white flight," as African Americans began moving into their neighborhoods.

Most celebrated in this regard were the efforts of Peter and Alma Fitzpatrick and their family of sixteen children. The Fitzpatricks were a pioneer CFM family, having accompanied Pat and Patty Crowley on some of their earliest travels. They had been instrumental in the spread of CFM throughout Chicago, especially on the South Side, where they lived. When their own neighborhood began to be integrated, they helped to form an Alinsky-style group, the Organization for a Southwest Community (OSC). The OSC sought to prevent whites from "panicking" and to allow "integration to occur without turmoil."[9] Peter served as president of the OSC for twelve years. He also served on the Chicago Commission on Human Relations for thirty years, fighting racism within the city. The example of the Fitzpatricks is typical of many CFMers. While their many actions were not CFM-sponsored, CFM pushed them into the community, where they became leaders in the fight against racism.

In 1956–57, CFM examined the racial question in its most concentrated set of inquiries, entitled "Social Harmony." By 1956, the repercussions of the *Brown* decision were already becoming evident. CFM upheld the notion of "integration" as an ideal worth striving for. The program book observed that "social disharmony" not only affected "Negroes," it also affected "Latin Americans, Indians, Chinese, and poor whites." CFMers were asked to observe the extent or lack of integration in their many spheres of community life—neighborhood, city, schools, parish, social groups. They were asked to examine their own prejudices: What would your attitude be if someone of another race moved into your neighborhood or tried to attend your school or club? CFMers were reminded of their role in the Mystical Body. "If charity is the bond that unites Christians, racial injustice and hatred are the greatest evil. They tear the Body of Christ apart."[10] As many other Catholics had come to see, discrimination and segregation were not simply misguided cultural norms, they were sinful.

Six inquiries were provided to investigate attitudes as they applied to minority groups: "Civil Liberties," "Housing," "Economics and Employment," "Recreation and Entertainment," "Education," and "Communication of Attitudes." Again, CFMers were urged to replace assumptions with facts. Interestingly, CFM received a letter from distinguished NAACP lawyer and later U.S. Supreme Court justice, Thurgood Marshall, congratulating the movement for this set of inquiries.

At the 1956 national convention at Notre Dame, the yearly program received an enormous boost with the address given by Archbishop Joseph Rummel of New Orleans. Rummel had gained national attention for his push for integration in Louisiana. On one occasion he "publicly denounced Louisiana parishioners unwilling to allow an African-American priest to celebrate mass."[11] In a dramatic speech at the grotto on the campus at Notre Dame, Rummel expressed the Catholic understanding of race: "We are all one in origin, nature, and destiny."[12] Rummel's plea for social harmony was greeted by a standing ovation.

Implementing the program was not so easy, as CFM groups across the country came to grips with the problem of race on home ground. Omaha CFM reported, "Many couples are not prepared to take up topics outside family life, much less segregation."[13] Nonetheless, the program inspired a flurry of activity. Omaha groups invited black couples to their meetings, sponsored or went to "talks by minority speakers," and read John La Farge's *Catholic Viewpoint on Race Relations.* Some members joined the Urban League, some couples attended Mass at the black parish, St. Benedict the Moor, and supported St. Benedict's fund-raiser for a new church. Others developed a handout on the pros and cons of the Fair Employment Practices Commission. Yet another group investigated the Knights of Columbus, which had refused to accept three black applicants; another congratulated the president of Mutual of Omaha for opening white-collar jobs to blacks, while others worked for a FEPC ordinance.

CFM groups throughout the country responded in similar manner, joining Catholic Interracial Councils, inviting African Americans to come to their meetings, attending civil rights lectures. A CFM group in suburban Chicago investigated the real estate market to see if blacks were prevented from buying homes. At St. Gregory's in Chicago, CFM got a local company to change their personnel policy regarding African Americans. Mount Prospect, Illinois, CFM formed an "Opportunity Council" which worked to break down restrictions in housing and employment. In Oak Park, Illinois, CFM investigated various stores' hiring policies. If they found the policy to be nondiscriminatory, they wrote letters congratulating the stores. They also established a housing association to attempt to prevent discrimination in housing.[14]

Despite all the activity, the program was not successful everywhere. Louisville CFM reported that there were "too many lessons on the problems of the Negro to maintain interest."[15] A member from Brooklyn CFM complained that the "recent study of social harmony has aroused some dissatisfaction and criticism among CFM members."[16] Others complained that the "problem was too great," while Chicago CFM complained that it was hard to develop actions from the inquiries. Perhaps the most telling criticism came from an all-black CFM group in Chicago. They wrote, "We think of all the CFM people all over the country studying discrimination, discussing its immorality, and we wonder what so many of them would do if a Negro actually moved next door to them."[17] The group went on to urge CFMers to make personal contact with black families, to break through the stereotypes.

CFM would not choose race an as an area of inquiry concentration again until 1964. Nonetheless, CFM did not neglect the issue. From 1958 to 1964 the civil rights movement exploded across the United States. Sit-ins, freedom rides, protest marches, bombings by

Klan members and their ilk, the ubiquitous Martin Luther King, civil rights bills, and the extraordinary March on Washington made it impossible for CFM to neglect the civil rights movement. Pat Crowley wrote Hillenbrand in 1963, "Many CFM groups have been very active in the racial problem. . . . We have found that almost every group we have visited has been preoccupied with the race question."[18] Responses to the annual program survey revealed the same. One respondent wrote, "The Negro question seems to creep into virtually every meeting."

Reports were not always positive. One respondent wrote, "Our group is in personal conflict over civil rights and segregation."[19] And veteran CFMers Bill and Laura Caldwell confirmed, "Our race relations activities . . . haven't particularly endeared us to most of the community."[20] A chaplain from Green Bay wrote of his group, "We are in personal turmoil over Civil Rights."[21] Another CFM chaplain in Muskegon, Michigan, was censured by his bishop for his advocacy of interracial justice. He "was way ahead of the other priests," which got him into "hot water."[22]

Despite the tensions, CFMers felt compelled to confront the issue. At the CFM national convention at Notre Dame in 1963, a special, unscheduled meeting was called to discuss what CFM groups had done to "further interracial justice."[23] The reports were impressive. In Baltimore, a CFM group had joined with a couple from CORE and another from the NAACP to establish a city Human Relations Committee. The group prodded the commission to integrate a local amusement park. They were successful. Of special note, priests and ministers were arrested in the protests.

In Alexandria, Virginia, a tutoring service was established for grade and high school blacks who were transferring into previously all-white schools. Transportation was provided when necessary. CFMers in Greensboro, North Carolina, were asked to support the sit-ins (1960). Many did. Following that, CFMers worked to help integrate the town's businesses. In Downer's Grove, Illinois, CFM gathered a long list of people in their locale who said they would not protest if an African American moved into their neighborhood.

The group then presented the list to local real-estate agents. In Chicago, CFM made a survey of housing and unions and then sponsored a forum on housing. In many other CFM groups, lectures were sponsored, interfaith groups set up, housing committees established, and human relations councils supported. Still many CFMers were uncomfortable with the topic. Milwaukee CFM reported that they "found that many in their section were hard to convince when it came to seeking civil rights and equal opportunities for Negroes." This recalcitrance was encountered in many other locales the following year, as CFM's national program directly confronted the race issue.

Those who fought for racial justice began to realize that racial justice could not be achieved by one denomination alone. Cardinal Albert Meyer of Chicago had said that "establishing a really integrated community is by its very nature a task for us all: not separately and alone, but jointly as well."[24] In many cities, CFMers established and worked with interfaith groups that were working towards integration. Nationally, CFM responded positively to a call from the National Catholic Conference for Interracial Justice for a national conference at which all faith traditions would examine the problem of racial injustice. On January 14, 1963, the centennial anniversary of the Emancipation Proclamation, 657 delegates from 67 national religious organizations met in Chicago to establish the National Conference on Race and Religion. Among the various religious leaders who addressed the conference was the Reverend Martin Luther King, Jr.[25] In the spirit of King's philosophy, the conference made "An Appeal to the Conscience of the American People."[26] CFM actively participated in the conference, sending six couples as official delegates.[27] Following the national conference, CFMers in many different cities worked to create local conferences.

The racial issue was of such great importance to CFM that it caused the movement to break its long-established policy of not taking an official stand at the national level. Policy stands were on the whole left to the grass roots to decide, and the CFM name was to be used with only the greatest caution and deliberation. Once the civil rights issue came to the fore—many in the CFM leadership considered it "the single gravest moral problem" confronting the U.S.[28]—that policy was questioned. In 1963 the National Coordinating Committee passed a resolution endorsing Dr. King's March on Washington: "Resolved, that the Christian Family Movement join with all men of good will in identifying themselves with the Negro families who are now seeking their full national rights, that we support and identify with them also in the national civil rights demonstration in Washington, D.C."[29] Many CFM groups participated in the March on Washington, including groups from Portland, Oregon, Indianapolis, Chicago, Detroit, and elsewhere.

While support of the March was innocuous enough, a number of CFMers protested when *ACT* published a call for CFMers to write their congressmen on behalf of the Civil Rights Bill of 1964. "This Bill is absolutely necessary for progress in race relations in this country and your support is vital."[30] Letters of complaint pointed out that this violated the CFM policy of not taking a national stand. Others believed CFM simply misunderstood the nature of the bill. One woman wrote, "I am shocked to read that a Catholic publication is actually supporting a move to remove from our laws an incentive to a better way of life by granting to the government the right to review all firing and hiring practices."[31] CFM responded that not only did morality and justice compel them to support the bill, the clear teachings of the bishops and the pope did as well.

In 1964, the national program again focused on the racial question. In one of the most controversial yearly programs ever, *Encounter in Politics and Race*, CFMers were given "a bold call to action." At the heart of this program was the concept of "personal encounter." CFMers would be expected to encounter an African American family, a civil rights organization, a politician, and a political organization, but the most challenging part of the program was the encounter in race. A flyer publicizing the new program read, "Every member of CFM must also seek out and come to know a Negro (Every Negro member must seek out and come to know a white person.) He must have this close personal encounter with a

Negro or Negro family, so that he will finally see not a person distinguishable by color, but a man in his God-given individuality. Every CFM member, beyond this act of friendship and love, must take on an active part in the original movement of equal civil rights for all."[32]

The program followed up along the same line: The premise of the program was that "to effect *change* within ourselves and on the world around us, we must *involve* ourselves with persons—not with 'the race issue' or 'the world of politics,' but with Mary and Jack Blake, Negro parents and fellow citizens."[33] Underlying the CFM program was the belief that black and white were absolutely equal. As an article in *ACT* observed, "there is only one race, the human race."[34] Differences between the races were artificial, culturally and societally created and enforced. Personal encounter with the opposite race would break through racial stereotypes—"from encounter will come understanding."[35]

The new program book was produced by the Program Committee chaired by Joe and Madelyn Bonsignore.[36] When Joe presented the topic at the national convention he used these words, which were written into the annual program: "If not me, who? If not now, when? If not this, what?"[37] The issue was too important to be neglected. The same message was conveyed on the cover of the April 1964 issue of *ACT*—a young black face in the shadows was depicted with the words, "If not now, when?"

The booklet itself is filled with powerful statements from bishops, civil rights leaders, civic leaders, and various authorities. Sprinkled among the inquiries are such moving testimonies as "Who's to Blame in Birmingham?" a reflection on the recent bombings there, published with a photograph of an injured child; a checklist from the Catholic Interracial Council entitled, "When the First Negro Family Moves into a Previously All-White Neighborhood." Included in the advice is "get the facts," "don't panic," "avoid violence," 'live your religion," and "organize."

The initial inquiries involved a personal encounter with an African American and with a civil rights organization. Later inquiries used the encounter as a base from which to examine a series of crucial issues, including civil rights, education, housing, jobs, community organizations, public facilities, direct action, social services, urban renewal, and even interracial marriage.

The most basic action inspired by the program was the home visiting program, in which a white couple visited the home of a black family. This program of home visiting was actually begun by Friendship House in 1955 in cities across the United States and had been tried by many CFMers prior to the 1964 program. But the 1964 program multiplied the number of home visitations manyfold. For many white couples, it was the first time they had ever been in the home of an African American. Many spoke of how "uncomfortable" they felt; this was new terrain. One veteran South Bend CFMer remembered, "Well, we went into black homes. We had never done that before. . . . My husband Ralph and I, and several other couples from our group went into this black couple's home. The husband was a schoolteacher, and he and their home broke all the stereotypes. It was a really nice home, well-furnished. The couple met us at the door and the wife greeted us and then immediately left, left the husband to carry on with the guests, and I think for the first time we knew what rejection was—it was reversed."[38] For many of the thousands of CFM couples who visited black homes and engaged in frank discussions over the division between blacks and whites it was a transforming experience. They would never look at the racial issue in the same way again. As Milwaukee CFMer Cathy LaChapelle concluded, "For many of the members it was a breakthrough. This was only a start, but a start that has given many members a sense of conviction."[39]

Others commented on how "artificial" the program was, but as one CFMer observed, Yes, it was artificial, but "it was a start, and you've got to start somewhere."[40] The executive director of the NCCIJ, Matthew Ahmann, echoed these sentiments: Although the program was artificial, it was "very useful."[41] Ahmann then urged couples to move beyond the simple encounter to more significant actions for equal civil rights.

The program did indeed inspire a host of actions. The annual program survey reported the following as the "best actions": potluck dinners for interracial groups, essay contests, establishment of human relations committees, civil rights marches, establishing African American CFM groups, fair housing committees, interracial dialogues, economic opportunity councils, support of Head Start programs, support of the Urban League and other inner city groups.[42]

CFM groups in the Chicago federation sponsored a variety of actions similar to those mentioned above. Most interesting, however, were attempts to come to grips with the problem of neighborhood transition, attempts to prevent white flight. In Queen of All Saints parish, CFM initiated a series of six lectures, which were sponsored in conjunction with an ecumenical group. The lectures were "designed to prepare the Lincolnwood-Sauganash area for integration." The lectures drew more than 200 people each night. In St. Sabina's parish, the CFM group sought to assist and welcome African American families new to the parish. They invited them to join CFM. Other Chicago actions included an "interracial cocktail party" hosted by Sacred Heart parish in Hubbard Woods (Hillenbrand's parish). Several groups attempted to recruit more black members, while an all-black CFM group at St. Isaac Jogues in Morton Grove invited white couples to join its group. *ACT* also reported that "St. Viator's is continuing to work in the Cabrini Green project. They have rented a store on Franklin St. which is named Damien House which is open five days a week. Activities have consisted mostly of providing food and clothing to destitute people. . . . It is hoped that soon, help can be given to solving basic problems such as finding jobs for unemployed, etc."[43] Several years earlier CFM had become acquainted with the problems of Cabrini Green, when they provided the workers to conduct a census of the housing project.

Many CFM groups joined the battle for fair housing. In Oakland, California, CFM rallied to work on behalf of the Rumford Fair Housing Act. In 1964, Proposition 14 was placed on the ballot to overturn the Rumford Act. CFMers sponsored lectures and handed out literature in an attempt to maintain Rumford. They were unsuccessful. Other cities, including Chicago, Milwaukee, and Alexandria, Virginia, had groups working to ensure fair housing legislation. These efforts turned out to be quite difficult and at times explosive. Gabriel and Kathleen Fay, members of a CFM group in Larchmont just outside New York City (and later members of the Program Committee) shared their rather frightening experience in working for fair housing. Their efforts began with a meeting at a local Catholic school to form a fair housing committee. Shortly into the meeting things began to deteriorate. The leaders were challenged "Who are you?" while another person asserted, "We're not prejudiced, but we're not helping Negroes to move in." Over the course of the next several days, angry crowds began to gather, spurred by the rumor that the committee was raising money to enable a black family to move into the neighborhood. Committee members began receiving hate mail and obscene phone calls. According to the Fays, "the community was on the verge of hysteria," though it seems from their report that the community had already passed that border. What particularly depressed the CFMers was the large numbers of Catholics in Larchmont who appeared to be no more tolerant than anyone else. Nonetheless, the Fays continued to work for the fair housing committee.[44]

CFMers also pushed for low-cost housing. Notable in this regard were the efforts of Charles and Cathy Scalise from an Erie, Pennsylvania, CFM group, who created a nonprofit housing group called HANDS (Housing and Neighborhood Development Service), with the purpose of enabling low-income families to purchase their own homes. In 1966, they helped six families—four black, one white, and one mixed—obtain "decent, low cost housing."[45] HANDS grew out of a "senior CFM" group that was focusing on interracial relations. Typical of CFM, once they started HANDS, they allowed it to develop into an independent organization. CFMers continued to support HANDS financially and through volunteer help, and Charlie Scalise remained president for many years.

Other CFMers became involved in various civil rights marches, local and national. A number of CFMers journeyed to Alabama to participate in the famous Selma to Montgomery march. Among others, groups from Chicago, New York, Louisville, Alexandria, and San Francisco flew to Selma to join the protest. The experience in the march, like the experience in the battle for fair housing, was an eye-opener for the CFMers. Michael Ambrose and Charles Moran of Virginia CFM recounted their experience for *ACT*. They were unprepared for the hostility of the crowd and the "hate stares" they received. They observed "For most of us, it was our first encounter with hatred." They now had some inkling of what it was like to be black in the South.[46] Another CFMer who had gone south to work in Mississippi reported, "Now I know what it feels like to be an outcast in my own nation."[47]

Detroit CFM chaplain Father Jerome Fraser shared his personal experience of Selma with many CFM groups. One couple, deeply moved by his account, wrote him, "The difficulties facing the Negro in the South and in our community are much more real to us because of the facts you were able to present. It is our hope that being better informed ourselves we may in some concrete manner be instrumental in changing the unchristian attitudes of some of our fellow Catholics."[48]

The experiences in the fair housing battles and the protest marches were at the heart of the encounter program. Participants gained real insight into the problem of prejudice and discrimination, not textbook knowledge. True to the CFM commitment, they encountered the real experience and were not allowed to be content with abstractions. Once the hatred and discrimination were experienced, it was impossible to go back to life as if nothing had changed.

Another participant in the Selma march was not so sanguine. In a letter to *ACT*, Sallie Troy of Evanston CFM spoke of the march as a "heart-opener." Evanston easily filled a bus to travel to Selma. However, to Sallie's dismay, when she attempted to recruit participants to go to the state capitol in Springfield, Illinois, to demonstrate on behalf of pending open housing legislation, she was unable to garner much support or enthusiasm. She reflected, "Is it possible that what occurs in the south seems more unjust than what happens in our own neighborhoods?"[49] People's own neighborhoods remained a problem. The Caldwells of Cleveland's CFM concurred. They observed that people talk of how terrible the South is, "but we feel it is far more important to discuss racial problems in Cleveland and the housing situation in particular." However, they discovered that there was "not the same eagerness to discuss the local situation . . . it is easier to solve problems far away, than those close at hand."[50]

While the encounter with race dramatically affected many CFMers positively, it was not universally well-received. In the first place, many groups did not use the race inquiries. In an end of year survey, respondents indicated that about 50 percent of the groups conducted the inquiry on making personal contact with an African American, while just 25 percent conducted the inquiry designed to encounter a civil rights group.[51] The program chairs, the Bonsignores, later lamented the lack of involvement on the part of many CFMers, who chose simply to ignore the inquiries.

The racial inquiry placed enormous stress on many federations. Federation after federation reported a significant loss of membership as a result of the race inquiry. Gary, Joliet, Mobile, Erie, South Bend, Chicago, to name a few, all reported losses. Others simply described the difficulties the program generated. Gary reported that the inquiries were the "most demanding" ever. Mobile reported, "Our encounter with race has been rewarding, just a little jittery." Joliet reported with pun intended, "This is the year CFMers showed their true colors."[52] Group after group reported the pain and conflict created by the inquiry. The use of the terms "turmoil," "conflict," and "strife" became repetitive in the annual reports. The inquiry, when used, had touched a nerve.

The inquiry was also undercut by many clergy and bishops who were unwilling to have their people confront such a sensitive topic. In Los Angeles, the Chancery blocked the use of the race inquiry.[53] This is not surprising inasmuch as Cardinal McIntyre did not understand the depth of the racial problem in Los Angeles. Some chaplains refused to use the book. Many clergy seemed unwilling to support interracial projects. By and large, however, the clergy and bishops were in advance of the laity on this issue. It was the laity who dragged their feet over fair housing, integrated schools, clubs, and so forth.

While the race inquiries generated much conflict, they also generated new attitudes and, on occasion, profound personal transformation. One respondent, assessing the annual program, wrote that the booklet "forced us to confront the race issue in a personal way. . . . I know for sure one whose opinion and attitude has changed very much on integration as a result of CFM this year."[54]

After 1965 many groups continued to work on the racial issue, but relations between blacks and whites in the United States were becoming increasingly strained. Selma proved to be the last major peaceful march of the Southern civil rights movement. The same year Los Angeles exploded in the worst urban riot since World War II, in what came to be known as the Watts riots. The following year, James Meredith's "March against Fear" would turn violent and Dr. King's search for "Freedom Now" was superseded by Stokely Carmichael's call for Black Power. King learned the difficulties of segregation in the North as he and his marchers were pelted with garbage as they walked in protest through Cicero, a suburb of Chicago with a substantial Catholic population. Eight major riots rocked inner cities in the United States during the "long hot summer of 1967." In 1968 there were more of the same. A nadir was reached with the assassination of Dr. Martin Luther King, Jr., in Memphis. Many blacks despaired of nonviolence and the integration model so eloquently advocated by Dr. King. The assassination itself led to riots—riots that, ironically, destroyed mainly black city neighborhoods. Many younger black leaders advocated a new model—black self-determination, black pride, black assertiveness, and black separatism became the watchwords.

Despite the disappointments, the riots, the shift in models which made white participation less and less welcome, CFM remained committed to the vision of an integrated America, where white and black could live side by side. CFMers across the country continued to work to bring housing and job discrimination to an end. Many CFM groups became involved in the NCCIJ's Project Equality Program, an interreligious, interracial program, begun in Detroit in 1965, that worked to create fair employment programs. In Wheaton, Illinois, twenty-eight miles from Chicago, one CFM couple joined an ecumenical group to investigate discrimination in their town. When discrimination in housing and employment became evident, a human relations commission was established, as was an educational program, which prepared for the breaking of the color barrier in housing.[55] Ultimately, a fair housing ordinance was enacted.

South Bend CFM worked aggressively to end discrimination. Several groups supported the St. Peter Claver Interracial House. St. Augustine's CFM sponsored an interracial housing program that encouraged the creation of an integrated neighborhood. Little Flower CFM supported a black community newspaper, *The Reformer.* CFMers handled subscriptions, took the newspaper to the printer, and distributed it. The editorial direction of the paper was left in black hands.[56]

New York CFM engaged the increasing racial violence head-on. In the summer of 1967, a riot in East Harlem exploded. A New York priest organized a march through the riot area, easing tensions and bringing the riot to a halt. More than 200 of the 800 marchers were CFMers. The following summer CFMers returned to the area, helping to rebuild some twenty-seven houses in East Harlem.[57]

Not all CFM experiences were so positive. CFMers were continually distressed by the viewpoints of their fellow Catholics, even some of their fellow CFMers. The Chicago CFM newsletter of July 1967 reported an interview with a black state senator from Chicago's South Side. He observed, regarding the fight for fair housing legislation, "Those with the most vitriol were, you will be interested to know, for the most part Catholic."[58] According to the senator, the opponents of fair housing had a hate list that ranked Martin Luther King, Jr., first, with Cardinal Cody close behind in second place. CFMers were learning first-hand about the capacity for violence, white violence for the most part, generated by the integration issue. CFM continued to advocate the integrated parish, urging the merging of separate white and black parishes, though one priest warned "blood would flow." Despite the possibility of violence, integration had to be pursued.[59]

At the national Executive Committee meeting in 1967, the difficulties of CFM and race were discussed. In an eloquent plea, Don and Marilyn Burton of Oklahoma called for CFM "to awaken awareness of the racial situation. . . . We must quit spoon-feeding the people."[60] The Burtons called for CFM to challenge its members.

Challenge it did. In 1967 and 1968, *ACT* published a series of articles that laid out the new ideology of black power. One article defined black power as "to bargain from strength rather than beg from weakness."[61] More than a decade of struggle had brought relatively few significant gains for black people, it was argued. The new strategy called for the raising of black consciousness and pride, and "an aggressive assertion of blackness." Blacks had to be "empowered." This empowerment might evoke violence, since whites did not seem inclined to give up or share power. As one article observed, "The only way they can get it, is to take it."[62] Another article in the series cautioned, "Has Time Run Out for the White Man?"[63]

By 1970, CFM's advocacy of integration had been modified. In South Bend CFM, a specific couple was designated to introduce CFM to black couples. They were to "adapt" the introductory booklet "to the particular needs of black people." African Americans, they discovered, "wish to be in predominantly Black groups to emphasize particular challenges to Black families."[64]

CFM had never been very successful in recruiting black members. Chicago had a significant number of groups (they presented a striking picture at one of the national conventions wearing dashikis). Blacks had also served at the national level, most notably two Program Committee couples, William and Gladys McCoy, in the early 1960s, and Bishop and Jocelyn King in the early 1970s. Bill McCoy became the first black ever elected to the Oregon House of Representatives.. He later served as a state senator. Gladys served on the Portland School Board and chaired the Multnomah County Board of Commissioners. Together they raised seven children.

Irrespective of numbers, CFM continued to identify the racial question as one of the nation's most serious moral questions. In several cities, CFM became involved in extensive actions. Let's turn to the experiences of Milwaukee and Detroit CFM.

MILWAUKEE

Like most other northern cities, Milwaukee's African American population increased dramatically following World War II, nearly tripling to more than 60,000 by 1960. And, as in other cities, ethnic Catholic neighborhoods and parishes showed open hostility to the new arrivals.

CFM responded in Milwaukee as it had elsewhere, trying to ease people's fears. One group established a community organization named Cooperation West Side in an effort to stabilize a "racially changing neighborhood," to stop white flight and end the violence directed at their new black neighbors. In the early 1960s, the Milwaukee CFM federation established an Interracial Committee to provide a greater focus on race relations. The committee was given a threefold task: "1) To promote and foster the social doctrine of the Church in the area of race relations; 2) To convince CFM groups of the necessity of educating their neighbors, parish, and community in the area of race relations; and 3) To establish a program to prepare their parish and neighborhood for integration, and if possible, develop a method of welcoming minority groups."[65] The committee encouraged CFMers to participate in Catholic Interracial Councils, the Conference on Religion and Race, and other interfaith groups. It enthusiastically endorsed the 1964–65 inquiry program on race, and encouraged personal contact between blacks and whites through the home visit program.

As Milwaukee's program year came to an end, many CFMers were discouraged by their lack of success in changing the racial attitudes of Catholics. CFM was stung by the harsh assessment of a local civil rights worker, Lloyd Barbee. He commented that CFMers were "naive, but eager." He continued, "I do feel that most of the CFM people tend to feel they are helping their little brown brother—a condescending type of help. . . . [In addition, CFMers believe] that talking about the problem is tantamount to solving it." These were damning words to a movement that prided itself on promoting real action. More damning was the response Barbee received at a CFM meeting on the South Side in which he met with "hostility, bigotry, and ignorance." He did qualify his critique by saying many CFMers were "open-minded" and were making a "sincere effort to understand."[66]

CFM leadership was equally troubled. Federation president Don O'Connell lamented, "We had a greater than normal dropout during this period." However, O'Connell pointed to the magnitude of what had been attempted. "[Some] activities were monumental for some individuals in that they had never done anything like this before . . . .[Many couples] had a change in attitude about race problems . . . .[U]nfortunately some haven't moved into the area of action."[67] Past federation president Bill Connolly also concluded that CFM's efforts had been "poor. A number of people did get tied up in it, but the Negroes involved expected much more. This was discouraging to them. They saw that our books were committed, but we weren't. We let the Negro down."[68]

Despite its shortcomings, Milwaukee CFM did not despair. Instead it redoubled its efforts. In Spring 1965 a special St. Martin de Porres group (SMDP) was established, superseding the Interracial Committee. The SMDP started with twenty couples in two action groups plus a research team. Their purpose: "The SMDP is a CFM group in the specialized area of civil rights, formed to give inspiration and guidance to its members. They will study and act as individuals, small sections, or as a whole group." Chairs for SMDP were Bill and Mary Connolly, who noted that the group was not a civil rights group per se; it was to promote "Christian leadership in the community."[69] SMDP would focus its efforts in the areas of education, housing, and politics.

SMDP immediately joined with fourteen other civil rights

groups to protest the "de facto segregation" of Milwaukee's public schools. Three CFM families joined the NAACP suit against the public school district, which argued that de facto segregation was harmful to the children involved. The protest escalated when activists called for a boycott of schools to be coupled with the establishment of "freedom schools." SMDP supported the boycott with several CFMers, including Mary O'Connell, serving as teachers in the freedom schools. The boycott highlighted the rift within the Catholic Church when Auxiliary Bishop Roman Atkielski, acting in the absence of Archbishop William Cousins, forbade any church or parish facilities to be used for the freedom schools. Nor were any priests or sisters to teach in the schools. Many defied the order, most notably the young Father James Groppi, curate of St. Boniface, an old German parish now located in the heart of the ghetto. Groppi led a celebrated protest in which Atkielski's home and the Chancery were picketed.

By 1967, CFM was still active in pushing for school integration. Now they decided political involvement was necessary. SMDP approached Don O'Connell with a proposal that he run for the school board on a platform calling for the integration of Milwaukee's public schools. Don, a forty-year-old newspaper artist for the *Milwaukee Sentinel*, was convinced by his CFM experience that he had to run. "As a CFMer, although we can be very active on the fringe of politics by exerting pressure as private citizens, it is only when we actually become a member of the power structure itself can we exert our maximum Christian impact. If we want to change the situation, we have to get in there."[70] O'Connell reflected a commonly held CFM attitude. With the help of CFMers, O'Connell won a seat on the board.

The following year, 300 CFMers endorsed a slate of nine candidates running for city offices including a mayoral candidate. An endorsed candidate had to support school integration and open housing. They succeeded in electing one alderman.

Open housing increasingly took center stage in 1967. The call for an open housing ordinance was highlighted by Father Groppi's dramatic marches into the Polish South Side. Many CFMers participated. CFM had been instrumental in forming a South Side Committee for Equal Rights. The Milwaukee federation board openly endorsed the call for a housing ordinance, ignoring arguments that CFM should not take a public stand on an issue. This issue was too important.

Though Milwaukee CFM did not resolve the race issue, the efforts of so many CFMers was impressive. With so many Catholics aligned publicly against integration and fair housing, the witness of Milwaukee CFM was all the more important.

DETROIT

Like Milwaukee, Detroit saw its black population grow significantly after World War II. During the 1960s Detroit's inner city became one of the nation's best known ghettoes when it exploded in a violent riot in summer 1967, resulting in 43 dead, more than 2,000 injured, and hundreds and hundreds of buildings destroyed by fire. By the time of the riot CFM had virtually no presence in the inner city. In 1966 the Detroit federation had reported, "CFM in the inner-city is dead."[71] Even so, several CFMers remained in the inner city and were directly affected by the riots. Detroit CFM's newsletter, *CFM Observes,* reported that one couple fled from their apartment to the home of another CFM family when looters broke into the cleaners below them, and another couple reported police used their back porch in a gun battle with snipers.[72]

Beyond these personal experiences the riots jolted Detroit CFM into action. CFMers Joe and Mary Beth Hansknecht organized Project Commitment, "an unprecedented relief operation," which "changed from an adult education program to a relief operation."[73] Suburban CFM set up relief centers; St. Gertrude's served as a center for clothing; Queen of All Saints, a center for food. One parish sent eighteen station-wagon loads of food including 400 half-gallons of milk, 200 loaves of bread, 60 dozen eggs, and 7 crates of fresh fruit.

Following the initial relief efforts, CFMers joined other community groups in helping riot victims. CFM became involved in the "Homes by Christmas" program, which helped families who had lost their homes in the fires to find new ones. By Christmas more than twenty families had been resettled. Ultimately more than 250 people were helped.

The following summer, Dr. King's Poor Peoples' March arrived in Detroit. CFMers Jim and Betsy Carr organized welcome and lodging for more than 2,000 marchers. CFMers responded most generously, offering their homes for hospitality.

The most significant program created in response to the riots was Focus: Summer Hope, organized by CFM chaplain Jerome Fraser and Father William Cunningham. The program was intended to "heal the wounds between the black and white communities." Its initial project was an intense educational program explaining the Church's teaching on race relations. Fifty priests were trained, then sent into the parishes to give sermons on racism and urban issues. The sermons were followed by home meetings. More than 90,000 participated.[74] The program, now called Focus: HOPE, moved beyond education to food programs for low-income families and the elderly, and later to job-training programs. In 1997, a report on Focus: HOPE read, "Focus: HOPE is an astonishing success story, part factory, part college, part vocational training center, part food bank, and part child care center and Montessori school. Today Focus: HOPE employs 850 staff members and involves over 45,000 volunteers, contributors and participants. It funds a more than $100-million, 33-acre high technology campus primarily serving low-income blacks in Detroit."[75] Though this was not a CFM-run program, CFM contributed to its early success. According to co-founder Jerome Fraser, "Many CFM people were involved from the very beginning and accepted leadership positions in several early efforts."[76] As with other projects, it was CFM's job to get the ball rolling, then allow others to run the program.

As in other cities, Detroit CFM participated in open housing drives and other civil rights protests, but their response to the riots was the high point of their efforts.

CONCLUSION

For more than two and a half decades CFM grappled with the race question. Critics might dismiss CFM's efforts as insignificant, but in communities across the United States CFM made a difference. They provided public witness to the Church's teaching on race, often at great personal expense. When a black family moved into a suburb of Detroit, CFMers rallied to their support, throwing "a sod-laying party at their home, even as others were harassing them." The lead couple of St. Cletus CFM in Warren, Michigan, Bob and Theresa Kozak, "suffered a lot from their involvement." Though more might have supported them, they were afraid to be publicly associated with them, afraid of the repercussions.[77] While no doubt experiencing some fear, CFMers stood up and were counted for what they considered the most important moral issue of their time.

The most profound change that came from CFM's involvement with civil rights is that which occurred in the hearts of thousands of CFMers who had to come to terms with their own racism. Did CFM change the world? No, but it did change a lot of people.

Sadly for the movement, taking the high moral ground was costly. Though the movement remained vigorous through 1970, its decline from its 1964 membership peak began with the issue of race.

NINE

Becoming Ecumenical

Vatican II not only urged Catholics to become more deeply involved in the world, as CFM had done with the racial issue; it also encouraged Catholics to establish better relationships with their non-Catholic brothers and sisters. CFM's involvement in the civil rights movement had given members experience in practical ecumenism as they had joined with other faith communities in the struggle for equal rights. By 1969, CFM had taken the ecumenical movement much to heart. It declared that it was no longer solely a Catholic movement; it was now "ecumenical."

In the lore of the movement, CFM had always been open to interfaith groups; that is why the term "Christian" was chosen rather than "Catholic" in the movement's name. Several early actions do suggest that CFM was more expansive toward non-Catholics than other Catholic organizations. In 1950, chaplain Gerard Weber reminded CFMers that the parish, on which CFM groups were based, meant all people, non-Catholic as well as Catholic. As early as 1951, the Coordinating Committee dealt with the question of whether a Protestant could belong to a CFM group, a point that arose repeatedly, given the reality of mixed marriages. The answer was Yes.

Despite these gestures of openness, CFM was a thoroughly Roman Catholic movement with a priest present as chaplain at each meeting. The movement's introductory book, *For Happier Families,* spent a good deal of time reflecting on the Roman Catholic Mass and the Roman Catholic interpretation of the sacraments. The early annual inquiry books followed suit, with a frequent sprinkling of quotes from papal encyclicals.

The earliest inquiry to take a look at "Our Non-Catholic Neighbors" appeared in the 1955–56 annual inquiry book. The inquiry asked CFMers to observe the percentage of non-Catholics in their parish, to give examples of Catholic and non-Catholic cooperation in the community, whether or not non-Catholics were invited to parish activities, and whether or not their parish had a "convert" class. The members were then asked to judge, "Does our role in the Mystical Body require lay people to cooperate with non-Catholics? In what activities should we cooperate?"[1] As reported in *ACT*, this inquiry did generate some contact between Catholic and non-Catholic groups, particularly in actions to improve the neighborhood and community, such as playgrounds and other recreational outlets. However, as mention of a convert class indicates, if Catholics had their druthers they would have preferred everyone to be Catholic. It was an outlook that was alive and well in CFM as late as 1960, when the annual program book quoted the "Chair of Unity Octave Prayer" with its plea for "the return of all the 'Other Sheep' to the One Fold of St. Peter."[2]

In the 1960s the Catholic Church under the leadership of Pope John XXIII, moved towards a greater openness to "our separated brethren." Pointedly, Pope John addressed his 1963 encyclical *Pacem in Terris* to "all men of good will." Then came the Second Vatican Council (to which several non-Catholic observers were invited). Its *Decree on Ecumenism (Unitatis Redintegratio)* issued in late 1964, called for the "restoration of unity" among all Christians and directed all faithful, clergy and lay, to work toward restoration. After centuries of ill-concealed animosities, the Church was opening a dialogue based on a more loving, more embracing worldview. CFM responded most positively.

Even before the council's decree, CFM had caught the "spirit" of the council. The 1961–62 program book contained an inquiry "Christian Unity and the Family," which observed that "the Pope has called a Council with the unity of Christendom in mind."[3] The Observe included the question, "Are there any attempts in your area to increase understanding among people of various religions? For example, by working on some common project to improve race-relations, housing, political activity." These in fact became the major areas of interfaith activity.

The 1963–64 inquiry book encouraged action along the same line. Included in this book were "Suggestions for Interfaith Dialogue," based on a sermon by Archbishop John Heenan of Liverpool, which showed an openness to other Christian denominations, but which also demonstrated the difficulties that lay ahead. The suggestions advised Catholics to stay calm, explain doctrine, admit differences, but "never accuse non-Catholics of being in bad faith." Catholics were encouraged to work with non-Catholics for the "good of the community." On the other hand, Catholics were counseled, "Don't deny that the Catholic Church claims to be the one true Church. Non-Catholics know that is our claim. . . . But . . . don't allege that only Catholics can be real Christians. That is not only absurd, but false." And Catholics were warned that charity did not require them to take part in public worship with non-Catholics, though "We may pray with them in private."[4] Many Catholics still thought it a sin to venture inside a non-Catholic church. The issue of worship proved to be the major obstacle in the ecumenical movement.

The suggestions were followed by two inquiries on "Interfaith Approaches to Community Problems," an approach that avoided the thornier issues of interfaith worship. The inquiry stated the problem in the following manner. "Leading church figures have stated strongly that one of the best ways for laymen to take part, at the parish level, in the ecumenical efforts of the Church is to join with persons of other faiths in solving community problems." However, Catholics suffered from "dual disabilities: they do not see community problems as part of their Christian concern and they do not, if they do recognize a community problem, readily join with persons of other faiths in seeking solutions."[5] The inquiry tried to lead CFMers to become involved in civic and community affairs and to consider interfaith action on a community problem. Groups were particularly encouraged to support the National Conference on Religion and Race, and the National Conference of Christians and Jews. CFMers did become involved in both programs at a local and national level.

By 1964 and 1965, CFMers had reached a fairly sophisticated level of interfaith activity, in caring for refugees, in community groups, and in fair housing battles. In Denver, CFMers joined with the Jewish Anti-defamation League to combat anti-Semitism.

Some groups even began experimenting with interfaith worship. A CFM section in Clinton, Iowa, sponsored common worship services in a Presbyterian Church and in a Catholic church. One member reflected, "We were praying for our separated brethren when someone got the idea, 'Why not pray with them?'"[6] The result was the creation of an interfaith, interracial council and common worship. Elsewhere, many other CFMers were engaged in "deep dialogue" with people of other faiths. Providence, Rhode Island, sponsored a "Unity Week" and stated that they had had dialogue groups since 1962. In Schenectady, a CFM action resulted in the creation of "The Dialogue Coffee House," which began in the basement of a Methodist Church. The Coffee House sponsored interfaith speakers and encouraged ecumenical dialogue.[7] Kalamazoo reported two interfaith CFM sections—one a Catholic-Presbyterian combination, the other a Catholic-Lutheran group. Atlanta reported an "ecumenical group," which contained an Episcopalian, a Presbyterian, a Baptist, a Roman Catholic, and a Lutheran; however, mixed groups were still a rarity in 1966.

EPISCOPAL CFM

More common was the creation of denominational CFM counterparts, notably Episcopalian CFM. In the early 1960s, the Episcopal bishop of the diocese of Chicago, James W. Montgomery, and a lay couple, Fred and Adena Stitt of Evanston, Illinois, began exploring the possibility of adapting CFM for Episcopal couples. They adapted several of the inquiries from *For Happier Families,* mimeographed them, and began spreading CFM for Episcopalians throughout the Chicago area. By late 1964, an Episcopal version of *FHF* was printed with the approval of the CFM Coordinating Committee, the Stitts, and Bishop Montgomery. The book had been adapted with the assistance of Program Committee chairs, Joe and Madelyn Bonsignore.

The Stitts began traveling from parish to parish, Crowley style, to spread CFM. They proclaimed that the "aims" of Episcopal CFM "were the same as Catholic CFM—to make Christ the center of our lives. . . . we are all Christians united through love."[8] They were assisted in their efforts by Robert Leonard Miller, canon for education of the diocese of Chicago, who persuaded priests to become chaplains, especially younger priests. One glaring difference between Catholic CFM and Episcopal CFM was that many of the Episcopal clergy were married. This simple fact created a different dynamic between the group and its chaplain. It also created some difficulties for Catholics. One Episcopal chaplain remembers a Catholic Sister asking him how he reconciled his "higher vocation" with the married state!

One young couple the Stitts corralled for CFM was a recently ordained (1963) Episcopal priest, Donald Jones, and his wife, Margaret. Don had been assigned to Rockford, Illinois, and there he met the Stitts and CFM. He began establishing Episcopal groups in his own parish and had four groups operating by 1966. The groups operated in the same manner as Catholic CFM, using the Observe-Judge-Act formula for Catholic Action, and beginning each new group with the "little yellow book" (albeit in mimeographed form). Similar actions resulted. One CFM group seeing the need for Saturday recreation for children started a Saturday swimming program at the community pool. Other acts of neighborliness, similar to those of Catholics groups, were also undertaken. Like Catholic CFMers, Episcopal CFMers regarded themselves as part of the avant garde within their church.[9] During these early years, however, Episcopal CFM, though connected with the national headquarters in Chicago, acted as a "separate" movement; that is, groups were not mixed but were made up solely of members of the Episcopal Church. In 1967, Joliet CFMers Joe and Jodie Adler, chairs of CFM's Interfaith Committee, acknowledged that CFM was "primarily a Catholic and Episcopal movement (kind of separate but equal)."[10]

As was the case with Catholic CFM groups, by 1967–68 Episcopal CFM was becoming interested in authentically ecumenical groups. By 1968, Rockford had two interfaith groups, which included Methodists, Presbyterians, and a Unitarian. Together they worked with the ecumenical community group, the Westside Cooperative Ministry.

LIVING ROOM DIALOGUES

The primary tool used in encouraging ecumenical CFM was the "living room dialogue." The dialogues were developed by the Paulists, an order long engaged in ecumenical work, and the National Council of Churches Division of Christian Unity in New York. Subtitled as "A Guide for Lay Discussion: Catholic—Orthodox—Protestant," *Living Room Dialogues* was presented as "a program of informal discussion by groups of Protestant, Orthodox, and Catholic church members meeting in each other's homes."[11] The program guide, written by Paulist William B. Greenspun and the NCC's William A. Norgren, was published jointly by Paulist Press and the NCC. Significantly, CFM was closely associated with the dialogues. At the press conference announcing the publication, brochures for CFM were also passed out. Less than two weeks later, Father Greenspun sent the Crowleys 200 copies of the dialogues.

Living Room Dialogues, for use by groups of between twelve and fifteen people, were based on a series of seven themes:

1. Concern, prayer, love: Foundations for dialogue
2. Good conversation in Christ
3. How do we worship?

4. Our common Christian heritage
5. Renewal of God's People
6. Our common Christian witness
7. Why we don't break bread together[12]

Along with the dialogues, Bible study and discussion were used. The group then prayed together. *ACT* reported that CFM groups across the country made use of the new book to begin ecumenical CFM groups. For instance, in Los Angeles a CFM group consisting of Presbyterians and Catholics used the dialogues. Repeatedly, CFMers spoke of "grass roots ecumenism."

CFM GOES ECUMENICAL

An article in *ACT* in 1968 asked the "perennial question, 'Where is CFM going?'" The answer: "CFM is going ecumenical. While the trend in recent years has been in this direction—from essentially Catholic to truly Christian—the ecumenical look will be real in future CFM programs."[13] Besides the *Decree on Ecumenism* issued at the Second Vatican Council and the grass-roots ecumenism of the *Living Room Dialogues,* the major forces behind ecumenical CFM were two couples—the Adlers and the Joneses. The Adlers, in particular, kept the pressure on traditional CFM, which was already moving, though slowly, in that direction.

In 1966, a revised version of *FHF* was published to incorporate the new documents of Vatican II. Despite the new openness to interfaith CFM, the revised *FHF* remained decidedly Catholic. Though Catholics were encouraged to cooperate with non-Catholics on community projects, the interfaith dimension of the book was recessive. In Meeting 19, in the Liturgy inquiry, "Our Link with Other Christians" was examined. The inquiry was introduced with a long quote from the *Dogmatic Constitution on the Church,* which emphasized that though others "do not profess the faith in its entirety," they did possess many things in common with Catholics, including our faith in Jesus, and that "in some real way they are joined with us in the Holy Spirit." The discussion then asked "What do we have in common with Protestants? What Christian practices should we do with our Protestant neighbors?" Meeting 20 expanded the discussion, examining "For Other Believers, Love and Esteem." Moslems and Jews were presented as worthy of respect; they were searching for answers to the fundamental questions of life, as were Christians. The discussion questions asked, "What do we know about non-Christian religions? What can we learn from them?"[14]

The openness expressed in the two 1966 liturgy inquiries, the Adlers believed, was the type of openness the whole movement should demonstrate in all of its programs. In 1967, they began to lobby hard for CFM to become an openly ecumenical movement; a truly ecumenical CFM—not an Episcopal CFM, a Lutheran CFM, and a Catholic CFM. Their formal proposal, which was distributed to CFM's Executive Committee for discussion, stated, "It seems clear that the present and continuing renewal of the Church in the world calls for the expansion of the Christian Family Movement into an inter-faith Movement." If CFM was to be effective in the larger community, it could not limit itself to Catholics. "As societies and communities are composed of families of various faiths, realistic and effective study and evaluation of and solutions to community problems must come from all the people in the community; not just from the Catholics present. To suppose that a group entirely, or even primarily, composed of Catholic members can bring about effective change is a continuation of the ghetto mentality we have been working to eradicate. It furthers disunity and divisiveness among all the people of God (if we may be permitted to coin a Vatican II phrase) and unrealistically and unjustifiably puts up barriers to positive attitudes that are imperative to any really meaningful civic progress. We feel CFM should be composed of couples from various backgrounds and faiths meeting together to work on community problems. The more varied the membership, the more realistic the solutions and more effective the actions and results." The proposal concluded by urging the Executive Committee to encourage interfaith groups and to form an ecumenical committee to work with the Program Committee to create a "program for use by interfaith groups."[15]

The 1967–68 inquiry program, *Building Community . . . Through Religious Life . . . Through Politics,* included several inquiries aimed at ecumenical action and interfaith dialogue. In one inquiry, entitled "Widening the Circle," CFMers were urged to "Plan an action to improve and continue building community among the parishioners or between parishes or (leading into the next inquiry) an ecumenical action."[16] The following inquiry examined the difficulties experienced when "religious people" try to collaborate. Often, religion was the source of division in a community. The inquiry sought to reduce the division. The Observe asked, "Describe the inter-faith dialogue going on in your area." The Judge asked "How far should ecumenical dialogue go—all faiths?" And the Act asked, "What action can we take to lessen the obstacles to unity in our area?" The book also included guidelines for an interfaith "Program of Renewal" to be sponsored by CFM groups.

Again, although the inquiry book encouraged ecumenical action and interfaith dialogue, it did not go far enough for the ecumenical activists. At an interfaith meeting held at the 1967 Notre Dame convention all denominations were urged to use the *Building Community* book but to adapt it to their particular tradition. The Adlers made a series of suggestions including eliminating the word "non-Catholic," and replacing it with "Christian"; using fewer quotes from Vatican II; using the term "clergy" instead of "priest;" and eliminating the Alternate Meeting 11 section (a group of inquiries on particular Catholic topics—Catholic schools, parish councils, vocations, priests, the role of the laity). It was suggested that groups use the Living Room Dialogues as a means of getting ecumenical CFM begun, then go on to use an adapted inquiry book.[17]

A committee of Protestant ministers from Joliet and Chicago was convened to adapt the book to make it usable for ecumenical groups. Included in the panel was Edward Gatson of Mount Olivet Baptist Church, Bruce Hesse of Messiah Lutheran, Edmund

Williams of Grace Methodist, all from Joliet, David McCreath of the Church Federation of Greater Chicago, and Canon Robert Miller of the Episcopal Diocese of Chicago. The ministers made suggestions as to how the inquiry book could be used for ecumenical groups. Ecumenical CFM was not to "be construed as an official action of any particular church organization."[18]

The Adlers continued to push for ecumenical CFM and continued to expand their contact with non-Catholics. One such contact was Harold Belgum, National Lutheran Family Life Education Director. The Adlers wrote Belgum in September 1967, "Interfaith CFM must not be delayed any longer for either lack of a program booklet or money."[19] They also kept stretching the notion of ecumenical. In another letter to the Executive Committee, the Adlers suggested CFM reach beyond Christian groups to include Jewish groups as well. They asked, "How can we presume to use the title 'Interfaith CFM' in a movement so heavily reliant on New Testament and Christian thinking?" Even this they stretched, suggesting that CFM should consider changing its name to the "*Community Family Movement*"(emphasis mine), in order to include all couples in a community.[20] To some CFMers this suggestion was too extreme. However, in Bethlehem and Allentown, Pennsylvania, two experimental groups were formed made up of Jews and Christians.[21]

At its February 1968 meeting, the Executive Committee firmly committed CFM to ecumenism. While not going so far as to accept the notion of becoming the "Community Family Movement," the Executive Committee did commit the movement to becoming truly interfaith. A statement "On Ecumenism" issued by the Executive Committee proclaimed, "As early as 1949, we chose to call ourselves the Christian Family Movement. Implicit in this choice of name was a potential openness to all Christians. The time has come to make this openness explicit by 1) Directing the program committee to produce an annual inquiry book suitable for use by Christians of all denominations. 2) Updating all CFM publications ecumenically. 3) Encouraging the start of more ecumenical groups by employing the total resources of the Christian Family

Movement."[22] With CFM officially ecumenical, the Interfaith Committee was disbanded. (It would be revived a year later, when the switch to ecumenism proved to be more difficult than originally thought).

The first fruit of the new ecumenical thrust was the publication of the 1968–69 annual inquiry program, *Shalom: Peace in the City, in the Family, in the World.* The first ecumenical book was produced by a Program Committee chaired by the Joneses. No separate edition was to be published for Protestant groups. All groups, Catholic, non-Catholic, and interfaith, were to use the new book. A notice in the introduction of the book read, "This inquiry book, written by the national CFM program committee, has been edited by an ecumenical commission for the purpose of assuring its usefulness to couples of all faiths in the work of the Christian Family Movement."[23] The book used a variety of non-Catholic sources in its "gray pages," pages that included thoughtful insights into current affairs, culled from contemporary magazines, sociologists, theologians, and other scholars. The quotes were to provoke reflection on the topic being investigated. Each group was encouraged to become involved in some community organization and/or program—a natural way to work with non-Catholics and non-Christians.

The following year, 1969, a new "yellow book" entitled *People Are . . .* replaced *FHF* as the basic introductory manual for CFM. In 1969–70, all CFM groups were to use *People Are . . .* as the yearly inquiry program. The new book was advertised as no longer having a "Roman Catholic thrust."[24] Donald Jones underscored the point, saying that CFM was now "an ecumenical movement" and that "two years ago at the National Convention, CFM officially broke formal ties with the Roman Catholic Church. This was to make possible truly ecumenical CFM."[25] The same claims were made in a letter sent out to all CFMers.

The book itself stated, "This book, the basic or 'beginning' book for CFM groups, does not have religion, faith or doctrine as its central theme. It does not deal with 'ecumenical issues' or theological differences. It does not have anything to say about conformity to or rebellion against any form of authority, religious or political, and it is not the arm of any organized church body."[26] As the Joneses stated, "The *People Are* . . . book uses our common experience as married couples within families as its primary emphasis . . . . The reason the Family is the main emphasis is to enable the Christian part of the Movement to spring from the common experience of Christian families. This means the new 'Yellow Book' is not parochially orientated as was the old."[27]

The Scripture-Liturgy inquiries had been replaced by a section called "Reflections" made up of quotes from Scripture and other, contemporary sources. This shift represented a significant change. In content, the book was an adaptation of the time-tested subject matter of *For Happier Families* without the heavy Catholic perspective and use of exclusively Catholic source material.

ECUMENISM: KEEPING CFM AVANT GARDE

Many believed that by providing leadership in the ecumenical encounter, CFM would retain its tradition of leading the way. Moreover, CFM would be at the forefront of the redefinition of Church as initiated by the Second Vatican Council.

CFM would also provide sustenance to those who believed the changes called for by Vatican II were being implemented too slowly. In an address to the CFM chaplains, CFM pioneer Louis Putz approved the break from the association of CFM with the parish. "Parishes and dioceses have hindered your development. You are the People of God. You have your own work cut out for you."[28] His position was supported by the assistant national chaplain, Ed Kohler. Like Putz, Kohler believed the ecumenical approach was in keeping with the Council's *Decree on Ecumenism*, but that it also pushed CFM beyond the "institutional Church"—thus offering institutional support for being anti-institutional. Kohler asserted that the ecumenical approach "will help couples overcome the parish orientation, and . . . live in the real world. CFM will be freed of rigid ties to an institutional base, i.e. the parish and the diocese.

CFM will lose ultimately its image as 'right arm' of the bishop, the old notion of Catholic Action."[29] The movement was henceforth to seek its identity with the community of which it was a part, not with the parish.

The move to become ecumenical did indeed represent a major break with CFM's past. Though CFMers in the past may have been open to working with non-Catholics in their community with a pragmatic ecumenism, CFM was a Catholic movement. Especially as defined by Monsignor Hillenbrand, the Mass was central to the movement, as were the many inquiries designed to help CFMers understand the Mass better and to participate in it actively. So the move to become truly interfaith signaled the creation of a radically different identity, an identity that dismayed many members and the priests who worked with them.

PROBLEMS WITH ECUMENISM—INTERCOMMUNION

Despite the bold policy decisions, the membership of the movement remained largely Catholic. Separate groups of Protestant CFM continued to spring up—(Episcopal, Lutheran, and Methodist being the largest)— all across the United States. Peoria had a new group which included a Methodist, a Lutheran, a Presbyterian, and an Episcopalian, as did Joliet.[30] San Diego under the leadership of Al and Lillian Macy had six ecumenical groups by 1968.[31] New York CFM hosted an ecumenical weekend at Graymoor, the mother-house of the ecumenically oriented Friars of the Atonement. Though issue after issue of *ACT* reported similar developments, in truth the ecumenical concept never had widespread success. Most groups remained separated according to denomination.

The greatest obstacle to the ecumenical movement taking hold was the "problem" of the Eucharist. While groups readily came together for common prayer services, things fell apart when the topic of shared communion between faiths was raised. From the Roman Catholic perspective, communion in another church was strictly forbidden. Nor were members of another faith allowed to share the Eucharist at a Catholic gathering. Similar, if somewhat more fluid, prohibitions existed in most Protestant denominations. This barrier was referred to as "the agony" by a speaker at a CFM area convention in New Hampshire.[32]

Nonetheless CFM became actively involved in the dialogue on intercommunion. In 1970, CFM participated in the National Workshop for Christian Unity held in Kansas City, Missouri. The two major topics of dialogue were "ecumenical marriages" (what Catholics used to call mixed marriages), and intercommunion, with the latter topic receiving the bulk of the conference's attention. At one point, delegates agreed that there were certain situations in which intercommunion could be "beneficial." Catholic delegates were reminded by the bishops present that intercommunion remained forbidden, but they were encouraged to continue to "study" the matter.[33] Delegate Katherine Burgraff of New York CFM summed up her view of the conference in the title of her report, "Christian Unity: Why 'Later' Rather than 'Sooner.'"[34]

The divisiveness of the Eucharist first became a critical problem for CFM at the Program Committee meetings, when Hoyt Hickman, a Methodist minister, and his wife, Martha, joined the committee in 1969. At the committee's annual meetings, the Eucharist was celebrated daily. When Hickman and Jones were asked to preside at one of these, several Catholic members felt in conscience that they could not receive communion. The decision was an agonizing one, with several committee members breaking down in tears. As chaplain Ed Kohler remembers it, the "lived experience of feeling one" was undercut by the feeling of disunity created by the Eucharist, the sacrament that was supposed to signify unity.[35]

The intensity of discussion and feeling at the Program Committee meetings moved Kohler to wonder how the struggle of the Program Committee could be shared with the larger CFM community. His decision: invite Donald Jones to celebrate the Episcopal Eucharist at the 1971 National CFM convention to be held in

August at Notre Dame. The decision would generate a tremendous tempest. CFM once again found itself well in advance of the institutional Catholic Church.

At the 1971 national convention, by now called the "National Seminar on Family Life" at Notre Dame, Jones celebrated the first non-Roman Catholic liturgy in convention history at the Friday evening Eucharist. He also invited all those present, close to 800 people, most of whom were Catholic, to receive communion. Before the service he had stated the two churches' position on intercommunion. Jones said, "Officially the Roman Catholic Church would prefer that you didn't receive Holy Communion. Officially the Episcopal church would prefer that I didn't invite you publicly to receive Holy Communion. Anyone who wishes to receive and presents himself will be given Holy Communion."[36] Jones's invitation was in keeping with Kohler's intent. In planning the Eucharist, Kohler had told the Executive Committee when explaining the possibility of intercommunion, "It will be up to the conscience and personal opinion of each person to decide on the degree of participation."[37] Of the estimated 800 present, all but 50 received communion. Jones was assisted by CFM Catholic chaplains Kohler and Ed Hamel, O.S.A., in distributing the communion.

For the participants the intercommunion was a most positive event. Of the close to 200 responses to the postconvention questionnaire, all but six people gave the Episcopal liturgy a rating of good or excellent. No response gave the most negative rating. Jones recalls nothing but positive comments from convention attendees. He recalled that at least ten couples who were in mixed marriages approached him to thank him for the Mass, telling him that this was the first time they had received communion together in their lives, and it was wonderful.[38] Generally speaking, the mood of the convention was upbeat and positive. The controversy that erupted soon after came as something of a surprise to Jones.

As news of the Episcopal liturgy and intercommunion spread, Jones and CFM were roundly attacked for their "unauthorized liturgical innovation."[39] Jones was vilified in some Catholic newspapers as a "radical priest who had come in to raise a ruckus." Particularly upset was the Roman Catholic bishop of the diocese of Fort Wayne-South Bend, in whose jurisdiction the Mass had taken place. The Episcopal bishop of Northern Indiana took an enormous amount of criticism for allowing this to happen, even though he had not been formally asked for permission. (The Episcopal bishops of Milwaukee, where Jones was stationed, and of Chicago had given him their permission.) The controversy reached the highest circles of the Catholic Church, with inquiries received from the apostolic delegate, Cardinal Luigi Raimondi. An official statement of the diocese of Fort Wayne-South Bend concluded with this condemnation, "If CFM is moving in this direction, it is time to pause and reconsider its position. Meanwhile, somebody is responsible. Who?"[40]

The magnitude of the outcry also surprised the leadership of CFM. The liturgy had not been conducted as "an act of defiance." True, CFM's leadership was discouraged by the pace of ecumenical reform, but the action was not meant as a challenge. Kohler observed, "We have wrestled with this and debated and tried to make as conscientious and responsible a decision as we could," but the ecumenical commitment of CFM demanded that such a liturgy be celebrated. Kohler went on, "We felt that the symbolic value alone was essential to counterbalance the image of our being only a Roman Catholic movement. We're still predominantly that, but we felt we had to say in a public way at a national convention that we have become a movement of couples of all different churches."[41]

Similar sentiments were expressed by a *National Catholic Reporter* editorial, which was endorsed by CFM and reprinted in its own official newspaper, *ACT*. The editorial pointed out that "CFM is not a radical group. . . . [It is] ahead of, but not in conflict with, authority." It went on to note that Jones had been involved with CFM for many years. "In sharing communion with him, other CFM delegates were celebrating the unity that was clearly felt.

Their action was a mature recognition of reality at a basic level, and an undefiant acknowledgment that reality need not wait on curial approval."[42] CFM's president couple, Ray and Dorothy Maldoon, reiterated the same point, arguing that authentic change could not wait on the clergy and that CFMers were "trying to show that we are mature Christians and that we must move forward and we're not really waiting for the clergy to say we must do this or must do that. It was spelled out in Vatican documents about ecumenism and we've decided to take that step."[43]

Despite the brave comments, that single Episcopal liturgy placed CFM under intolerable stress at a critical point in its evolution. Jones himself would later reflect that it was the "issue of the Eucharist," the issue of intercommunion, that "broke the back of ecumenical CFM."[44] The ensuing uproar made plain to CFMers the broad gaps between grass-roots ecumenism and the official Church. Little progress seemed forthcoming. From the other side, Father Louis Putz saw the liturgy as the final split between CFM and the bishops. In his estimation, with the liturgy "CFM lost the bishops," and the movement's further decline was ensured.

One final result of the liturgy: The commitment of CFM's national leaders to ecumenical groups seemed to lessen, and once again denominational CFM was emphasized, signaling a return to what the Adlers had called separate but equal CFM. By 1972, the Maldoons wrote to Putz, "The present membership of the Executive Committee seems to lack confidence in the decision to be ecumenical in fact as well as in name."[45]

Still, the ecumenical dream did not die easily. The Maldoons and Kohler attended a meeting of the Family Ministries division of the Department of Christian Education of the National Council of Churches, an action *ACT* heralded as a "step forward for ecumenical CFM."[46] In addition, CFM's Ecumenical Committee was transformed into the Christian Unity Committee, (headed by John Laurich of Helena, Montana) on the grounds that the movement was already ecumenical; it made no sense to have an ecumenical committee. Not only that; in 1973, CFM created a national chaplaincy team that paired a Protestant minister with Father Louis Putz, then rector of Moreau Seminary for the Order of the Holy Cross at Notre Dame. Appointed with him was Methodist minister Hoyt Hickman, and his wife, Martha. (Martha later wrote the distinctly non-Catholic book entitled *How to Marry a Minister.*) The Hickmans were from Nashville but had lived in Erie, Pennsylvania, since 1965, when Hoyt became pastor of the United Methodist Church there. In the same year they had joined an ecumenical CFM group, via the Living Room Dialogues. In 1969, they had become members of the national Program Committee, and now, they became co-chaplains of the movement. The following year they were replaced by Don and Margaret Jones, thereby keeping the chaplaincy ecumenical.

Despite the best efforts of the CFM leadership, ecumenism never really caught on with the rank and file. The ecumenical movement came precisely at the time CFM's membership rolls were heading toward a new low. By 1971, CFM claimed only 9,000 couples nationally, the lowest number since the early 1950s. This decline became a near-obsessive concern of the movement, an obsession not entirely understood by many of the ecumenical groups that were just beginning. Rightly or not, the fear that ecumenical CFM was turning off Catholics caused CFM to retreat from its ecumenical commitment.

TEN

Gender and Sexuality

Beyond ecumenism, the volatile change in the status of women in society and within the Church bore earthshaking implications for CFM. Between 1950 and 1970 an extraordinary transformation of the sexual identities and gender roles for men and women in the United States took place. In the 1950s the clearly defined nuclear family was celebrated in the churches and in the media as a model. The "cult of domesticity" flourished, with women depicted as enjoying their "God-given tasks" of taking care of home and children. The postwar best-seller *Modern Woman: The Lost Sex,* by Ferdinand Lundberg and Marynia Farnham, touted the prevailing wisdom: Women were unhappy because they were fighting their "biological destiny" of being wives and mothers. They should leave the workforce, where their services had been valued during World War II, and return home. It was the man who should go out into the world, to provide for his family and run its affairs. Sexual matters were not to be discussed in public.

All this changed dramatically in the 1960s. The sexual revolution, fueled by the introduction of "the pill," called into question the old sexual taboos and made forthright discussion of sex more common. Simultaneously, the status and image of women and men underwent a significant change. In 1963, Betty Friedan's *The Feminine Mystique,* also a best-seller, suggested that many women were frustrated by being limited to housework. Women needed more expansive areas in which to act if they were to be "fulfilled." By the early 1970s "feminism" had become a household word, and the old notions of "man," "woman," and "sexuality" had been shattered.

These changes profoundly affected CFM, even though it was a movement in which husbands and wives had, almost from the start, participated together as equals. By the late 1960s, CFM was embroiled in disputes over birth control, the status of women, and abortion.

CFM AND THE STATUS OF WOMEN

From its inception, CFM taught traditional concepts about the roles of men and women. Men and women were different, but equal. In God's great plan, man and woman had been created to complement and fulfill one another. Marriage created a unity. CFM regularly sponsored and supported Cana Conferences that clearly articulated the differences between, and complementariness of, men and women. According to *The New Cana Manual* (1957), man was the head of the family, the center of authority; woman was the heart, the center of affection. Man was the protector, the provider, who must earn his living in the world: aggressive, courageous, interested in "objects and projects, facts and figures," more interested in things than persons. Man analyzed and put things in logical order. His biggest problem was that he was prone to self-doubt and discouragement. Woman was the homemaker, "spontaneously and easily" given to the service of another, i.e., husband and children: more sympathetic and sensitive than the male and with an intuitive faculty whereby she was able to take a wider view of things. Woman was more interested in persons than in things. Her biggest problem was that she was prone to loneliness.[1] The *Manual* provided a simple list of the complementary traits of men and women.

Male Traits	*Female Traits*
physically stronger	physically weaker
more realistic	more idealistic

logical	intuitive
more emotionally stable	more emotionally volatile
objective	subjective
more factual	more fanciful
slow judgment	quick judgment
literal	tangential
seeks love	wants love
self-assured	less self-assured
holistic thinking	grasps details
less adaptable	more adaptable
less possessive	more possessive[2]

The manual did acknowledge the simplicity of the listing, but there was nothing radical, innovative, or reactionary in their list. Most Americans would have concurred with it.

CFM likewise expressed this standard view of men and women. In a talk billed as "Three Big Advantages of CFM," the Crowleys stated that CFM's first big advantage was, "It recognizes and utilizes the complementary abilities of husband and wife: man's thinking and generalizing; woman's quality of heart and capacity for details and for being practical."[3] Interestingly, Pat and Patty complemented one another beautifully, according to this definition, in their own lives. Pat continued his analysis of the male role in the family, emphasizing that "the man comes first in the home" and that the wife should "encourage and help her husband to assume his proper leadership; that she lean toward conformity with his way of managing affairs, and try to develop interests similar to his." Patty concurred, noting that "a husband's work keeps him away from the home for long hours. He returns fatigued and often irritated. Unless the wife has a deep appreciation of his needs and some understanding of the psychological difference between man and woman she is likely to widen the gap instead of bridging it. Of course, the husband should try and reciprocate."[4]

This same analysis was presented in various articles in *ACT* and in the annual program booklet throughout the 1950s. In 1958,

CFM chaplain Forrest Macken, c.p., asked the question, "Must a wife obey her husband?" His answer: Yes. He asked further, "Why is the wife not the head?" The answer: "The fundamental reason lies in the husband's God-given roles to provide and protect." The woman needed to be protected and provided for, particularly after childbirth and during child-rearing. Ultimately, the different roles were assigned by God.[5]

The father was also the spiritual head of the family. The husband was required to "guide his family to Christian perfection."[6] He was to initiate "pious practices" in the home, and work to transform the environment. The woman was to inspire. In an article entitled "Woman's Role in Next Year's Program," Canadian CFMer Lettie Morse reflected on the tension between the social thrust of the program and the mother's responsibility in the home. The program's goal of bringing "Christ to the market place" would "take both husbands and wives." Morse then asks, "What does this mean to the women members of CFM?" Clearly, their families could not take second place to the program—the wife first had to take care of her husband and children. Morse suggests three ways for a woman to move the program forward. First, she can read to more deeply understand the issues. Second, she can encourage her husband. Finally, she can instill in her children the proper Christian ideals. The essay concluded, "If the heart cares, the head will try harder to think of what to do."[7] This sentiment of the wife pushing her husband into the world was regularly repeated. Another article concludes, "The leadership the husband exercises will set the moral tone for the capture of a neighborhood for Christ. And complementing the husband is the wife, whose faith and confidence will inspire the husband to perform his role."[8]

The ideology of husband and wife as presented by CFM prescribed what was necessary for successful home life. Men and women had to understand their purpose and nature, and act accordingly. CFM couple Tom and Kay Gaudette reflected on the reality of home life and the CFM directive to transform the environment. Tom served as chairman of the neighborhood council in a section of Chicago. Kay, mother of four, observed, "I don't think a husband's place is in the home every night of the week. As a family we should project ourselves into the community, and Tom's active participation in the council enables him to do exactly that."[9] Though it was the husband acting outside the home, he represented the family.

The woman's place was in the home and neighborhood taking care of her family. This was not a denigration. *ACT* reminded, "The work of the mother is a true vocation; creative, spiritually fruitful, and of primary importance in a day when family life is being attacked from every quarter."[10] Several of the social inquiries in the annual programs dealt with working mothers, and the message was clear: a system in which women were required to work outside the home was a disordered system.

In the 1952–53 inquiry booklet, the topic of working mothers was examined in the nineteenth meeting. The inquiry began with a long quote from Pius XI's encyclical *Quadragesimo Anno* that articulated the standard Catholic teaching on working wives: the primary responsibility of the mother was the home. If a woman was forced to work because of her husband's poor wages, it was as an "intolerable abuse." The husband should be paid a family living wage that allowed the wife to stay at home to take care of their children. In the Observe section of the inquiry, couples were asked to observe the number of working mothers and the reasons for their working. "How does the absence of the mother affect the family? Does her absence cause her children to be a problem in the neighborhood?" The Judge section asked a series of probing questions, including "Does the wife working develop a false standard of living?" The implication is clear—the wife should not work simply for luxuries. "Is the independence a woman develops when she works a good thing for her family?" Again, it is clear from the phrasing that the wife's independence would undermine family unity.[11]

In the 1958–59 program, the topic of working mothers appears again as an elective inquiry. The inquiry is almost identical to the 1952–53 inquiry save for the loaded question, "What are the possible bad effects of a mother's working outside the home?"[12] No mention is made of the woman's independence.

In 1962–63 the topic was addressed once more in light of Pope John XXIII's encyclical *Mater et Magistra*. The inquiry begins with a long quote from Pope John, which emphasizes the shared responsibility of parents in the rearing of children. The Observes are more rigorous than in the earlier inquiries on working mothers, calling for statistical studies of working women, but the inquiry as a whole is no more enthusiastic about working wives than the previous ones. The inquiry states the problem simply, "It is difficult to reconcile the homemaker's responsibilities with an occupation outside the home." Among the questions in the suggested "Discussion Starters" are: "When a wife has a job does a husband lose some of his importance as the head of the house?" "What about the religious and cultural formation of the children of a working mother?"[13] If the questions seem open-ended, one of the suggestions for action makes the implication of the inquiry clear. "Protest efforts by business and government officials to encourage the practice of women working."[14] The inquiry also encourages groups to battle the ongoing denigration of the role of housewife that was occurring in the schools and the media.

While CFM's ideology spoke of the distinctions between men and women and of a limited sphere in which wives could work, the experience of CFM undercut these distinctions. Essential to this was the simple fact that the CFM was a movement of *couples*. In an era in which most organizations were separated by gender, in CFM husband and wife met together as equals, with other couples. For the first time, many women found themselves speaking openly in public on an equal basis with their husbands. Many CFM women spoke of the "confidence" this experience created in themselves and their capabilities. Alma Sternik of Toronto noted that "CFM brought you out of yourself,"[15] and Isabelle Leroux concluded, "CFM worked wonders for women." Women who entered the movement "quiet and docile," developed into strong, confident women, unafraid to take a public stand.[16]

Many found themselves in a variety of public undertakings they previously would not have imagined they could do—civic groups, school boards, even politics. Eileen Sullivan, a ten-year CFM veteran, became the first woman judge in the Albany County Family Court in New York. Marion Dewar became mayor of Ottawa, Canada. Joanne Farley founded and became the first director of Citizen Advocacy in the Montreal Area.[17] The list goes on and on. CFM prepared women for public service.

To a large extent, the success of CFM depended on its women. Women shared the leadership of groups, and, more often than not, prepared the meetings. Since most CFM women did not work outside the home, they had the time to do the necessary work. As veteran CFMer Fran Muench observed, "Women did all the work, and the men got all the credit!"[18] The experience of CFM propelled many women into paying jobs. Their ability to handle significant responsibility and action within the movement convinced them they could work outside the home without damaging the family. An Oregon CFMer concluded, "Many CFM wives in the mid-60s made a major change in their lifestyle. Although early CFM had been much against working mothers, CFM training led women to realize that their responsibility to themselves and to society did not end with raising a family. So, many returned to college, entered new careers, or found other means of self-fulfillment."[19]

The lived experience of CFM undercut the gender stereotypes which the movement endorsed. When the questioning of gender roles erupted during the 1960s, CFM women were ready, though not all CFM women were equally ready to be "liberated."

Even in the 1950s, CFM was modifying gender stereotypes. The first edition of *For Happier Families* included an inquiry on the "Family Obligations of the Father," which prodded fathers to spend more time with their families and to actually speak with their children. More significantly, women were encouraged to investigate serious issues. Even before CFM began, the Young Mothers' Catholic Action cells in Chicago were examining "woman's place in the world" and such "male" concerns as race relations, labor relations, and unions.[20] Patty Crowley often laughs as she recalls the early days of the movement—the men talked of family and the women talked unions. Many clergy, including Hillenbrand, did not believe real Catholic Action could occur in mixed groups. Catholic Action sought to transform the world outside the family; they feared that with women involved men would be trapped within the family. Moreover, it was feared the presence of women would trivialize the inquiries. Such was not the case, as evidenced by the yearly program books and actions.

CFM AND THE NEW WOMAN

By the mid-1960s CFM began to reevaluate the role of women in society as a result of the experience of women within the movement and in response to the large-scale cultural shift that was taking place in the United States. As the women's movement grew through the 1960s, the idealized notion of the happy housewife, working contentedly within the home and raising her children, began to fade. Women began to demand access to jobs hitherto restricted as "men's work." Women began speaking of work outside the home as necessary for the full development of all their capacities and talents. Discussion of the need for good child care became commonplace.

CFM was not immune to these currents. By 1967, *ACT* was publishing commentaries that openly questioned the traditional Catholic teaching on working mothers and the role of women. CFMer Trudie Barreras wrote an article entitled "Career or Family— Is Motherhood the End for the Educated Woman?"[21] On the back cover of *ACT*, sociologist William D'Antonio was quoted as saying, "I think we are past the stage where we can maintain or want to maintain the aphorism that a woman's place is necessarily or only in the home."[22] More radically, scholar Sidney Callahan was quoted as saying, "By the time we have women priests, I think the Church will be so changed that no one will even notice."[23]

The new attitude toward woman was reflected in an inquiry in the 1967–68 inquiry program entitled "Madame President!" Women were encouraged to run for political office; men were encouraged to support women candidates, possibly even their wives![24] In a dramatic dinner speech to a group of CFM women, former Program Committee co-chair Madelyn Bonsignore gave a vivid description of a new understanding of women's role. "Christ seemed to think active, involved women were fine. . . . So take courage; you are firmly within the fold if you feel more useful at a city council meeting than at a bridge benefit, though you may never get chosen Catholic Mother of the Year." Madelyn went on to suggest that suburban women had a special duty to become politically involved: Their husbands were too busy between work and the long commute. Suburban women had the time. So she urged, "Get out and work!"[25]

CFM continued to redefine its attitude toward women. In the 1969–70 inquiry book and the new introductory book *People Are . . .* the topic of working wives was once again examined but with a much different tone than had been the case in the 1950s. Gone are the papal quotes; the inquiry entitled "A Woman's Place . . . ?" begins with a quote from *Marriage* magazine which discusses the increasing number of working women, and then goes on to assert that though the woman who desires to stay at home is still to be highly respected, the woman who chooses to work outside the home is also accepted. The Observe section again explores the reasons why wives work, but it also examines the availability of child care facilities. The Judge section again asks the motivations for working; beyond materially improving one's lifestyle, the Judge also asks "To what degree did work, paid or volunteer, seem motivated by a desire for personal fulfillment? As a change from the home environment? In response to a community need?" The couples are also asked, "How much weight do you feel should be given to these factors in determining a wife's role: Her own needs as a developing person/ Her obligation to any talents or abilities she may have/ Her husband's needs and feelings/ The family as a whole."[26] These terms—needs, feelings, developing person— are definitely new to CFM and suggest a dramatically different understanding of women and men.

The 1971–72 inquiry program continued the discussion, asking CFMers to examine current definitions of femininity and masculinity and to reflect on the reevaluation of woman's role that was occurring in the modern world. In the inquiry "Women and the New Feminism," the introductory paragraph states, "There is, indeed, a growing feeling on the part of many women that they do not fulfill themselves in the traditional homemaker role fully, if at all." If these women took jobs in the business world, what was to become of the children? Rather than asserting that the woman's place was in the home, as in the 1950s inquiries, this book suggested looking into the adequacy of day care and encouraged husbands to become more involved in the home. The next inquiry examined changing notions of masculinity, pointing out that as women changed their roles, the roles of men also had to be reevaluated. The inquiries encouraged CFMers to break through traditional stereotypes, to arrive at new understandings of gender roles.

Included in the Observes of this inquiry was an "opinionnaire," developed by the American Association of University Women, that couples were asked to fill out themselves and then use to ask other couples their opinions. Couples were asked whether they agreed or disagreed with such statements as these: "A woman's first responsibility is to be a feminine companion of men and a mother." "Women who wish to develop their potential have adequate opportunities to do so." "Children of non-working mothers are better adjusted than children of working mothers." "Women are by nature more mediating than men."[27] The questionnaire and the inquiry generated a good deal of debate in the pages of *ACT* and within local CFM groups.[28] Many articulated a vision of women in keeping with the new feminist movement. Other CFMers were not as supportive, seeing in the new feminism the destruction of the family and of everything CFM had worked for over the years.

The differences between CFMers surfaced again when several women asked the Executive Committee to develop a new symbol for CFM that would be more in keeping with modern thought about women and the family. The old CFM symbol was an amalgam of four separate symbols representing Christ, man, woman, and child, superimposed on one another. *For Happier Families* gave this explanation:

Y *Man*—shown with his arms lifted up to God, standing as a tower of great strength, exemplifying his place as head of the family.

⟑ *Woman*—reaching toward the earth, beautifully demonstrating her likeness to the earth in her fertility—the place she holds in the divine plan of creation, fulfilled in the family unit.

O *Child*—the circle, as a sign of life, represents the child, showing the closeness of the power of man and woman to God's supreme power of creation.[29]

A new symbol proposed by Program Committee member June Smith of Erie, Pennsylvania, sought to reflect new understandings of men, women, and family by merging a symbol for man and woman, a symbol for life (children), and a new symbol for the Christian family. Along with the new logo came a new explanation: the symbols would suggest that husband and wife were "each a unique person with a full range of needs and talents, each helping balance the other" and the Christian family would be shown to be "supportive and open to each of its members and also to all the family of God."[30] The proposed new symbol faithfully reflected the new attitudes toward the family that had been circulating in CFM over the preceding several years.

The ensuing debate revealed the division within CFM's rank and file. *ACT* published a series of letters responding to the proposed symbol. Several supported the old symbol and attacked Smith's "feminism." Burnie Bauer came out strongly against the change and stated that June Smith "has blurred vision." Others supported Smith. One letter read, "It's [the new symbol] much more meaningful for today's world than the old interpretation."[31] This split in CFM mirrored the split that was growing within American society. For many the expansion of roles and opportunities for women was occurring too slowly; for others it was occurring too rapidly. These tensions were increasingly evident within CFM.

How did all this reverberate at the international level? The issue of women's role in the family and in the world was even more pressing, given the abominable treatment of women in many countries. ICCFM addressed this issue and began to tout CFM as a cure for the inequities inflicted upon women. In preparing for Familia '74 (see below), promotional literature observed that CFM's "most unusual contribution is a long insistence that married people should share in meetings as a couple. Thus the proposed Assembly will not and cannot be a male dominated one."[32] And as a delegate to the assembly put it, "In CFM, women and men are equal."[33]

ICCFM turned its attention to "sexism within the Church," which was chosen as the area for inquiry at the international level for 1973. The inquiry asked "[W]hat role has the church played in liberating the woman?" The tenor of the inquiry was that the Church has not done enough. The introductory comment reads, "All acts of suppression and discrimination are contrary to God's will. In examining the present situation it is imperative to acknowledge the suppression of and discrimination against women in past ages. The Church has played a dual role in this area. While preaching equality and love, it has subtly failed in theory and practice."[34]

The inquiry called upon couples to examine the actual condition of women in the church in their own locale. The Observe question leaves little doubt about what will be found: "Examine neighborhood churches to see how women are denied access to positions of authority, are subtly repressed, and underrepresented." There was nothing subtle in the phrasing of the question. By 1973, CFM, at least in its international form, was questioning the status of women in the world and within the Church. The movement had come a long way since 1949.

SEXUALITY AND BIRTH CONTROL

As CFM reevaluated the role of woman in the modern world, it also began to reevaluate the issue of sexuality. As had been the case with women, CFM's attitude toward sexuality in the 1950s followed traditional lines and was not much different from that of mainstream America. The primary purpose of marriage was the procreation and the education of children. On sexual issues, CFM was ardently conservative, joining the fight against indecent literature, immoral movies, and other manifestations of filth that were cluttering the modern world. Birth control was condemned in no uncertain terms, following Pope Pius XI's 1930 encyclical *Casti Connubi,* which condemned birth control as intrinsically evil. Birth control violated the natural law, as a 1960–61 inquiry instructed, "Why is artificial birth control wrong? Would it be wrong even if the Church did not exist?"[35] The answer, of course, was Yes.

Early CFM had no difficulty accepting this teaching, offering the ideal of the big family and counseling couples to accept as many children as God sent them. Even the rhythm method, which the pope had approved, had to be used with caution, if at all. In a 1959–60 inquiry, couples were asked, "Why is it wise to seek the advice of one's confessor before using rhythm?"[36] The answer was ready to hand. Birth control undermined strong family life by introducing selfishness and individualism into the family. The Planned Parenthood Association (PPA) was repeatedly singled out in CFM literature and actions as an enemy of good family life. Several early actions of CFM groups consisted of protesting PPA-sponsored events and making sure good Catholic literature was available to counteract PPA propaganda.

CFMers were also concerned over the growing reliance on birth control as an answer to the problem of world overpopulation. A standard strategy, abhorrent to CFM, was to solve the problems of developing nations by introducing birth control programs. CFMers were reminded that this was not a Christian solution. Instead, the root causes that led to the use of contraception had to be addressed and corrected.

By the mid-1960s, CFM had begun to reconsider its attitude toward birth control and sexuality. As early as 1963, CFM moved to the forefront of the growing debate over birth control and the growing perception that the Church was going to modify its traditional teaching and approve some form of birth control. For too long, several articles in *ACT* complained, the Church offered nothing but a negative theology of sex. The conjugal act was seen primarily as a means of procreation, with little attention given to its unitive aspect. In June 1963, *ACT* published a provocative statement by Bishop William K. Bekkers of the Netherlands, entitled "Birth Control: Viewpoint of a European Bishop." Bekkers stated that the couple "and they alone . . . must decide what God requires of them concretely . . . how large the family should be and how the children should be spaced."[37] Family limitation did not necessarily entail artificial contraception; Pope Pius XII had approved the rhythm method of natural family planning. Many CFM groups began supporting rhythm clinics, and national CFM supported research into making rhythm more effective and reliable. In 1967, the Executive Committee would endorse the creation of a CFM Laboratory for the Study of Reproduction, though this project never came to fruition.[38]

With the Second Vatican Council, the ends of marriage and the marriage act were expressed in a more positive light (in part as a result of CFM efforts—see chapter 7). The love expressed and engendered by the marital act was of equal importance to its procreative aspect. The council also addressed the issue of "responsible parenthood" and the need of some couples to limit their families. Birth control was not directly addressed, but the issue was to be studied by a special papal commission, the Pontifical Commission for the Study of Population, Family and Births, popularly known as the Papal Birth Control Commission.

In 1964, Pat and Patty Crowley were asked to become members of the commission, one of only three married couples to be appointed. The story of the Crowleys and the Birth Control Commission has already been clearly told by Robert McClory in *Turning Point* and need not be elaborated here. The impact the issue had on the movement and the effect the Crowleys' position had will be considered below.

In 1965, CFM leadership engaged the question of artificial contraception more directly. A series of articles published in *ACT* in the last half of 1965 suggested not only that change in the Church's teaching on birth control was possible but that that it was probable. Typical of CFM, *ACT* invited all viewpoints to be expressed, and a debate ensued, but the viewpoint of *ACT* was definitely in favor of a change in the teaching.

In July 1965 scholar John Noonan published a small essay in *ACT* entitled "Catholics and Contraception: How the Church Reached Its Present Position," which was a brief summation of his massive and definitive history, *Contraception: A History of Its Treatment by Catholic Theologians and Canonists* (Harvard University Press, 1964). Noonan placed the development of the Church's teaching in a historical context, showing how it had evolved over the centuries in response to various crises. In responding to the crises the negative, defensive posture was emphasized to the detriment of the positive. He concluded by asking the important question, "Are rules once necessary to protect procreation, life and personal dignity (of the spouse) now necessary for the community of Christians?"[39]

In the same issue, Father Walter Imbiorski of the Chicago Cana Conference, and editor of *The New Cana Manual*, called for a dialogue between Catholics on the issue of birth control—a bold proposition in itself. In his article, "What We Should Ask Ourselves," Imbiorski asserted that "as baptized Christians we must participate in its [the Church's] charismatic search for a richer and fuller understanding of marriage, procreation, and sexuality."[40] This was new thinking. Even more startling, Imbiorski cited the Patriarch Maximus who said it was time to listen to married couples "rather than celibate theologians." Imbiorski cautioned that he did not want the dialogue to become "adversary proceedings—conservatives against liberals, 'new breed' against 'old guard'." Rather, he hoped the dialogue would result in a deeper understanding of the

Church's teaching so it could be better presented to the rest of the world.

Imbiorski proposed ten provocative questions designed to stimulate discussion, among which were:

> 1. If contraception is forbidden by natural law, "the law graven in the hearts of all men" why is it that in Western society only Catholics by and large recognize and acknowledge this proposition?

> 4. Is frequent and continued physical expression of love in marriage truly a necessity for the fostering and deepening of love and for the good of the marriage, or are we drifting with a cultural situation that overemphasizes sexuality and denigrates control and asceticism?

> 9. Are those who suggest wider approval of various means of birth control denying God's providence and forgetting that He will provide?

> 10. Do you find your Catholic friends who practice contraception against the stated law of the Church in other respects exemplary people or is their contraceptive behavior part of a pattern of selfishness?[41]

Questions concerning contraception and premarital chastity, the proper rearing of children, and overpopulation were also asked. While the questions were ostensibly objective, Imbiorski's bias for change was not hard to detect.

The following issue of *ACT* featured a response by Canadian CFMers (and former Program Committee members) Grant and Vivian Maxwell entitled, "Love and Contraception in Marriage—A Response." The Maxwells acknowledged it was time to reexamine the Church's official teaching in "light of new knowledge and new realities." They called for a "move to a new (but not final or absolute) consensus, which the Pope and Bishops will some day confirm officially." Typical of CFM, the movement was to be out in front of the official Church in this matter. As the matter was under consideration by the papal commission, now was a time for "responsible public opinion." The Maxwells concluded that they knew good Catholic couples that practiced contraception.[42]

Finally, Trudie Barreras checked in, in the October 1965 issue of *ACT,* with "Let's Rid Ourselves of Negative Theology," which, as the title suggests, called for a more positive theology of sex. She derisively referred to what she called the Eleventh Commandment— "Thou Shall Not Commit Contraception."[43]

The articles generated a barrage of letters to the editor, pro and con. Several letters objected to the tone of the articles, claiming that the old teaching was still in force, despite current discussions. One letter claimed contraception "undermines premarital chastity," while another suggested CFM really meant "Contraceptives For Me." Another cautioned, "Disobedience, civil or moral, is in the end productive only of chaos."[44] A writer from Illinois complained, "I fail to understand why you insist on presenting CFMers with such half-baked, pro-contraceptive propaganda."[45] A letter from El Paso, Texas, objected, "Why not simply say, 'Do as you damn please' (with the accent on damn)."[46] Many readers canceled their subscriptions to *ACT,* according to the editor, Larry Ragan, who felt compelled to address the growing controversy in a special editorial, "Birth Control and *ACT.*" He stated that many critics told him that as "editor of a Catholic magazine, you are expected to carry only the truth" and that his policy had produced confusion among the faithful. Ragan countered, "Yet we believe in free speech or we don't,"[47] arguing that any kind of discussion was better than no discussion at all.

The Maxwells responded by saying they were "surprised there was such a reaction."[48] They answered that their position had been based on the notion that doctrine could and did develop in the history of the Church. Many letters sided with the Maxwells and urged that the birth control doctrine be modified. Several letters attacked those who criticized the Maxwells as being "so smug with their pat answers," while another called it "hysterical anti-intellectualism."

A couple from Erie, Pennsylvania, asked, "Is it necessary to be unquestioning to be a good Catholic?"[49] This latter question was at the crux of the issue. CFM taught lay Catholics to think—to observe, to judge, and to act. It was asking too much, many CFMers argued, to turn off discussion and wait indefinitely for the Church authority to dictate an answer. This was not CFM's style.

Emblematic of this was the planning of the 1966 Midwestern area convention. Ralph and Reggie Weissert scheduled a panel discussion on the issue of birth control at the convention. A priest from Columbus attempted to block the panel, claiming that "this topic was strictly forbidden by the Pope for open discussion." The Weisserts, however, believed that "this was a subject CFM must discuss."[50] They discussed the issue with their CFM chaplain, John Sheehy, who was an outspoken social activist but also a faithful CFM chaplain. Sheehy responded, "That priest in Columbus sounds weird to me. How can you suppress discussion in the so-called open Church? Let him go to the Bishop if he wants. Let's have our panel as planned."[51] The panel did take place as planned, but the episode suggests the tensions that were present within the movement on this tricky issue.

The debate picked up steam in 1966. The issue of responsible parenthood (a code word for birth control in Catholic circles, since Catholic publications were forbidden to discuss the topic openly) and family limitation was incorporated into the 1966 edition of *For Happier Families,* and in the 1966–67 yearly inquiry program, *The Family in a Time of Change.* In addition, *ACT* consistently presented news on the subject in such a way as to suggest that change was imminent. In December, *ACT* reported that Pope Paul VI had delayed his pronouncement on the subject. Many expressed disappointment; others felt that most Catholics had already made up their minds, making papal comment irrelevant. But *ACT* reported a comment by John Leo of the *New Republic* that the delay was intentional, to give a "new consensus time to grow."[52] In May, 1967 *ACT* suggested that the papal encyclical *Populorum Progressio* (On the Progress of Peoples) represented a breakthrough. "Did he [the pope] change, ever so slightly, the Church's traditional teaching on birth control?"[53] In July, *ACT* reported that the *National Catholic Reporter* had leaked the papal commission's report, with the majority report calling for a change in the Church's traditional teaching on birth control. In September, Larry Ragan harkened back to the 1965 National Convention, at which there had been enormous interest in the issue of birth control. (During that event, a *Chicago Daily News* story claimed that a "high Church official" had approved the use of the Pill created quite a stir. Chaplain James Halpine had to announce to the convention that the report was wrong.).[54] By the 1967 convention CFMers seemed embarrassed by the issue, indeed, by the very fact that it was still an issue. In Ragan's assessment of the convention crowd, pro-birth control feeling predominated.[55]

The bias of *ACT* and CFM leadership did not go unnoticed by a minority of CFMers who continued to protest. A couple from Clinton, Iowa, charged, "CFMers are being 'led' by an unrepresentative leadership into questionable 'political' areas."[56] Another letter from Ontario, typical of its genre, complained, "Your whole treatment of the Birth Control issue seems to be very slanted and there appears to [be] . . . a tendency on the part of your editorial staff to 'sell us a line' rather than discuss the issue objectively."[57] The writers closed by canceling their subscription. All in all, this viewpoint, though a distinctive point of view within the movement, was a minority viewpoint. The majority of CFMers, as did the majority of Catholics in the United States, hoped for and expected a change in the teaching.

CFM AND *Humanae Vitae*

According to Robert McClory, CFM made a major contribution to the Papal Birth Control Commission's deliberations. When Pat and Patty Crowley were appointed to the commission, they reached out to their CFM connections throughout the world to obtain the lived experience of couples who had to deal with the Church's teaching on birth control and the use of the rhythm method. The Crowleys conducted an international inquiry on birth control using the Cardijn method. They managed to collect more than 3,000 letters from couples, many of which told of the stress the rhythm method put on their relationship. McClory contends that these personal testimonies were influential in prodding a number of members of the commission to vote to change the traditional teaching. When the final vote came, the Crowleys sided with the majority report, which called for a substantial change in the Church's traditional stance on birth control.[58]

Much to the shock and dismay of the Crowleys and many CFMers, Pope Paul VI rejected the majority report, deciding instead in favor of the minority report in his encyclical *Humanae Vitae*. He did soften the language, but the teaching remained the same: The use of artificial contraception was forbidden. The Crowleys were astounded and were later quoted as saying they were "happy it [*HV*] was not infallible."[59] They joined with Bernard Haring and other theologians and churchmen in dissenting from the papal encyclical. The Crowleys' dissent was respectful. Patty said, "I'd like to agree that we listen with respect to Pope Paul. Pray that somehow his decision is correct, but continue the discussion, the study and the research in all the relevant areas hoping that a solution is reached that will accord with reality."[60] Despite their disappointment, the Crowleys went ahead with their ICCFM-sponsored conference on world population in La Prée, France, though the conference had lost episcopal support (see chapter 11).

ACT reacted in a manner that became standard for those who opposed the encyclical. An article entitled "A Matter of Conscience" pointed out that the encyclical was not infallible and suggested that birth control was "a matter of personal conscience."[61] CFMers had been prepared for this the previous year at the annual convention. Speaker Gregory Baum had assured them that it was "licit for loyal and obedient Catholics to disagree with the Church."[62]

Humanae Vitae, far from resolving the issue of birth control, touched off a series of conflicts and created deep divisions within the Church. By the end of 1968, *ACT* reported that theologian

Bernard Haring called for an end to the "declarations and arguments against *Humanae Vitae.*" He called for an end of conflict and for further study.[63] Haring was one of the most respected theologians of the era and had been at the forefront of the efforts to redefine the ends of marriage. He had sided with the majority report of the commission and had initially signed a declaration dissenting from the encyclical. Now, perceiving the strife, he called for an end to dissension.

The issue was now beyond the stage where it could be simply resolved by such a statement, even by a theologian as respected as Haring. The division within the American Church was also reflected within CFM. The Crowleys tried to separate their personal disapproval of the encyclical from their public position as heads of CFM. They tried to make it clear that they were not speaking for CFM in this matter. Their distinctions were lost on a number of CFMers, who abandoned the movement as a result of the issue. One protest arrived from two CFM groups in Princeton, New Jersey. In an "Open Letter to Pat and Patty Crowley," Don and Connie Shipley wrote, "Our two CFM groups have undergone a severe reappraisal of our association with CFM. All of the members of our two groups are dissatisfied, to different degrees, with the liberal attitude continually expressed by *ACT,* and by the public statements made by yourselves on Pope Paul's encyclical on birth control." The letter concluded that they could no longer support CFM.

Again, Burnie Bauer joined those who disapproved of the Crowleys' dissent. Bauer repeatedly emphasized that the goal of CFM was not to change the Church and its teachings—those were God-given. The Church was not a democracy. The CFMer was to accept the teaching, respect authority, and work toward changing the environment in which the family functioned and the institutions that affected family life. CFM was to support families and work to create an environment that supported Catholic family life. Church teaching might be difficult, but it could not be changed. Bauer contends that the Crowleys' dissent from *Humanae Vitae* undermined CFM and led to a massive exodus from the movement.

The evidence does not support Bauer. The majority of CFMers supported the Crowleys, as did the majority of U.S. Catholics. For example, at the 1968 Area 4 regional convention, the delegates approved a resolution of support for "those who have publicly expressed dissent with the papal encyclical on birth control" and those who had been disciplined. The resolution was "vigorously applauded" by the convention.[64]

CFM did decline after 1968, but not merely as a result of the dissent of the Crowleys. In fact, the contrary case might be made—that the papal ruling was the last straw for many Catholics, including many CFMers. One wonders what might have been CFM's fate if the simple common sense of Pat Crowley had been followed. In many ways Pat proved a prophet. At a meeting of the papal commission he observed that "the sense of the faithful is for change . . . change is anticipated and great problems will arise if no change is made. If the Church fails in this, much of the progress made by the Council will be lost."[65] If Andrew Greeley's sociological studies out of the National Opinion Research Center are correct, Pat was right. Greeley cites the birth control encyclical as the single most important factor in recent dissatisfaction with the Church.

Pat also proved accurate in his belief that the Church needed to get the birth control issue behind it, so it could address more pertinent issues. Pat stated, "This problem seems to have been escalated into a position far beyond its importance. War, peace, poverty, social justice seem more urgent. So let us help the Holy Father scuttle this question so we can get on to the work of being Christ to the world with his law of love."[66] Once again, Pat was right. Over the past three decades the Church has been involved in what seems to be an endless and fruitless discussion that has distracted it from preaching the essential Gospel message.

ABORTION TAKES CENTER STAGE

Even before the birth control issue was resolved, a much more serious issue loomed on the horizon—abortion. While the birth control issue aroused the passions, it was generally resolved on a personal level that made debate irrelevant. This was not the case with abortion. The Church's clear teaching on the issue was never significantly challenged, nor was there any reason to believe the Church would change its teaching on abortion. The passions aroused by the abortion debate dwarfed those aroused by birth control. The feminist demand that women have ultimate control over their bodies and their demand that women have the right to choose an abortion was diametrically opposed to Catholic teaching. The issue heated up during the late 1960s as several states passed laws permitting some form of abortion. In 1967, California passed a therapeutic abortion law that allowed women to have abortions for medical reasons with the approval of their doctors. New York soon followed suit, as did other states. The issue was thrown into the courts, culminating with the U.S. Supreme Court landmark 1973 decision, *Roe v. Wade,* which endorsed a woman's right to abortion. Catholic outcry was immediate and vocal.

CFM addressed the abortion issue as early as 1962, when it was discussed at CFM area conventions in Virginia and Iowa.[67] Of immediate concern was a law proposed in Arizona to allow the aborting of "deformed fetuses." The issue became more passionate by the mid-1960s as abortion legislation was proposed in several state legislatures. In 1966, Los Angeles CFM began to gear up for the coming struggle. In November, their newsletter outlined the anti-abortion position. By March 1967 they were supporting the formation of Right to Life Leagues. Syracuse CFM promoted similar activities, urging CFMers to stand up and be counted. Detroit CFM did the same.

By 1970, CFM was active in the pro-life movement at the grassroots level. Pittsburgh CFM sponsored a Human Life Sunday to alert Catholics to the problem, as did other locales. Several groups established branches of Birthright, an agency that counseled pregnant women on alternatives to abortion. Information evenings were also sponsored. CFMers were becoming increasingly concerned by reports that a growing number of American youth accepted abortion. Chicago CFM reported that 46 percent of all youth between sixteen and twenty-one years of age approved of abortion.[68] Chicago CFM advocated the creation of Right to Life committees and initiated a letter-writing campaign to Illinois legislators.

By 1972, the intensity surrounding the issue increased as pro-choice efforts seemed to have gained the upper hand in the national debate. The September 1972 *ACT* published a passionate plea by Larry and Mary Little of Phoenix, Arizona, entitled "Thou Shalt Not Kill." The Littles expressed concern that a new ethic was emerging which did not consider abortion killing. If abortion was reduced to a simple medical procedure, the profound moral issues would never be considered. The whole issue came down to one question, "Is the being within the mother human life?" Yes, answered the Littles, and they pleaded that "We Must Act Now!"[69] The October issue of *ACT* contained similar appeals.

Following the *Roe v. Wade* decision in 1973, CFM pro-life activity exploded. The 1973 federation reports document pro-life actions taking place across the country: Richmond, Virginia; Altoona-Johnstown, Pennsylvania; Des Moines, Iowa; Youngstown, Ohio; Newark, New Jersey. Virtually every federation reported some pro-life activity ranging from sponsoring information nights to creating speakers' bureaus to creating Right to Life Leagues to supporting Birthright and other pregnancy counseling services.[70] In 1974, many CFM groups supported the proposed federal human life amendment to outlaw abortion. Minnesota CFMers joined the march on the state capitol in support of the amendment.[71]

Despite the clear commitment of CFM at the grass roots to the pro-life movement, many accused the CFM leadership of dragging their feet on the abortion issue, or, more troubling, they accused CFM of being soft on abortion. In 1967, a couple from Monroeville, Pennsylvania, accused, "CFM has ignored abortion as an issue."[72] Part of the neglect was that CFM's national leaders did not yet perceive abortion as an urgent issue, being preoccupied with birth control and social conflicts such as race, war, and poverty.

CFM may also have been inhibited by the ecumenical character of the movement—they hesitated in stressing the Catholic position. The inquiry on abortion in the 1970–71 inquiry program suggests the difficulties. Titled "Abortion, An Agonizing Question!" the inquiry began with: "The Constitutional Question: Is There a Right to Abortion?" Several excerpts from *The Terrible Choice: The Abortion Dilemma,* edited by Robert E. Cooke and others, are then presented, followed by a series of questions such as "In the matter of abortion, where should the ultimate decision be made? Is it strictly a private issue? Must the unborn continue to have the protection of the law? Do present laws against abortion force an alien ethical or moral system on many citizens?" The Observe section required the couples to ask three neighbors or friends several questions, including "Is abortion always immoral? Why or why not? . . . Is abortion the killing of an innocent person? . . . If not, at what time in the life of the embryo or fetus can life be ended? . . . Why force a woman to bear an unwanted child?" The Judge section then asked, "Do you think that the abortion laws in your state or province should be kept? Abolished? Liberalized? Why?" And the suggested action, "Take proper political action to defend, abolish or change the existing laws on abortion as you judge in this matter."[73] The neutrality and apparent absence of Christian values upset many CFMers. In what many considered *the* moral issue of the day, the inquiry seemed to suggest one option was as good as the other.

CFM leadership was also accused of consorting with groups that supported abortion. One letter criticized the use of a quote in the program book from Elizabeth Janeway, who supported "unrestricted abortion." CFM's participation in world population studies involved it with groups that advocated abortion as a policy strategy. Especially singled out for chastisement was the World Council of Churches, which had approved the use of therapeutic abortion. Typical of hostile letters received by *ACT* is one from a couple in Murraysville, Pennsylvania, which complained that the pro-life argument was not receiving enough attention: "we have noticed a very one-sided approach to population and abortion issues. . . . Last year's *Quality of Life* study book managed to suggest anti-life groups should be investigated as to their goals. This is true, but it is meaningless unless coupled with the objectives of pro-life groups."[74] The letter concluded that CFM needed to support strongly the Right to Life movement.

The claim that national CFM's early treatment of the abortion crisis was rather tepid is accurate. Part of the leadership dilemma lay in the fact that many of CFM's traditional allies, who had sided with CFM on issues ranging from race to birth control to women's rights, advocated a liberalization of abortion attitudes and laws. CFM now found itself on the other side of the fence, allied with a variety of conservative groups. Nonetheless, CFM came to support the Right to Life position, reflecting the concerns of its rank and file. The abortion issue drove the movement—as it drove the nation's political life—in a conservative direction.

Indicative of this was a renewed interest in the rhythm method of birth control or what was called natural family planning.[75] On the one hand, the side effects of the Pill were being publicized. On the other, a connection began to be seen between artificial birth control and abortion. In many instances, abortion seemed a simple extension of birth control. While some argued that more efficient birth control would make abortion unnecessary,[76] others argued that the use of birth control created a "contraceptive mentality" that increased the resort to abortion. Natural family planning was more healthy physically and psychologically, they argued. The June 1974 issue of *ACT* published an article that gave a ringing endorsement to natural family planning. "Our sharing is simple—we want you to know—Natural Family Planning works for us, for hundreds of couples we know, and we suspect, for thousands of other couples, who hesitate to say anything about it."[77]

The abortion issue continued to inflame passions for many years as the search for an acceptable alternative continued. The dilemma remains to be resolved.

CONCLUSION

In the period 1949 to 1974 CFM's attitude toward women, sexuality, and birth control changed dramatically. Starting with very traditional attitudes towards women and sexuality, CFM changed over time to respect greater avenues of activity for women. It also advocated a more positive theology of sex, seeing the couple's sexuality as a gift that enriched marriage love and not simply a tool for procreation. Despite CFM's liberal bent, the issue of abortion in the early 1970s propelled CFM in a more conservative direction.

ELEVEN

ICCFM:
The International Confederation
of Christian Family Movements

While CFM in the United States and Canada grappled with issues of race, ecumenism and sexuality, the movement continued to expand throughout the world. By 1965, CFM had spread to more than fifty nations; however, in the process, "CFM" had become a generic rubric under which a variety of family organizations were placed, some of which did not follow the Cardijn method. For instance, the Spanish family movement, which affiliated with Mexican MFC, never used the Observe-Judge-Act formula. Veteran CFMers Dan and Rose Lucey observed of an early gathering of world CFM groups, "Each of the national groups has its own approach to the philosophy of CFM." By the mid-60s there was a growing consensus that there needed to be greater communication between international CFM groups. Jose and Luzma Alvarez Icaza of the Mexican MFC were the driving force behind efforts to join the Latin American MFCs and the U.S. movements—the first step in what was to be a worldwide linkup.

The Alvarez Icazas were a remarkable couple who had risen quickly to prominence within the Mexican Church. In 1964, the Mexican bishops appointed Jose director of their new information center, the National Center for Social Communication (CEN-COS).[1] The same year the Alvarez Icazas became the first lay couple to serve as auditors at the Second Vatican Council, representing married couples and families.

Alvarez Icaza was not content to be a simple tool of the Mexican hierarchy. In 1968, he denounced their extreme authoritarianism and called for a more democratic Church. In addition, he supported elements of the student protests that were erupting throughout Mexico as the nation prepared for the summer Olympics to be held in Mexico City that year. He argued that the students were "idealistic," not "Marxists," and that to repress them would merely throw "gas on the fire."[2] In 1969, he severed the relationship of CENCOS with the Mexican hierarchy after a series of disputes including "the hierarchy's refusal to allow single mothers to join the MFC."[3] For the next two decades Alvarez Icaza played a major role in Mexican church and political affairs. He continued as director of CENCOS and in 1992 he served as vice president of the "Zapatista-convened" National Democratic Convention (CND) held in Chiapas.[4] Alvarez Icaza's rise began with CFM.

Alvarez Icaza began to see the need for some sort of exchange between CFM groups in different countries as early as 1961. That year in an article in *ACT,* he called for an "Alliance for Understanding" to complement President John F. Kennedy's "Alliance for Progress." Alvarez Icaza made his case from two converging perspectives. On the spiritual plane, the notion of the Mystical Body demanded a better flow of understanding between the United States and Latin America. At the practical level, the United States as the supreme world power would inevitably influence the development of Latin America, for better or for worse. To make sure it was for the better, the United States needed a better cultural and ideological understanding of Latin America. To achieve this, more direct communication was needed between families.[5] The two family movements were ideally suited to the task.

Alvarez Icaza's efforts came to fruition in the summer of 1965. At the CFM national convention, U.S. CFM (which still included Canada at this point) and Latin American CFM (or MFC) entered into a "confederation agreement" creating the Christian Family Movements Confederation, or the Confederacion de Movimientos Familiares Cristianos, to promote the "unity of the Family Movements of the Americas, and [to aid] joint project development especially in international fields."[6] Both movements would retain their "own individuality and independence in their respective areas. The Confederation shall only act as a coordinator in the achievement of the joint projects."[7] Both groups would assist in taking care of Latin American families living in the United States and Canada as well as North American families living in Latin America. Both groups would seek to expand CFM into new areas. This agreement, established "ad experimentum" for one year, had already been ratified by the General Latin American Assembly of the MFCs in Mexico City, August 17, and was ratified by the CFM Executive and Coordinating Committees at Notre Dame, August 25, 1965.

The following year, 1966, the first meeting of the confederation took place in Caracas, Venezuela, in conjunction with the fourth Inter-American Assembly of Latin American MFC. Included in the confederation were family groups from Spain. The Alvarez Icazas were elected general secretary couple of the confederation with headquarters in Mexico City. The meeting confirmed the confederation agreement of the previous year but stated its purpose in slightly different terms. With the addition of Spain, the confederation had burst its inter-American bounds, and its name was changed to the International Confederation of Christian Family Movements (ICCFM). The purpose: "to promote and develop communications between the Christian Family Movements around the world and to support each other's objectives, programs, methods, plans, etc."[8] The ICCFM was not a "superstructure" but a cooperative movement, "a unity of equals" that would show the world a "unified family movement." In practice, the purpose of ICCFM came to be communication between the family movements and research into a variety of areas affecting family life.[9]

The ICCFM convened again the following year, in October 1967, in Madrid. At this meeting, the Crowleys were elected to replace the Alvarez Icazas as general secretaries, and the headquarters of the confederation was moved to Chicago. In addition, a nine-couple executive committee was established with three couples each from Spain, North America, and Latin America. The first executive committee was made up of the Crowleys and Dan and

Rose Lucey (U.S.), Charles and Kathleen Connolly (Canada), Jaime and Mercedes Ferrer, Rafael and Conchita Ruiz y Ruiz, and Jose Antonio and Margarita Pich (Spain), the Alvarez Icazas, Alberto and Blanca Rodriguez, and Federico and Hortensia Soneira (MFC).

Beyond the structural developments, the Madrid meeting stressed that the ICCFM was to be ecumenical. U.S. CFM was already in touch with the National Council of Churches in New York, and the ICCFM was soon to make contact with the World Council of Churches in Geneva. The Crowleys had already worked out an international ecumenical prayer with the Taizé monks in France. The meeting called upon the assistance of "experts" to conduct research into areas pertinent to family life around the world. The ICCFM would then seek to disseminate this information.

To effect this consultation, ICCFM planned a conference for 1968 at Lake Como, Italy, among family experts, family leaders, and the hierarchy. Underwritten by a grant from the Rockefeller Foundation, the meeting was planned to "be small, private and without publicity."[10] Its stated purpose was "to develop a pedagogy on marriage in the light of the Council Documents."[11] The featured speaker was to be noted scholar John Noonan, discussing "Education for Responsibility in Love and Marriage."

Before the gathering could take place, several interesting developments occurred. First, the Marriage Encounter of Spanish Father Gabriel Calvo was brought to the United States. ICCFM was a major supporter of the expansion of the Marriage Encounter and, later, owned the ME name (see below). Second, the ICCFM became truly international, as Japan and the Philippines joined the movement. Finally, and most important, Pope Paul VI issued the encyclical *Humanae Vitae*, reaffirming the Church's traditional teaching on the use of contraception.

As noted before, the Crowleys, who had been members of the papal birth control commission, openly dissented from the encyclical. The fallout directly affected ICCFM. The Lake Como conference was postponed, then rescheduled for La Prée, France. With the encyclical, hierarchical support for the conference dried up. The topics to be discussed were much too controversial. Undeterred, the Crowleys forged ahead with the La Prée conference, but significant tensions emerged as a result of the encyclical.

Conflict between the Crowleys and the Alvarez Icazas on the issue of birth control had surfaced the previous year when the Alvarez Icazas had issued a statement on behalf of the ICCFM with which the Crowleys strongly disagreed. They were "upset" particularly by its implication that ICCFM did not support a change in the Church's teaching on birth control. "It sounds like we're for the status quo, and we're not. . . . it is not an answer to the industrialized nations."[12] Shortly after the promulgation of the encyclical, at a meeting of the directors of the ICCFM in Bogotá, Colombia, Spanish and Latin American MFC issued a statement publicly and officially supporting the pope's stand. The Crowleys explained their dissent but pledged not to "compromise CFM."[13] Nonetheless, the Alvarez Icazas withdrew from the La Prée conference, arguing that the topics to be discussed were "too sensitive."

Despite their withdrawal, the La Prée conference convened in November 1968. If the Alvarez Icazas were nervous about the conference, it was a good thing they stayed away. The conference contained an open and forthright discussion of *Humanae Vitae,* world population, and contraception. Many of the papers openly questioned the papal encyclical, but birth control was not the only topic. Twelve nations presented reports on the condition of families in their countries.[14] Thus, the La Prée conference, despite the controversy, succeeded in meeting the two most important objectives of ICCFM—dissemination of expert information and communication between the families of the world.

In 1969, the first General Assembly of Families was held at the University of Notre Dame in conjunction with the annual convention of U.S. CFM. By this time, India, New Zealand, and England had joined the ICCFM. At the meeting, six research areas were assigned for study: responsible parenthood, human sexuality, the socioeconomic basis of family development, education for family life, marriage encounter, and the birth-baptism event. Reports were to be made at the next ICCFM gathering.

In 1970, the ICCFM Executive Committee met in late September in Auckland, New Zealand. All the continents except Africa were represented: Jose and Margarita Pich for Europe, Antonio and Cristina Alcocer for Latin America, Sito and Sony Sison for Asia, Des and Margaret Nolan for Oceania, and Dan and Rose Lucey for North America.

All the various committees made reports, but the spotlight was on another topic: how the families of the richer nations could help families in poorer nations. The Pichs of Spain suggested a world questionnaire to investigate this topic. Of special concern was how best to implement the challenging social encyclical of Pope Paul VI, *Populorum Progressio* (On the Progress of Peoples). The Executive Committee passed a resolution that called "the whole church into a more active and direct leadership against oppression, exploitation and poverty."[15] The committee also agreed to support the goals of the United Nations in this regard.

The following October, twenty-five couples, eight priests, and two Protestant clergymen from twenty nations gathered again in Kilkenny, Ireland, for ICCFM's second General Assembly of Families. Six continents were now represented. Edi and Magdalene Barnor from Ghana were added to the Executive Committee to represent Africa. The World Council of Churches also sent representatives, namely, Rex and Caroline Davis and Leslie and Mona Clements; the Clements were included in Executive Committee deliberations. ICCFM continued to expand its membership at this meeting by admitting to its ranks Ghana, Cameroon, Belgium, Malaysia, Korea, Singapore, and Australia. In another administrative action the term "general secretary" was replaced by "president-couple" and the Crowleys were reelected to lead ICCFM.

National representatives reported on what their governments were doing to assist families, on ecumenism, on migrants, and on other topics. At this 1971 meeting, ICCFM emerged as a truly international body, a "United Nations for families," as one delegate called it. World issues were discussed in an open exchange. Topics such as apartheid in South Africa, the conflict in Northern Ireland, the tension in India and Bangladesh, and other world concerns were addressed. The meeting also considered the needs of different types of families throughout the world. Lola Vidal of Venezuela called for the ICCFM to take up the issue of single-parent families. A social inquiry on the topic was suggested. Reggie Weissert, representing U.S. CFM, observed, "CFM should include more than just 'neat families.' We should reach out to one-parent families, divorced people, and married clergy."[16] The Barnors of Ghana pointed up the difficulties of traditional tribal marriage customs and their conflict with Catholic teaching.

While the international discussions generated much enthusiasm, one of the more moving events of the conference was provided by Nicaraguan priest-poet Ernesto Cardenal, s.J., who celebrated Mass for the delegates. Cardenal presented his *Psalms of Struggle and Liberation,* a rewriting of the Book of Psalms based on his experiences in Nicaragua.

The most significant action of the conference arose from Pat Crowley's proposal that ICCFM develop a long-range plan. The result: the conference produced a five-year plan on the spot. In 1972 ICCFM was to focus on ecumenical development, with contacts to be made with the World Council of Churches and the U.S. National Council of Churches. The movement was also to make efforts to expand in Asia and Africa, assist families behind the Iron Curtain, and take a variety of other actions to assist families everywhere. In 1973, ICCFM was to concentrate on the family and socioeconomic development, population awareness, and responsible parenthood. "ICCFM should become involved in social and political action and encourage cooperation with concerned national government agencies and UNESCO." ICCFM would also work on marriage and family-life education, and plan the first World Conference of Family Movements. In 1974, ICCFM would obtain reports on family research centers and work to establish "a central repository for information on family life." In 1975, ICCFM would examine the social and political involvement of the family movements and the problems of the poor and needy. At the close of

1975, an evaluation of the first ten years of the international move-ment was to be made.[17]

To carry out the plan, a host of committees were established: on Marriage Encounters, premarriage, young couples, family therapy and counseling, population education, responsible parenthood, so-cial and political involvement, the ecumenical family, the one-parent family, parent education, mass media, cooperation in international organizations, a world congress on the family, and a research center. These committees ably reflected the interests and concerns of ICCFM; however, little concrete action ever resulted. The strengths of ICCFM remained dissemination of research and communication between groups throughout the world.

The next ICCFM meeting took place in Tarrytown, New York, in September 1972. Again, ICCFM gathered couples and family experts to examine the topic "Friendship, Families' Answer to Loneliness in the World." Among the participants was noted scholar Margaret Mead. She praised CFM for being one of the few movements that was "paying attention to spouses as human beings, when everyone else regards them as parents." CFM considered the "relationship of adults . . . something nobody else is doing much about."[18] The scholarly exchanges at this and several other sessions were well received by the Executive Committee.

The meeting then turned to the work of the ICCFM itself, with reports from around the world, and several significant initiatives were set in motion. The ICCFM agreed to sponsor the first interna-tional Marriage Encounter seminar to be held in Barcelona, Spain, in 1973. It also responded to the Barnors' eloquent plea for assis-tance to Africa by choosing Africa as the site for its world assembly in 1974.

Finally, the ICCFM Executive Committee unanimously passed this "Resolution for Family Action." The resolution read,

> We condemn the universal exploitation of the family as a social unit. This exploitation is steadily deepening, and family life and the human values which family embodies are everywhere seriously

threatened . . . .[We] deplore, in particular racism . . . especially apartheid, economic exploitation . . . especially of families in the Third World . . . , misuse of the world's resources . . . particularly by rich nations of developing countries . . . , war . . . the oppression of children . . . , the enforced migration of peoples . . . , conspicuous consumption . . . , the subjugation of women . . . , the plight of the powerless, the poor, the imprisoned, the aged, the handicapped and those disenfranchised. . . . This exploitation is violence. It embodies a lack of respect for human life which undermines the core of family life everywhere. We therefore resolve to use all the family power of our international and local groups to confront this situation. We will encourage governments to promulgate laws and programs which will enable oppressed peoples to achieve their just expectations of life. We will unite the great power of the family which springs from its love and solidarity with those who strive for justice, peace and equality because these are basic to a complete human life. We will resist those actions, those policies which either explicitly or implicitly impede a viable family life. The power of the family should be felt at all levels of society, government, religion, commercial, trade unions, education—wherever necessary. We do not believe that other choices remain.[19]

This resolution was a powerful statement of policy and of the philosophy underlying the ICCFM—reflecting a totally different strategy than that of U.S. CFM, which avoided making statements or resolutions.

ICCFM spent most of the next two years planning for a major World Assembly of Families to be held in Tanzania in 1974. They had been invited by the president of Tanzania, Julius Nyerere, to hold their assembly in his country. Years before, Nyerere had dined at the Crowley dinner table. He had not forgotten. Planning for the event was extensive and detailed.

Preparation for what came to be called Familia '74 was the main topic of discussion of the Executive Committee when it met in Barcelona, Spain, in October 1973. A steering committee for

Familia '74 was established, with Father Charles Vella of Malta appointed executive secretary. Also included were Rex and Caroline Davis and the Clements of the World Council of Churches, the Crowleys, the Barnors, and Chief Patrick Kunambi and Stanford Shauri of Tanzania. What they aimed for was "an assembly of people representing the family, meeting to experience in movement and action studies, the frustration and hope of men and women as the family of the world."[20]

Emphasis was placed on people. In contrast to previous ICCFM meetings, this meeting was not to be "a meeting of experts; it is to be a meeting of those who live out the day-to-day problems of the family in a world of major and minor conflicts."[21] The people were to be the teachers—they were the real specialists on family life.

As Familia '74 was being planned, other business items were tended to. Pat Crowley reported that the ICCFM had been incorporated as a nonprofit organization in the state of Illinois. The Crowleys and Father Vella had also made contact with the Vatican. Before coming to Barcelona, they had spent several days in Rome, where they met with representatives of the newly created Papal Family Committee, with the Laity Council and with the Secretariate of Christian Unity. The secretariate complimented the ecumenical character of ICCFM and encouraged it to continue to develop its ecumenical program. A process for regular communications between ICCFM and the Secretariate of Christian Unity was established.

Father Vella had also made contact with the United Nations, which had declared 1974 to be World Population Year. Vella was able to obtain two grants from the UN—one to plan for Familia '74 and the other to partially underwrite the Tanzania gathering. For its part, ICCFM developed a survey form to enable its members to gather facts on the population policies of their nations' governments.

One final note to the 1973 gathering. The Executive Committee interrupted its sessions so the committee could attend the first International Marriage Encounter seminar being held in Barcelona at the same time. Quite appropriate, since the seminar was sponsored by the ICCFM, which owned the trademark to Marriage

Encounter. The seminar was attended by more than eighty people from twenty-four countries.[22]

The planning for a world assembly culminated in June 1974. From June 16 to 30 more than 250 delegates from 56 nations gathered at the University of Dar es Salaam in Tanzania for Familia '74. The event was cosponsored by the ICCFM and the Family Education Office of the World Council of Churches. For Pat Crowley, the assembly was to be his crowning achievement. His tireless efforts and determination overcame obstacle after obstacle to ensure its success, even as he was conducting his own battle with cancer, a cancer that would kill him less than five months after the assembly ended. According to Father Vella, without the Crowleys and Les Clements, the event probably would have been canceled, but it was a triumph. Patty Crowley remembers Familia '74 as "the climax of his [Pat's] life. Never before had he brought together . . . so many people of so many colors from so many places on earth."[23] The Crowleys' leadership was affirmed as they were reelected to serve another term as President Couple for ICCFM.

At the heart of Familia '74 was direct contact with the people of Tanzania. After the delegates arrived in Dar es Salaam they were taken, in groups of eight to fifteen people, to different rural *Ujamaa* villages, where they were to live and work for two to three days. They were there to observe President Nyerere's "experiment in village socialism." *Ujamaa* was translated as "familyhood" or "extended family." Nyerere's experiment of cooperative village life was based on the traditional extended family, in contrast to the nuclear family of Western, industrialized nations. The socialism was thus based not on Western political doctrine but on traditional concepts. Delegates were urged to withhold judgment and simply observe and experience village life. As the prospectus for Familia asserted, "the best learning results from experience, and the best insights emerge from such learning."[24]

By all accounts the village visits had a profound affect on the delegates. As the *ICCFM Newsbulletin* reported, "Most of the delegates . . . said their eyes were opened, their values shaken, and their approach to life changed."[25] During their stay in the villages the delegates went to work beside the villagers. One delegate reported going to fields and cutting sisal with a machete. Another reported that "our job for the day was to help make bricks for the village . . . the bricks are made from sand (which was hauled from nearby in a Land Rover), cement, and water (which must be brought from a nearby well). The women in the team helped in carrying the water from the well. The village women carried the bucket full of water on their heads, often with their babies on their backs at the same time. We made 81 bricks that day. We only stopped because we ran out of cement."[26] Another delegate reported that they "worked together for two days, opening furrows to plant tomatoes, or gathering maize." After work, the leisure moments and sharing of cultures were also important. An Uruguayan woman delegate related, "At the end of each day's work we sat down on a carpet of sisal, and this moment was the climax of our experience. They told us about their rites, their folklore, the ways in which the family is organized . . . .We played and sang with the children, seeing in each of them our own children far away. And just as we taught our own children children's songs, we taught the same songs to them."[27]

Many delegates came away from the visits with an ecstatic, if somewhat uncritical, vision of the transformation of Tanzania. In rhetoric typical of the end of the sixties several delegates spoke of "liberation," of seeing "history" being transformed. One observed "women proud to be in the vanguard of the dedicated people of Tanzania working through *Ujamaa* to build a new world." Others were not so carried away with the experience. U.S. delegates Ray and Dorothy Maldoon were "disturbed" by the eating customs in the villages. First the delegates ate, then the men, then the women, and finally the children. "We were disturbed to see that the children were served last and only rice was left for them."[28]

Upon the delegates' return to the university, the second phase of the conference began—the "Market Place," an open exchange of ideas, combined with a series of workshops and presentations. Included in the presentations were Daniel Mbwenze and Janet

Mondlane, describing the "liberation of Mozambique." Paolo Freire, author of *Pedagogy of the Oppressed,* gave three seminars on education. He put the whole village experience in perspective. "In an educational exercise such as this, the consequences of actual visits to the heart of the Tanzanian experience, the *Ujamaa* villages, together with sufficient time for people to reflect on that experience as well as their own, offer fantastic opportunities for everyone to discover new levels of critical awareness about themselves, their society and the world."[29] Other seminars dealt with topics ranging from the status of women around the world to sexuality to population and development.

The exchange between delegates was frank and, at times, contentious. The Maldoons reported, "The expected emergence of 'Family Power' did not occur, at least not in a way that our Western eyes could recognize."[30] The extremely disparate groups found it difficult to reach consensus. Tensions were particularly evident between First and Third World contingents, between the haves and the havenots. The Latin American delegates were upset that all the proceedings were in English and that the translators provided were inadequate. According to the Maldoons, "papers on population, liberation, and development were especially disputed."[31] The Latin American delegation was so upset with the conference's statement on population that they issued their own. In their assessment, Latin America was "under-populated," and attempts to limit their population was another form of "colonialism"—one more attempt by the First World to keep Third World nations in dependence and subjugation.[32]

Despite the conflicts, the delegates left the meeting forever changed. From Familia '74 on, ICCFM would be sensitive to the issues of Third World families and continue to work at exposing ICCFM members to the plight of these families. The next world assembly, to be held in Manila, would contain an "exposure program" similar to the *Ujamaa* experience.

Before Manila, ICCFM confronted several problems. First, the *Ujamaa* experience had left a sizable debt. Pat Crowley believed the debt was largely the fault of the World Council of Churches for bringing too many delegates, and they were billed accordingly. The result was a split between ICCFM and the WCC. No WCC representative would attend ICCFM for several years after this. More significantly, Pat Crowley died on November 20, 1974. Though Vernie Dale's history of ICCFM suggests there were some dissatisfied with the Crowley's leadership,[33] they were nevertheless re-elected, testimony to the fact that most ICCFM delegates valued their leadership.

Pat's death was a jolt the movement had to overcome. In so many ways, Pat and Patty Crowley *were* CFM. Their tireless efforts, their vast travel (over one million miles) had spread CFM throughout the world. Pat in particular had an extraordinary gift for bringing diverse groups and peoples together and enabling them to work together. Together, the Crowleys had ensured that the focus of CFM and ICCFM would extend beyond the family itself. In a speech they gave at the 1968 meeting they said, "We must not limit the family to conjugal communication, but rather communication and education between the family and the world."[34] The Crowleys, through their vision and example, transformed CFM into an international organization.

After Pat's death, Patty carried on as president until the assembly in Manila in 1977, where Rolly and Isabelle Leroux of Canada were elected as the next President Couple.

The ICCFM represented (and continues to represent) a unique experiment in international organization. Family groups from all over the world were brought together to explore common problems. As Dale put it, "[W]e are perhaps the first and only example of the worldwide domestic church, working to embody the hands and heart of Christ on all continents of the Planet Earth."[35] ICCFM has continued to prosper, with current membership estimated at over 200,000 couples worldwide. While this number is impossible to verify, it is interesting that while U.S. CFM was severely declining in the early 1970s, ICCFM was heading in the opposite direction. In 1974, ICCFM's growth had just begun.

OFFSHOOTS OF ICCFM

ICCFM was also successful in supporting the development of two other groups that enjoyed tremendous success in the late 1960s and early 1970s: Marriage Encounter (ME) and the Movimiento Cristiano Familiar (MFC) for the United States. Both of these groups were growing in numbers as the general membership rolls of CFM continued to decline in the United States and Canada. Both movements began with the assistance of CFM, but they both took a different approach to the family apostolate. ME and MFC believed that the family unit had to be solidified before social action could be undertaken. As a result, their focus was primarily on internal family relationships. As discussed before, this had been long debated within CFM—did one have to be formed before he or she could act? CFM had opted for the concept of "formation through action." ME and MFC believed formation must take place first. In theory, ME and MFC should have been natural feeders for CFM; couples once formed would naturally move into CFM. In practice this seldom worked out. Ultimately, ME and MFC were better suited to the era. Most Americans were tired of the nonstop controversies of the 1960s—race, war, Vatican II, etc. The inward, reflective style of ME was more appealing to this generation.

MARRIAGE ENCOUNTER COMES TO THE UNITED STATES

Marriage Encounter grew out of the family apostolate in Spain. In 1952, recently ordained Father Gabriel Calvo was approached by Jaime and Mercedes Ferrer, about serving as their spiritual adviser.[36] Calvo hesitated, as it was not customary to give spiritual counsel to a couple as a couple. Overcoming his initial hesitation, Calvo was soon meeting with other couples as well. Out of these meetings emerged a movement known as the Equipos de Pio XII or the teams of Pius XII, because the groups studied and reflected on Pius XII's writings on marriage. The basic meeting consisted of intense and honest communication, first between the couple, then with the other couples. Each couple reflected on their own marriage in light of the Gospels, then judged their marriage by the "mind of Christ"; they then acted to bring their marriage into "accord with God's plan." Though the Cardijn method was used, it was directed inward.

In order to make the experience available to more couples, the Equipos developed a weekend retreat that came to be known as an *encuentro conyugal,* or Marriage Encounter. The encounter duplicated in an intensive three-day period what the Equipos worked on throughout the course of the year. The Marriage Encounters became the primary action of the Equipos.

The Spanish family apostolate was drawn into the international scene during a visit from Latin American MFC founder Father Pedro Richards in 1958. Richards met with Calvo and other couples and began corresponding with them on his return to Latin America. In 1963, Calvo and several couples attended the third Inter-American meeting of Latin American MFC. Bonds were further strengthened in 1965, when the Alvarez Icazas visited the Spanish groups on their way back from attending the Second Vatican Council. Alvarez Icaza invited Calvo and the Equipos to attend the fourth meeting of Latin American CFM at Caracas the following year (1966), which was also the first meeting of the Confederation of Christian Family Movements.

At the Caracas meeting, Father Calvo and the Ferrers made a presentation on the Marriage Encounter. Deeply impressed, Alvarez Icaza brought Calvo and the Ferrers to Mexico City to conduct a Marriage Encounter weekend. Calvo and a Mexican couple who had made the encounter brought Marriage Encounter to three other regions of Mexico. Soon the encounters spread to other countries in Latin America. In November 1966 Calvo conducted the first U.S. Marriage Encounter in Miami. Like all the others, this Marriage Encounter was conducted in Spanish. Calvo left behind mimeographed outlines on how to conduct the encounter.

In 1965, the Crowleys became acquainted with the Spanish Equipos on their way back from Rome following a Papal Birth Control Commission meeting. Patty was deeply impressed by the "dialogue" concept that was present in the Spanish movement. She observed, "We picked up some new ideas on the importance of husband and wife discussing all their inner thoughts. . . . I remember how impressed we were on hearing of this idea of 'sitting down and learning the technique of dialogue.' As a couple we had done this. But the group in Spain had put dialogue into focus. We brought the idea back as an action item of the Christian Family Movement of Spain and pondered about how to use it here."[37]

The first Marriage Encounter in English was held in August 1967 in conjunction with the 1967 CFM national convention at Notre Dame. The ICCFM was holding their third meeting at Notre Dame at the same time, and here Father Calvo presented the Marriage Encounter concept. One Mexican couple, Alfonso and Mercedes Gomez-Benet, were so enthusiastic that they kept pestering Patty Crowley for time to present the encounter concept to the national convention. The convention schedule was already too full, but Patty asked university officials if a small group could remain on campus for several days following the convention. Ten couples did, and the Marriage Encounter was conducted by Father Donald Hessler, M.M., of Mexico City, and the Gomez-Benets. It was a great success. One of the couples, Robert and Mary Munson, returned to Florida, obtained Calvo's notes and had them translated into English. Thereafter, Marriage Encounter began to spread in the United States among English- as well as Spanish-speaking groups.

The real impetus to the development of Marriage Encounter in the United States came the following year. At the October 1967 ICCFM meeting in Madrid, the Crowleys and the Alvarez Icazas invited the Spanish Equipos to come to the United States to promote Marriage Encounter. Alvarez Icaza hoped that the group would engage the poorer Spanish-speaking couples in the United States and would thus generate the creation of MFC-U.S.A. The Crowleys and the Spanish groups formed the Encuentro Familiar America-España. The Crowleys insisted that one of the groups coming to the United States should be able to speak English so that English-speaking couples could enjoy the benefits of the Encounter.

The result was REDAR '68 (Receive and Give '68). On August 3,

1968, the Spanish group—made up of fifty-four married couples, twenty-three priests, and a number of teenagers—arrived in New York City, where they were greeted by the Crowleys, the Alvarez Icazas, and Antonio and Christina Alcocer, the current Latin American MFC President Couple.[38] The group then divided into seventeen teams and headed out across the United States "from Virginia to San Francisco, from Massachusetts to Texas." One team went to Mexico. As agreed, the Spanish couples paid their own air fares, but CFM-U.S.A. provided housing and transportation throughout the United States. Dozens of CFM families opened their homes to the traveling teams. Both Spanish and American couples were enthusiastic about the exchange. In all, more than sixty-five encounters were held in about thirty cities. One U.S. priest concluded, "The Encounter is a valuable device for dialogue and for deepening the values of marriage; we hope we can repeat it."[39]

Marriage Encounter came to Canada the same summer. Montreal CFMers Dave and Doreen Wright were introduced to ME by a Mexican visitor who was a guest of CFM Federation leaders Isabelle and Rolly Leroux during Expo '67. Montreal CFM sent the Wrights to upstate New York to experience an encounter weekend. When they returned they set about bringing ME to Canada, which they succeeded in doing on July 26 at Jean Brebeuf College in Montreal. The weekend was directed by U.S. couple Jamie and Arlene Whalen and Father Donald Hessler, M.M.

After the departure of the Spanish teams from the United States, Marriage Encounter continued to grow throughout the United States and Canada. CFM continued to support the Marriage Encounter movement, but unlike Spanish MFC, it did not endorse the Encounter as its primary action. As a result, Father Donald Hessler pushed for Marriage Encounter to establish a separate organization. A National Executive Board of Marriage Encounter was established in 1968 with Jamie and Arlene Whelan serving as the first executive couple. In August, 1969 the separation was made clear when the Executive Board of Marriage Encounter stated "that CFM and Marriage Encounter are two separate and independent Movements with different purposes albeit a common interest in families and the Church, and therefore [it was] decided that a liaison team would meet with the Executive Board of CFM when necessary on matters of mutual concern."[40]

Despite the separation, Marriage Encounter was enthusiastically received by CFMers across the country, and many CFM groups sponsored Marriage Encounter weekends, much in the manner that early CFMers promoted Cana Conferences. One CFM couple attested to the positive effect of the Marriage Encounter on their relationship by writing that after eight years of marriage and six children "we fell in love again . . . by the end of the very first day [of the encounter] we had discovered each other for the very first time."[41] And a headline in the April 1972 *ACT* read, "CFM People Are 'Into' Marriage Encounter—And Love It!"[42] The reason for Marriage Encounter's success was explained quite simply by the Whelans, "The Marriage Encounter is an opportunity for husbands and wives to examine their lives together through dialogue and to come to understand each other more fully and to grow in love."[43]

Relations between CFM and ME were not always so amicable. Scholar Robert White points out that though ME was promoted by the Crowleys, "the rest of the leadership of CFM did not seem to have much interest in ME."[44] Many CFMers were afraid that ME was draining members from CFM. Indeed, many involved in leadership roles in ME were previously active in CFM. In St. Paul, five of the six board members of Minnesota ME belonged to CFM.[45] Youngstown, Ohio, CFM printed an article entitled "ME and CFM—Rivals or Helpmates?" which stated, "[W]e have sometimes gotten the impression that ME was a rival to CFM and that CFM should not get involved with ME lest it steal them away from the movement."[46] Some CFMers were also fearful that the inward direction of ME's focus might undermine CFM's outward thrust. As one couple had observed, "We decided that all our outward-directed apostolic work would be one grand farce unless we were successful in bringing the love of Christ to each other."[47] The old debate that had plagued CFM once again reared its head.

While CFM groups supported ME, ME boards also promoted CFM. In 1973 the two groups came together to plan an inquiry book that would serve as a follow-up to the Marriage Encounter weekend. The result was the program booklet *The Encountering Couple,* published in 1973. The book consisted of eleven meetings to deepen the weekend encounter and to involve the couple in the community. Despite the promotion, ME never served as much of a feeder to CFM.

1973 was also an important year for international ME—the first international meeting of Marriage Encounter was held in Barcelona. Representatives from fifteen countries attended, as did the Executive Committee of the ICCFM, which was meeting in Barcelona at the same time. At the meeting controversy broke out between contending factions—one faction led by Father Charles Gallagher of New York argued that the Catholic dimension of ME should be respected, while another faction argued that ME should be ecumenical in approach.[48] The result: ME split into two groups—Worldwide Marriage Encounter and National Marriage Encounter, the first Catholic only, the second ecumenical. ICCFM continued to control the ME trademark, which it licensed to both groups.

MFC-U.S.A.

The introduction of ME to the United States also provided CFM with an entree into the Spanish-speaking communities throughout the United States. This had been precisely the hope of Jose Alvarez Icaza in inviting the ME teams to the United States. CFM had long had difficulty in appealing to nonwhite, non-middle-class groups. A variety of efforts had been made to involve Latino minorities. As stated elsewhere, Oakland priest John Garcia had been most successful in this endeavor; Father John Coffield in southern California had also enjoyed some success. As early as 1956, the Yellow Book had been translated into Spanish as *Por Una Familia Mas Feliz,* but through 1968 only two of the follow-up inquiry books had been translated. The result was that, despite scattered organizing efforts, very few CFM groups had developed in the Latino community.

This does not mean that CFM was uninvolved with Hispanics. Many CFM groups were leaders in helping migrant farmworkers, most of them Mexican. The spiritual care of these workers had long been neglected by the Catholic Church, as the workers simply did not fit into traditional parish structures. A special inquiry in the 1957–58 inquiry program triggered many and varied actions to assist the migrant workers. Actions varied: Joliet CFM sent couples to the fields to teach catechism; later, they created a "Spanish center" to distribute food, clothing, offer classes in English, and assist with jobs and housing; Kokomo, Indiana, created a day school for the children of migrants; Portland, Oregon, CFMers helped run a statewide survey of the housing and working conditions of migrant workers; Fond du Lac sponsored a clothing and toy drive for the workers; South Bend provided food, clothing, and appliances to migrant families. Southern California CFM groups worked not only with their own communities but also with the border towns of Mexicali and Tijuana, providing medical supplies, food, and building materials, as well as volunteer work crews.[49] All in all, many CFM groups became involved in some way—either providing transportation to Mass and to religious education classes or providing food and clothing. The trip into the fields was a real eye-opener for many CFMers, who were appalled by the "poverty and misery" of the workers.[50]

Actions continued in the 1960s. In Mount Prospect, Illinois, a senior CFM group made the needs of Spanish-speaking people in the area its focus. The group used the Gospel and Liturgy inquiries from the annual program book, but wrote their own Social Inquiries. They helped to create an Opportunity Council to try to improve living conditions. They also investigated housing and education and helped to establish summer school and adult education programs. They worked to promote low-cost housing, conducted clothing and food drives, and created a "clothing depot."[51]

CFMers were the driving force behind such community-wide migrant services as Head Start programs (even before Head Start existed) and legal services. In Chicago Heights, Olympia Fields CFMer Bernadette Remaly founded a one-stop service center called Respond, where migrants could get food, clothing, and help in threading through the social service maze.

In 1962, Saginaw, Michigan, CFM developed a special apostolate to migrant workers to provide the "corporal and spiritual works of mercy." As a result of their efforts, migrant families could go to a nearby Spanish-language Mass, get medical services, and use a day school and lunch program.[52] Milwaukee and Stevens Point, Wisconsin, created similar programs.

CFM's commitment to meeting migrant needs was no flash in the pan. Work continued through the sixties. St. John's Parish CFM in Winfield, Illinois, near Joliet, became aware of the plight of local Latino workers during a factory strike in West Chicago. The group developed an Opportunity Council, a self-help organization designed to provide needed services—English classes, job training, and other programs. On a personal level, the group helped one migrant family to settle by finding a job and a home, a house that was rebuilt by the CFMers.[53] In Tucson, CFM groups assisted a priest traveling among the migrants in a trailer.

In 1965 the migrant workers became national news with the dramatic strike of farmworkers against table-grape growers in Delano, California. Emerging from this strike was the charismatic Cesar Chavez, who called for a nationwide boycott of table grapes. CFM groups throughout California and the United States rallied to Chavez's banner, supporting the boycott, sending food and clothing to support the strikers. Many CFMers, including some from Oakland joined Chavez's "pilgrimage" from Delano to Sacramento. *ACT* joined the effort, publishing "The Sad Story of a Migrant Farmworker," which began, "Our tables are loaded with the fruits of his misery and despair."[54] The article laid out the injustices inflicted on migrant workers and urged CFMers to support their cause.

This considerable achievement did little, however, to forward the goal of developing CFM membership in the Latino community. It was hoped that the spread of Marriage Encounter would allow CFM "to widen acquaintances with Spanish-speaking people."[55] Hillenbrand told the CFM Executive Committee in 1967 that working with the Spanish-speaking was long "overdue."[56] As CFM had few materials printed in Spanish, the Crowleys invited Mexican MFC to come and establish the MFC in the United States. Norbert and Vivian Langer of Downer's Grove, Illinois, CFM veterans of ten years, served as the contact couple between the MFC and CFM. Norbert had made contact with MFC as early as 1962 and had worked on an exchange program with them. He and Vivian had also worked with Joliet CFM's migrant worker program. After the first encounters, the Langers realized that CFM "needed MFC to foster and sustain the encuentro experience."[57] The Langers were instrumental in helping the MFC spread under the aegis of CFM.

The tour of the Spanish Marriage Encounter teams in REDAR '68 did much to initiate MFC groups, but groups had begun to emerge even before their arrival. In Houston, Rafael and Berta Davila and a young priest named Patricio Flores, a future bishop, had established MFC groups following the first ME in Houston. By 1969, Houston MFC had twenty-three groups and the MFC had spread to Miami, San Francisco, Brooklyn, Chicago, Los Angeles, Detroit, Cleveland, Sacramento, Phoenix, and Dallas. The MFC tallied 1,000 couples, with Houston and Dallas accounting for 300 couples.

As MFC grew in the United States, so did a national structure. In August 1969, MFC held its first national meeting in conjunction with the CFM national convention at Notre Dame. The first MFC president couple elected was Gustavo and Isabel Erviti of Chicago. An Executive Committee was also established consisting of the Ervitis, Pablo and Esperanza Olivares, Hernan and M. Machicado of Boston, Benigno and Aida Galnares of Miami, Roberto and Consuelo Perez of Los Angeles, Rafael and Berta Davila, Pedro and Loretta Jurado of Chicago, (who were named national secretary couple), and the Langers, who served as liaison.[58]

The movement continued to expand in 1970. Soon MFC claimed more than 1,200 couples in twenty-three dioceses. Several MFC groups were started among migrant workers in Texas. In 1970, the National Executive Committee of MFC met in Denver. There they defined the general objective of MFC: "To promote the human and Christian values of the family so that it may be within the community a developer of persons, a shaper of the faith, and actively engaged in the total development of the community through its members."[59] A national newsletter, the *Carta Informativa* began publication as the official organ of MFC-U.S.A. MFC would continue to work closely with CFM, but with separate programs. The committee agreed to participate in CFM's national convention at Notre Dame in 1971.

In 1970 MFC was established in Canada as an outgrowth of the first Spanish-language Marriage Encounter ever held in Canada. It took place at a site near Montreal with CFM as sponsor. At the close of the encounter, the Montreal CFM area couple, the Lerouxes, told participants about MFC groups in the United States. Several couples wrote the Ervitis in Chicago for program materials, and MFC Montreal was born, with Father Aniceto Gomez acting as chaplain.

By the end of 1972, MFC claimed more than 3,000 couples as members in twenty-five dioceses. In the same year it held its first official assembly at the Mexican American Cultural Center in San Antonio. *ACT* called MFC's expansion "one of the great success stories," and by late 1972 proclaimed, "MFC Has Come into Its Own in 1972."[60] By 1973, MFC had published three program books and was firmly established throughout the United States.

MFC's path to success reminded many of CFM's early days, but its approach to the family apostolate was different. Taking its cue from Marriage Encounter, MFC focused more on internal family concerns. The Ervitis believed that couples needed three years of formation before they could venture into community action. The couple and the family had to be strengthened first. In 1969, Mexican MFC chaplain Donald Hessler had written the Crowleys,

"We are still too far away from politics and international life and race and social justice."[61] A similar assessment could be made of MFC-U.S.A.

Nonetheless, MFC enjoyed great success in Latino communities that CFM had found impenetrable. Part of its success lay in developing program materials relevant to the Latino situation in the United States. Several Latinos complained that the early translations of CFM materials were inadequate because they did not reflect an understanding of the "mentality, psychology, customs, 'needs' of the Spanish-speaking community."[62] Moreover, they did not reflect an understanding of the difficulties Latinos experienced living in the midst of an "Anglo culture."

To correct this, MFC developed its own bilingual program materials. By 1973, it had introduced three books: *Por Una Familia Mas Feliz* (1969), a first-year book; *La Familia: Formidora de Personas* (1971), the second-year book; and the third-year book, *Familia y Communidad*. The books began by focusing on "conjugal love," then moved to the family, and finally the community.

MFC also helped the Latino family confront a serious cultural problem—machismo. In MFC, as in CFM, the woman was seen as an equal to the husband, "a mode of family life not often practiced in Latin American countries."[63] The program of MFC helped the husband and wife come to grips with this cultural problem.

One final note on MFC-U.S.A.: One of its areas of greatest concerns was the abortion issue. MFC leaders felt that abortion laws were a "direct threat to Spanish-speaking families."[64] Abortion was regarded as an attack on racial minorities and therefore had to be vigorously opposed.

MFC as it developed in the United States was quite different from CFM, though it worked closely with CFM and was supported by CFM. MFC was more conservative than CFM and focused more on internal family matters than on social action.

Ironically, the three movements that CFM supported and promoted—ICCFM, Marriage Encounter, and the MFC—all prospered as CFM declined.

TWELVE

The End of the Sixties and the Decline of CFM

Through the 1960s, the issues that CFM focused on—race, gender and sexuality, ecumenism, international relations—grew out of the era. CFM's treatment of these issues was shaped by the yearly inquiry programs. Until the end of the sixties, the program continued to examine the seven areas of lay life as defined by Reynold Hillenbrand:

1961–62 The Family: Center of Social Rebirth
1962–63 Christianity and Social Progress
1963–64 The Parish: Leaven in the Community
1964–65 Encounters in Politics and Race
1965–66 The Creator Made the World: Come and See It: International Life and the Creative Use of Leisure
1966–67 The Family in a Time of Change: Family Life and Economics
1967–68 Building Community through Religious Life and Politics
1968–69 Shalom: Peace in the City, in the World, in the Family

The 1969–70 book, *People Are . . . ,* represented a departure from the cyclical format. As noted before, *People Are . . .* was an attempt to create an ecumenical introductory book to replace *FHF* and to initiate a more contemporary approach to programming. As will be seen below, once free of Hillenbrand's cycle, the Program

214

Committee experimented with a variety of approaches, none of which was very successful.

Beyond the larger actions and inquiries treated in the previous chapters, many CFM groups continued to carry out what might be called traditional actions. CFMers throughout the United States and Canada continued to host international students and to assist refugees, continued to support foreign and home missions and missionaries, and continued to improve their cities, neighborhoods, and parishes.[1] CFMers continued to staff parish programs. In addition to all these, and beyond the scope of the annual inquiry books, many groups also began addressing issues particular to the end of the 1960s. A group in Philadelphia set up a program to help men who were leaving the priesthood to make the transition to lay life. A group in Pittsburgh did the same for women leaving the religious life. Many groups took on the problem of drug abuse, while others explored the negative implications of the sexual revolution. Many groups established programs to assist senior citizens—Father Putz, for example, established Harvest House, an educational program for seniors. Many CFM groups supported the United Farmworkers' grape boycott, while others continued the struggle for fair housing and other civil rights. These actions fell within the typical actions of CFM groups over the previous two decades.

Surprisingly, the issue that was ripping the United States apart, the Vietnam War, received relatively little attention from CFM. Individual CFMers joined the chorus of antiwar protesters; the Crowleys worked for the presidential nomination of antiwar candidate Eugene McCarthy (who had addressed the CFM national convention in 1959), as did other CFMers. Individual CFM groups addressed the issue—Chicago CFM joined the 1969 moratorium against the war, issuing a statement that "surely we have the right to protest against the thirty billion a year, 50,000 lives outrage. The time to *act* is now!"[2] Green Bay CFM developed its own inquiry on the war, but no national inquiry was developed on this subject. Nor did national CFM take a public stance on the war, remaining true to the principle that CFM was a grass-roots movement, and the national office should therefore take no national stand.

This notable omission stemmed from a number of factors. First, like other people in the United States, CFMers, in general, initially supported the war effort. The war was understood as part of the worldwide struggle against communist aggression. Moreover, many CFMers had sons or husbands serving in Vietnam. A Virginia CFM group rallied to support a couple whose son had died in Vietnam. Other groups did likewise. In addition, the war, unlike the race issue, presented no clear moral imperative or consensus.

Even the annual inquiry book, entitled *Shalom* (1968–69), written at the time when antiwar protests were exploding, did not speak directly about Vietnam. Instead, via a fictitious Third World country named "Panolivia," issues related to Vietnam were indirectly dealt with, but the central issue of the morality of the war was never explicitly addressed. In the 1971–72 inquiry book, *Quality of Life,* meeting six was entitled "To End War," but, again, the Vietnam War was not expressly mentioned, although local groups undoubtedly did discuss and act on it.

ACT had a better track record. In 1966, it began publishing the occasional article on the Vietnam War. One such, a 1967 article by antiwar activist Gordon Zahn, "Catholics, War, and Pacifism,"[3] discussed the "limit to Christian patriotism" and the right of selective conscientious objection. That challenge set off a debate within *ACT.* Many letter writers continued to support the war effort. As late as March 1968 one letter stressed that "Vietnam IS worth the cost," and urged CFMers to continue to "fight against the red tide of communism."[4] Still, many others opposed the war. At the 1967 national convention, a petition calling for an end to the Vietnam War was circulated among the CFMers in attendance.[5] At the next convention in 1969, Mike Cullen, one of the "Milwaukee 14" who had committed civil disobedience in opposition to the war, addressed the convention, admonishing CFMers, "You must not be silent."[6] In Detroit, CFMers joined a national boycott of "all nonessential consumer goods" until the war was over.[7] Many opposed the war on a more personal level, counseling young men to flee to Canada or aiding them in their flight. Canadian CFMers were called on to provide a safe haven for the children of some U.S. CFMers. At the 1971 convention a special workshop on "draft counseling" was offered.

By the early 1970s, most CFMers, like the majority of Americans, had serious doubts about the U.S. effort in Vietnam. In 1971, Sister Elizabeth McAllister, then under indictment as one of the "Harrisburg 8" with Philip Berrigan, denounced the war in no uncertain terms at the national convention. Not everyone was pleased. In May 1973, *ACT* published a condemnation of U.S. policy issued by long-time CFM ally, the French La Vie Nouvelle, which condemned "the heinous bombardments . . . by the USA air forces" in Vietnam.[8] While many CFMers no doubt agreed and while many CFMers protested the war as individuals, even this powerful condemnation did not evoke a national CFM response.

More amenable to CFMers was a proposal brought forward by veteran CFMers Dan and Rose Lucey. The Luceys were a famous CFM family, starting out in CFM in Los Angeles in the 1950s, later becoming stalwarts of Oakland CFM. The Luceys proposed that a peace academy, styled after the U.S. military academies, be established "to train people for peace." The Luceys went national with their idea as early as 1967. In March of that year *ACT* reported that Robert F. Kennedy was interested in the Luceys' proposal.[9] At the 1967 Notre Dame national convention, the Luceys led a workshop entitled "Why Not a National Peace Academy?" that drew an encouraging positive response. Rose remembers, "We noted there were nine war colleges in the United States, many memorials to war heroes, but the nation had no national symbol to the serious work of building a world beyond war. Said Dan, 'Some day we may be faced with peace—who will work it out? The generals, the men trained in war?'"[10] The Luceys began to push their idea in earnest. Legislation for a peace academy was first proposed in Congress in 1975, but the Peace Academy or the U.S. Institute for Peace as it came to be called, was not passed into law until 1984. Ironically, it was passed as an amendment to the defense authorization bill. Nonetheless, it was a great and hard-fought victory for CFM and the Luceys, though Dan had died before the bill was passed.

Other CFMers became involved in protests to end the arms race. Most notable in this regard was Pittsburgh CFM chaplain Donald McIlvaine. He railed against "the bomb," warning that, "the arms race is an utterly treacherous trap for humanity, one which injures the poor to an intolerable degree. . . . Seldom do we hear of the gross immorality of piling up greater numbers of nuclear weapons. There is a serious 'lag' here. The same priest who backs the Pope in the fight on 'the pill' says nothing against 'the bomb' and the arms race."[11] Many CFMers and ex-CFMers became actively involved in the nuclear freeze battle a decade later.

THE NOTRE DAME CONVENTIONS — THE 1960S

Though shifted to a schedule of odd-year meetings (alternating with area conventions), the Notre Dame conventions continued to be remarkable affairs. As always, the conventions featured cutting-edge speakers—theologians, sociologists, activists— innovative liturgies, and of course, CFM families. Families from across America gathered to share their experiences and to greet old friends. The tremendous spirit of the conventions revved up the conventioneers, and sent couples home ready to undertake the coming year's program.

The conventions featured a tremendous lineup of speakers of which the following offers but a small sample: 1963: Bernard Cooke, Bernard Haring, Matthew Ahmann, and George Shuster; 1965: John Noonan, Mary Perkins Ryan, Monsignor Luigi Ligutti, and Haring again; 1967: John McKenzie, S.J., Paul Simon, Gordon Zahn, Harvey Cox, Gregory Baum, Sidney Callahan, and John Thomas, S.J.; 1969: Bishop Edward Crowther of South Africa, Seymour Halleck, M.D., Dr. Joseph Sittler; 1971: Sister Elizabeth McAllister, Michael Novak, Baum, and Noonan. The Berrigan brothers and Cesar Chavez also appeared at this convention.

The liturgies were spectacular. Particularly memorable were the liturgies of 1965 and 1967 organized by African American priest Clarence Rivers. CFMers practically floated out of these liturgies. Other significant liturgical singer/songwriters appeared—Ray Repp, Cyril Paul, and Carey Landry. The most famous of the liturgies has already been mentioned—the 1971 Episcopal Mass. Typical of CFM convention Masses was great lay participation, inspired preaching, and enthusiastic singing.

Still, what made the conventions was not the speakers or the liturgies, important as they were. What made the convention was the CFM couples, who for three days were immersed in the world of CFM. For three days they were painted a vision of what the Church was, what it and the world could be, and what they could do to contribute to the Church and to the world. Discussions, arguments, fruitful exchanges took place at the planned workshops and outside those workshops. The three days had the effect of a giant pep rally, a spiritual retreat, and an academic briefing, all rolled into one. Most CFM couples reported leaving in a state of euphoria.

The conventions had grown from the first simple gathering at Childerly to these extraordinary proceedings. The convention grew in number throughout the 1960s, peaking at the 1967 convention, the biggest ever held, claiming more than 1,200 couples. The lineup of speakers was also one of the most impressive. Reflecting the decrease in the movement's membership rolls, convention attendance declined in 1969, and continued to decline through the 1970s.

The convention speakers were not all upbeat. From Monsignor Hillenbrand rebuking the couples for their "double conscience" to Sister Elizabeth McAllister chastising them for their complacency over the war in Vietnam, convention speakers challenged their listeners. Elmer Zinn of Grand Rapids CFM published a daily mimeographed newsletter. In 1967, one bulletin read, "Father John McKenzie, S.J., said authority was in trouble, Father Robert Brooke, O.PRAEM., said the parishes were in trouble, and a local newspaper reporter said she has her lead for her story, 'EVERYBODY

Is in Trouble.' Really, it isn't that bad . . . .[Go out] and make things better."[12]

The sense of crisis that pervaded the 1967 and 1969 conventions seemed to have disappeared by 1971. *ACT* reported of that year's convention, "Gone it seemed were the endless questions dealing with 'where is CFM going?' . . . There was a calm acceptance, it seemed, among the regulars that CFM has been around a long time, has done its best, is now turning into new directions, and is hanging loose to see just precisely where the organization might best serve."[13] Whether calm actually prevailed or whether it was just wishful thinking on the part of the writer, CFM was facing its most serious challenges in more than two decades. If calm did prevail, it did not prevail for long.

THE DECLINE OF CFM

When CFM's decline came, it seemed to come swiftly, to the mystification of longtime CFMers. In reality, the movement declined over the course of a decade. The movement had peaked in 1964 with close to 50,000 couples involved in the United States and Canada. The 1964–65 program's frank inquiry into the racial problem in the United States resulted in a significant drop in membership. By 1967, membership had dropped to 32,000, with a dramatic drop of almost 50 percent by the end of the following year to 16,600. In July, 1968 the Crowleys reported that two areas—the southwest and the northwest—"have gone dead."[14] The numbers stabilized somewhat the next two years declining to only 14,160 couples by 1970.[15] The decline continued unabated through the early years of the 1970s, dropping to 8,866 couples in 1971, then to 4,313 in 1974, with one estimate going as low as 2,500 couples.[16] By 1980, only 1,100 couples remained in the movement.

As membership declined, the national leadership of CFM became more and more obsessed with the numbers. An Expansion Committee was established to promote new memberships. At the 1971 meeting of the Executive Committee one member warned,

"Our main concern is that CFM has to make some drastic changes soon or it may all be over."[17] Articles in *ACT* joined the chorus of doom, "Will CFM Survive?"[18] The chaircouple of the San Francisco Federation asked, "Is CFM as a movement passé? Has the quickening pace of contemporary life left CFM behind? Is CFM irrelevant to the Church and the World?"[19] Others repeatedly stressed that CFM needed to forget about the numbers and continue to bear fruitful witness to the Gospel through the observe-judge-act methodology. One chaplain warned the Executive Committee in 1973, "CFM was usually presented as an organization to be expanded rather than a cause to be extended."[20] These exhortations went largely unheeded.

In reality, CFM's main problem was not a loss of members. CFM had always lost members. Several surveys indicated that the typical CFM couple stayed in the movement for only 3.5 years. Yearly, it had lost 15 to 20 percent of its members. The problem in the late 1960s was that not enough new members were being drawn to the movement. This precipitous decline in membership resulted in an intensified debate over the future of CFM.

This debate did not, of course, begin with the loss of members. As noted earlier, a tension had always existed between CFMers who stressed social action and those who wanted more emphasis on the family unit itself, and this tension continued throughout the 1960s. The movement's perception of itself as part of the Church's avant garde also placed pressure on it. One couple expressed disappointment in the 1963 national convention liturgy: "It was a good example of how a Movement like CFM that once was avant garde can be passed up in the march of progress."[21] The status quo was unacceptable to CFM leadership—the movement's rightful place was at the forefront. Some expressed fears that CFM was becoming too complacent. One chaplain warned, "I fear that we are more interested in protecting CFM than helping man. We are becoming institutional."[22] Another recurring problem was what to do with CFMers who had been in the movement for more than three years and were looking for meatier challenges. All these concerns culminated in several celebrated controversies within the movement. The goals and nature of CFM were at the heart of these concerns, but a loss of confidence gave them a new edge.

WILLIAM NERIN AND THE END OF CFM

In 1966, when the movement still remained relatively healthy, William Nerin, CFM chaplain and family life director for the Diocese of Oklahoma City and Tulsa suggested that CFM had fulfilled its purpose and that it was time to disband the movement. In an address to an area convention in Cushing, Oklahoma, Nerin argued that CFM had "done its basic job of orienting Catholics toward the world." Further, he argued, CFM's activities should be taken over by "more specialized" organizations.[23] He had tried to push CFM in this direction four years earlier, arguing that the movement should eschew the shotgun programming and actions spawned by the national programs. "CFM['s] . . . basic purpose is not to form apostolic couples, but to assume the responsibility for Christ to secure 'a condition of life worthy' for sound family life."[24] Such a commission required that CFM focus on institutions that affected family life, and act to change those institutions. Many CFMers argued that this was what the movement was already about, but Nerin insisted CFM needed more focus. In many ways, Nerin suggested that CFM act as a pressure group, even a lobby, on behalf of couples and families. By 1966, Nerin gave up on CFM's ability to act in such a manner. He conceded that the movement had alerted "the Church to the crucial problem of interracial justice" and the need for an "active, meaningful liturgy." But in the post–Vatican II Church, "these goals had been taken over by the Church at large,"[25] and therefore CFM was no longer needed. He concluded by wondering "if CFM was one of those bureaucratic organizations which tend to perpetuate themselves whether they are needed or not."[26]

As might be expected, Nerin's talk generated some energetic counterpunches. The Crowleys responded by stressing that "CFM

these groundswells; indeed, CFM should be in the vanguard. First, the Mass had to be reformed, not in the manner prescribed by Hillenbrand, but dramatically and fundamentally. "Small, community-style Masses held in homes around the dining room table" should replace "the impersonal, anachronistic services still held in most parish churches [that] have little relevance to the banquet of love which Christ originally instituted." The Drishes had attended many of these home, "family-style" Masses, and suggested that CFM experiment with these new celebrations, perhaps incorporating them into the annual inquiry programs. Further, they suggested, the Mass could be shortened. "Certain irrelevant parts" could be omitted. "After all, if we have instant Christ in our brother, why is it necessary to spend an hour conjuring up Christ on the altar?" Further they encouraged the use of "folk songs" in the liturgy. The Drishes foresaw a time when the father of the family would say Mass "around his own dining room table for his family, friends, and neighbors."

The Drishes then addressed a number of sensitive issues, including the need to restructure Church authority, the right and need to question certain dogmas and decrees, the need to use small-group dynamics, the need to attract modern youth, and the need to understand the modern woman. They also called for an openness to new clerical styles, including a married clergy. The letter concluded with a list of CFM's weaknesses: a new *FHF* needed to be issued, updated with the decrees of Vatican II. "The old-church scripture and liturgy [inquiries] are an insult to a movement that declares itself to be a leader in the Church." Further, the movement had "failed in the civil rights struggle." CFM had "made practically no dent on institutional reforms." Leaders were not being trained. "[S]o far we have not come up with another Crowley couple to help relieve them of some of their tremendous burden." Members were not growing in depth. Issues of poverty and peace were not being addressed. Finally, the seven program areas of the yearly inquiries needed to be reassessed. The Drishes hoped that their letter would spur discussion and help CFM channel the spirit of Vatican II.

The letter did indeed generate a lively discussion among the Executive Committee, but national chaplain Reynold Hillenbrand "disavowed" the document.[31] His copy of the letter was filled with marginal comments such as "forbidden," "not allowed," "nonsense," "what is this?" "crazy," "have to accept"; to the comment that the "old-church scripture and liturgy are an insult," he wrote "I take exception."[32] To Hillenbrand, the document was totally incomprehensible.

THE PROBLEM OF HILLENBRAND

Hillenbrand's inability to understand or even tolerate the Drish letter reflected the growing distance between Hillenbrand and many CFMers. Hillenbrand's personality had never been what could be called ingratiating or popular, and he was a less than adequate public speaker. In fact, many CFM women found him absolutely impossible. Nonetheless, Hillenbrand had been the driving intellectual force in the 1950s and early 60s. Surprisingly, serious problems began to emerge with Hillenbrand during and after the Second Vatican Council. Hillenbrand, who had been so progressive liturgically and apostolically during the 1940s and 50s, seemed undone by the council. What many CFMers saw as Hillenbrand's vindication turned out to be Hillenbrand's undoing. By the end of the sixties most CFMers regarded Hillenbrand as hopelessly out of touch with the movement and with the laity.

Part of Hillenbrand's problem was his inability to accept the flux and process that followed Vatican II. Though he encouraged lay action, for Hillenbrand the spheres of priest and laity were clearly defined and distinct. The lay person acted in the world, and the priest formed the laity. As late as summer, 1965 Hillenbrand still maintained, "Without priests, no apostles are formed."[33] As the clear barrier between the clerical and lay sphere dissolved during the 1960s, Hillenbrand's vision became obsolete.

Hillenbrand seemed no more comfortable with the new type of lay person—educated, active, and questioning. To this new breed, the authority of the clergy and of the Church was not unquestioned. This viewpoint disturbed Hillenbrand, who for all his advocacy of an active laity still believed in the old notion of the Church teaching and the Church taught. One veteran CFMer pointed out the irony, " He is the one who turned us into the kind of lay people who could argue with him."[34] Hillenbrand did not much like the change.

By 1964, the complaints about Hillenbrand were increasing. He continued to edit each yearly inquiry book and continued to arrange for the imprimatur indicating that the book was free from doctrinal error. He insisted that *ACT* be read by a priest before publication. This domineering style alienated many of the new CFM leaders, who were impatient with the deference shown to Hillenbrand by long-time CFMers. As one couple active in the late 60s put it, "We knew Hillenbrand only as some 'mythical old ogre.'" Many urged that Hillenbrand be eased out of his role of national chaplain, a role he had played since the movement's inception in 1949.

Despite the criticisms, Pat Crowley remained intensely loyal to Hillenbrand; he was not about to abandon the man who had opened a whole new world to him. In October 1965 the Crowleys acknowledged, "[T]he present national chaplain has created problems, personality-wise, yet he has given us prophetic direction. As far as we're concerned he has never made a really serious mistake in judgment."[35] Many veteran CFMers felt the same way. They remembered what Hillenbrand had meant to the movement. Still, as the 1960s progressed, Hillenbrand became increasingly cranky and difficult to deal with. Some believed his physical ailments intensified his negative approach—he had never completely recovered from his near-fatal car crash of 1949, which had left him with a serious limp. One CFM chaplain observed, "He is physically suffering and worn out," and this added to his "emotional strain." It was left to the Crowleys "to be a buffer between Hilly and the movement, playing the prudential role all the time." The chaplain concluded by suggesting that this was the Crowleys' "cross" to bear.[36]

By 1967, Hillenbrand's control over the inquiry program began to wane. The program committee chose not to ask Hillenbrand to obtain an imprimatur, though the book was submitted to him for editing. That decision was a major step for veteran CFMers, but once again the need for it puzzled the newer members on the Program Committee. The following year the inquiry program was not even submitted to him. Though Hillenbrand officially remained the national chaplain until the early 1970s, his influence had completely dissipated by then. He had broken with the Crowleys, his major supporters, following their opposition to *Humanae Vitae,* and the breach was never closed. By the early 1970s, the man who had done so much to form CFM was isolated from the movement and seemed increasingly bitter. As one veteran CFM couple had so aptly put it, the fate of Hillenbrand in the late 1960s was "sad and disturbing."

THE NOTRE DAME STUDY OF CFM

In the fall of 1966, three sociology professors at the University of Notre Dame, John Maiolo, William D'Antonio, and William Liu, began an in-depth sociological study of CFM with the blessing and financial support of CFM's national leadership. The project, to be called "A Study of CFM in American Society," was to examine the movement's background and the social context out of which it grew, its appeal, its structure, and its accomplishments. CFM groups throughout the United States cooperated by supplying survey information. At the time, the movement was apparently thriving, and CFM leaders expected a most positive report. By the time the study was completed, CFM had lost more than half its membership, and the study concluded glumly that CFM "was on the wane." More disturbing was the finding that CFM was in danger of becoming "irrelevant" and that it had lost its appeal to young people. The study suggested that one way to regain members was to begin to act as a "pressure group" and take stands on national issues. The report predictably generated yet another serious discussion over the nature and future of CFM.

Overlooked for the most part was the study's positive analysis of the movement and its accomplishments. The typical CFM husband was in his mid to late thirties, was college-educated, of the business or professional class, and had an annual income about twice the national average. The typical CFM wife was in her early to mid thirties, a high school graduate with some college, and did not work outside the home. The average CFM family had four children. The average length of membership in CFM was 3.5 years.

The study revealed that CFM made a tremendous impact on the lives of the CFM couples and their families. Not only did CFM improve the personal relationships between the couple and within the family, it also increased the couples' participation in community, civic, and political affairs. Further, CFMers made a distinct contribution to the neighborhood and community of which they were a part. In general terms, CFM had to be considered a roaring success.[37]

The positive elements were overlooked in part because the negative aspects were emphasized in a press statement released by the three sociologists in December 1969. The bad press stung the Crowleys and other CFM leaders. The bad press was compounded by a lapse in courtesy on the part of the sociologists, who released the statement to the press without informing the Crowleys. The Crowleys' pique is reflected in a letter they sent to the sociologists, "We hope to hear from you on the final report of the CFM study. We'd probably prefer a letter or a phone call rather than a press release. Actually, we didn't mind it, but some people did. Maybe we are too easily pleased because we did appreciate that CFM was spelled correctly. In any event, we're still limping along, alive, well, and hoping to do some small work for the family's health, education, welfare . . . "[38]

The Crowleys also wrote a formal rebuttal to the study, and to the study's conclusions. The Crowleys wrote, "We do not agree that CFM is declining." They pointed to a number of CFM-supported programs that were expanding—Marriage Encounter, the Movimiento Familiar Cristiano, and International CFM—to demonstrate CFM's continuing vitality. The Crowleys were hopeful that the movement's new ecumenical orientation would spur new growth. In addition, "CFM still contains the ingredients of a social dynamic that can help to revolutionize the church as well as society." The Cardijn technique remained a powerful tool as did the small-group dynamic. "Beginning families" were still attracted to CFM.[39]

In the renewed debate, of special concern was D'Antonio's suggestion that to attract new members CFM should become a national "pressure group" and begin to take "national stands." D'Antonio thought one natural issue for CFM was birth control, and he suggested that CFM join forces with Planned Parenthood. The Executive Committee and most federation leaders rejected that suggestion, not so much for its substance but because it went against CFM's traditional position that the movement would not speak out on national issues.

As early as 1957, that point was underscored in an *ACT* editorial entitled "A Matter of Prudence," which warned against local groups using the CFM name to endorse their group's viewpoint. "No local group has the right to speak for the Movement as a whole."[40] In 1960, another editorial articulated why the national CFM committees would not take a particular stand on a national issue. First, CFM did not speak for the Church, whose official position was expressed by the bishops. Second, in temporal affairs there may be more than one right answer. Finally, "CFM is not a pressure group."[41] The editorial concluded that the movement would take a stand only when asked to do so by the bishop, or bishops.

By the mid-sixties many felt that CFM was violating its policy of no national stands, especially in regard to the issue of race. In 1965, the Crowleys came perilously close to signing a petition in response to the Selma crisis on behalf of CFM. Ultimately, they only signed their own names and did not commit the movement. Nonetheless, many complained that CFM was becoming "an ultra liberal organization,"[42] which was overstepping its bounds by making statements on national issues.

Larry Ragan, editor of *ACT,* argued that CFM did have a predisposition on many issues. For instance, the movement clearly supported the Civil Rights Acts, fair housing, the war on poverty, foreign aid to "have-not nations," and issues relating to the family. Why not admit it?[43] The Executive Committee responded with a statement that modified the traditional stance: "Given the goal of CFM that the movement is concerned with the growth of the person, the movement should generally avoid making public statements on national issues. However, it is recognized that exceptions may arise where the nature or urgency of an issue is such that CFM should speak. Such exceptions will occur only after the statement has been accepted by the Executive Committee or Coordinating Committee." Local groups and federations were also given greater leeway; they could take stands as long as they qualified their statements to indicate they were speaking for their own locality and not for CFM as a national movement.[44] Despite the innovation, neither the Executive Committee nor the Coordinating Committee ever issued a statement on a national issue.

It is scarcely surprising that D'Antonio's suggestion did not move CFMers toward more centralized decision-making. The study itself had underlined the fact that one of the movement's strengths was its decentralization; Maiolo marveled that "the capacity of CFM to hold a diversity of ideological moods is incredible—everything from the extreme left wing to the extreme right is seen in various communities throughout the country."[45]

THE TURN INWARD

More significant than the debate over a national stand was the continued debate and tension between those who saw CFM as a "family" movement, and those who saw CFM as a social apostolate. This tension, present in varying degrees since the movement's beginning, was generally resolved, in the first twenty years, in favor of the social action emphasis. An exchange between a Melrose, Massachusets, couple and the national Program Committee typifies the course of the dialogue. The couple asked simply, "What has become of the "F" in CFM?" A member of the Program Committee replied, "CFM is intended to help couples—and of course their families, because they are parents—see more fully the full range of their responsibilities as Christians, and to give them some practical experience in carrying out these responsibilities. The fact that a concern for world order, or for peace, or for poverty, is part of this responsibility is a fact not of our making."[46] CFM *did* benefit the family, not by focusing on it, but by pushing it beyond its own protective borders.

By 1969, the "family" focus was gaining ground. Marriage Encounter was flourishing, and the MFC was showing great promise. Both movements placed greater emphasis on internal family relationships than did CFM. Some CFM groups began to express interest in "sensitivity training," which had become enormously popular by the end of the 1960s. Indeed, Sister Gertrude Thomas (Dorothy Donnelly) conducted a "sensitivity session" for the Executive Committee at its summer meeting in 1967[47] and then presented a workshop at the 1969 national convention. In 1968, the Coordinating Committee was introduced to sensitivity training. The language of "interpersonal relations" and "group dynamics," "honest communication," "encounter," "positive think," and "feelings" was new to CFM. Obviously, CFM had used some of these concepts before—communication and group dynamics had been a constant concern—but CFM prided itself on its hard-headed demand for real action, not the introspective "navel-gazing" implied by sensitivity sessions.

Federation reports reflected the inroads being made by the new approach. In the Philadelphia CFM's newsletter one couple reported, in an article entitled "Sensitivity," "The longer Harry and I work and share with couples in CFM, the more conscious we become of a restlessness and reaching on the part of husbands and wives for deeper, more real, a creative, a more infinite relationship with each other. These feelings . . . are often . . . the motivating force drawing them on and outward to discover themselves more fully as lovers."[48] Similarly, the Chicago federation reported, there was a "greater need than ever before for the search for our own identity. . . . Couples are no longer fascinated with discussing just world problems, or even local and topical troubles. They want to find out more about themselves—Who are we really? What do we want out of life and each other?"[49] This fascination with the inner self struck several old-time CFMers as "dangerous views."[50]

Nonetheless, the new outlook was incorporated into the annual inquiry book for 1969–70, *People Are* . . . . As noted before, this book was the first fully ecumenical inquiry booklet, and it was intended to replace *For Happier Families* as the introductory book for CFM. Though it was to be the new *FHF*, all groups, even veteran groups, were to use it for the 1969–70 annual booklet. The introduction immediately set the tone, "*People Are* . . . is a book about *growth* and *development;* it presumes the dignity and value of every person; the need to *communicate* and to *care;* the necessity that we help each other to *grow* and *fulfill our potential* (emphasis mine).[51] In the new book, "formation" had become "growth". The book began with a series of inquiries examining the husband-and-wife relationship, then the parent-child relationship, the relationship of family to family, and, finally, of family to world. Significantly, the old *FHF* emphasis on neighborhood and the virtue of neighborliness was notable by its absence. Instead, more time was devoted to communication and interpersonal relationships, mostly between husband and wife. In many ways, *People Are* . . . seemed better suited as a Cana manual than as a primer for CFM. Meeting 7 programmed a rather explicit discussion of the couples' "lovemaking," decidedly new ground for CFM. Things outside the family were observed primarily in their relationship to the family. Only one or two of the inquiries pushed the family significantly out into the world.

People Are . . . received mixed reviews. Many felt the inquiries were "meaningful," "relevant," and "challenging." Others stressed that the book created better communication between couples and allowed a greater role for "feeling" and "emotion." On the negative side, many believed that the book was not conducive to action and therefore not a good beginning book for CFM. Others commented that the book was "too centered on the family" and "too personal." Several complained about the sexual content of meeting 7.[52]

Despite the complaints, *People Are . . .* continued as the introductory booklet for the next several years.

The following two years, the Program Committee returned to the approach of the mid-1960s with two inquiry programs exploring larger issues—*The Family in a Time of Revolution* (1970–71) and *Quality of Life* (1971–72). The books examined such issues as the aged, the poor, the unemployed, the working class, social revolutions, war, pollution, and overpopulation. The choice of "revolution" as a title caused some controversy. With all the protests, disturbances, and challenges to authority still in full stride, several suggested that it was not CFM's job to stir up revolution. Gary CFM commented, "Revolution is an extremely poor word to use for any program concerned with the Christian Family Movement . . . revolution is vile, repulsive and certainly not the correct term to use to effect changes in social injustices."[53] The choice of "revolution" was defended by Program Committee member June Smith, who placed a positive twist on the word. She called for a "CREATIVE REVOLUTION. A true revolution because that's absolutely necessary as the structures are irreformable, but a creative revolution, not a destructive revolution because otherwise no progress will result."[54] Though several inquiries dealt with the effect of revolution on the family, and within the family, the primary focus was outside the family.

Increasingly in 1971, the "family faction" grew in strength. *ACT* reported that at the winter Executive Committee meeting there was "much discussion about . . . more family centered programs, more concern for the family."[55] In March, the Executive Committee instructed the Program Committee to place greater emphasis and focus on the family. The Crowleys noted that while more attention needed to be paid to the family, they cautioned that "Family encounter should be developed but never lose sight of the need to help people develop by turning out to the community, relating to the needs and people of their community."[56] And National President Couple Ray and Dorothy Maldoon warned that it would be a mistake to let the program become "too family centered."[57]

By 1972, with membership numbers still in free fall, the faction calling for greater emphasis on the family was victorious. The Executive Committee instructed the Program Committee to "attempt to make OBVIOUS the tie-in of all inquiries to family life."[58] Later, at the winter meeting of the Executive Committee, *ACT* reported that the most significant thing that occurred was the "renewed dedication and emphasis of our movement to the family." In addition, a working committee on CFM's "relationship to the family" was established.[59] As Ray Maldoon recalled in 1974, " A few years ago, we made a calculated change in direction. We changed the focus of our programming from social problems, such as race and politics, to the subject matter of the family itself."[60] Inquiries still examined institutions outside the family, but their main focus was the family.

Besides shifting the focus to the family, the 1972 Program Committee offered four options. First, *People Are . . .* was to be used by all beginning groups. Second, groups who had not used *Quality of Life*, the 1971–72 inquiry booklet, could use that book. This was a practical decision—CFM was facing serious financial problems, and they had several thousand copies of *Quality of Life*, which they hoped to sell. Third, a new style of inquiry book entitled *Love Happens* allowed local groups to determine the focus of their meetings. *Love Happens* was divided into eight "clusters" of three or four inquiries. The eight clusters were further divided into four topics— family enrichment, community focus, reflection meetings, and ICCFM inquiries. The local CFM groups were to pick several clusters, thereby defining their own focus. Fourth, two new booklets consisting of eight inquiries each were produced, reflecting the new focus on family—*Family Commitment* and *Institutions and the Family*. These two "modules" were much like the old *FHF;* the former explored the husband-and-wife relationship, then children and the family, and then the neighborhood. The latter examined the effects of institutions such as schools, advertising, and government agencies on children and the family. The four options were to provide "greater flexibility" at the local level.

The following year, 1973, *People Are . . .* was replaced as the introductory book by a new eight-meeting program *The Encountering Family*. The eight meetings were designed to enable members to encounter (1) their children, (2) themselves, and (3) the world around them. The first four meetings examined "God's gift to us" and the final four, "our response to God."[61] Another module of eight meetings was also offered—*The Encountering Couple*. It was specifically meant to be a follow-up to Marriage Encounter and used the Marriage Encounter approach and subject matter. The following year, the most family-oriented of the modules was published—*Love Happens in Families*, a twelve-meeting program based on a Mormon "family enrichment program" that incorporated the notion of "family nights."

The Program Committee also planned a series of three thirteen-meeting units which mirrored the incremental approach of the MFC. *Discovering Christ*, published in 1973, examined the Gospel of Mark. Participants were encouraged to reflect on the life of Jesus, then apply it to their own life. The following year, *Discovering Me . . . A Challenge to Change*, was published. Participants were encouraged to look within themselves and develop a closer relationship with Jesus. Finally, in 1975, *Discovering Others* was published, where participants were encouraged to bear witness to Christ in the world. Even in this book, the first half explored the family; only the latter half was focused on the world outside the family and was geared to thrust the family outward. In Part II, groups were to choose one area of concern to explore in depth—killing, poverty and justice, or minority business. This three-year approach, it was hoped, would adequately prepare couples for action in the world. It was also hoped that CFM would benefit from the MFC approach, which was prospering while CFM dwindled.

Two more units were offered in 1975—Project FIND, and a program on world hunger. Project FIND (Families Involved in Nurture and Development) was a six-meeting drug prevention program funded by the Department of Health, Education, and Welfare (HEW). FIND believed that improving the quality of family life would reduce the attraction of and the need for drugs. CFM participated in the program for two practical reasons—money and publicity. The program was funded by HEW and brought some much needed funds into the movement. More importantly, CFM leaders hoped that participation would "build a broader public image for CFM" and help the movement regain some "national notoriety."[62]

Former members of the Program Committee were happy with the world hunger booklet, because it was a return to larger issues outside the family. One couple wrote that "these inquiries do fall within the definition of 'good, old CFM': in which the look was *both* inward to the family and outward to the world—and in which no conflict was seen in this dual emphasis."[63] They contended that this was the Crowleys' vision. Yet even for this theme, the Program Committee insisted that the "husband-wife dialogue" be employed in each meeting, using Marriage Encounter as a model.[64]

Plainly, this Program Committee was reflecting the change of focus of the entire movement. In 1974, the Board of Directors issued their "Mission Statement" and list of goals, which starkly revealed that the family focus advocates had won.

The Christian Family Movement

Mission Statement

To promote the Christian Family way of life in the family, in the families of the community, and in the institutions affecting the family by servicing, educating and representing the family.

Goals

1. To foster the reality that God's plan for the building of the kingdom is through the family, whereby individuals acquire the capacity to embrace one another in relationship.

2. To work for the development of responsible, concerned and happy families within the movement.

3. To offer opportunities for couples and their families to grow

in their personal relationships through social consciousness and involvement.

4. To establish a supportive network of families within every community in the United States.

5. To recognize and advocate the family as a basic unit in life.

6. To work for a society that not only recognizes but actively supports family life.

7. To reach out to any and all families that have a need to grow and to be supported in their family life.

8. To solicit cooperation of all groups concerned with family life in order to establish an alliance of family organizations.

9. To initiate, encourage and support research into family life in order to continuously respond to the actual needs of families.

10. To continue to foster the international spirit of the Christian Family Movement.[65]

The statement is an interesting mix of old CFM—the statement harks back to CFM's original purpose, which was "to serve, educate, and represent families," which in turn reflected the movement's YCW roots—and the new CFM, deeply affected by the success of Marriage Encounter, with focus on "relationships." Old CFMers were particularly disturbed by the unremitting focus on one's own family. In the old CFM, the family was an organic part of society that was deeply affected by the environment of which it was a part. If the family was to flourish, the environment had to be changed, which meant pushing out beyond the boundaries of one's own family. The new CFM focused on the family's own health—only healthy families could effect real change. Ray Maldoon later reflected on CFM's "transition . . . from a movement with actions on 'social issues' to a movement with actions on the 'family'. Was it, as I suspect today, that the younger parents joining the movement then knew what the *real* issues would be for them and their children? (Even though the 'old-timers' judged them to be dodging the action on social issues.)."[66]

The "family apostles" who moved CFM toward greater stress on the family itself, at the expense of social action, thought they had found a solid way to turn membership figures around. The 1972–75 program booklets incorporated insights from other successful programs—ME, MFC, and Mormon Family life—and experimented with new styles and formats. Nothing stopped the slide in membership.

STRUCTURAL AND PERSONNEL CHANGES

As CFM experimented with program changes, it also experimented with structural change. In 1967, Pat Crowley asked Father Ed Kohler of the archdiocese of Minneapolis-St. Paul to accept the position of assistant national chaplain for CFM. (Though Hillenbrand remained the national chaplain, his role steadily diminished.) Kohler was a professor at the minor seminary. He had worked as a CFM chaplain since 1958 and as St. Paul federation chaplain since 1963. He accepted the national role in 1967, and by the following year he had left his post at the seminary to work for CFM full-time. When he arrived in Chicago, he discovered there was not enough work at the national office to keep him busy, so he began touring the country, visiting CFM groups, encouraging them and promoting the movement. Kohler's travel left him optimistic about the future of CFM. Though the numbers might be declining, he saw that the movement remained vital in many locales. He expressed hope that it was beginning to develop among hitherto untapped groups such as the African American community. Kohler's travels and personal charisma soon made him a significant figure in CFM. He was irreverent, outspoken, and innovative. In 1971, he would mastermind the Episcopal Mass at the national convention. In style and substance he epitomized the avant garde image on which CFM prided itself.

The Crowleys remained the executive secretary couple. Their increasing responsibilities with ICCFM made them look for a way to withdraw from the leadership of CFM. This was difficult. Who could be found to replace the extraordinary blend of qualities that was the Crowleys, that enabled them to hold together such a diverse movement?

In 1969, to ease the Crowleys' burden, a new position, national president couple, was created. The first couple to fill this post was Dorothy and Ray Maldoon, fourteen-year CFM veterans from Indiana. They had served as chaircouple of the Executive Committee in 1968. In 1970, the Crowleys finally did resign. In that year Bob and Kathy Burgraff of Syosset, New York, became executive secretary couple, ostensibly to replace the Crowleys, but much of that work was already being done by the Maldoons. The Burgraffs' primary responsibility became running the national office in Chicago. Thus by 1970, a new leadership group made up of Kohler, the Maldoons, and the Burgraffs was directing CFM.

Unfortunately, this leadership team did not last long. Shortly after accepting the new role, Kathy Burgraff was diagnosed with cancer. She suffered through the remainder of the year, dying on June 27, 1971. Her death was a great loss to the movement. Following her death, Bob returned to New York. Father Kohler replaced the Burgraffs and became executive director of the movement, while the Maldoons remained president couple. Within less than a year, Kohler had married and left the movement. He was replaced in 1973 by Sister Bettye Lechner, a Sister of Providence, who lasted as executive director for more than a year. The same year, CFM formed a Board of Directors that replaced the Executive Committee.

None of these changes stemmed the decline of CFM's numbers.

THE KOHLER CRISIS

The quick turnover of executive directors after two decades of stability was typical of the turbulence at the end of the 1960s. Kohler's departure was equally typical of the unsettled state of the Church. Kohler decided to marry a woman he had met while doing CFM work. Rather than resign his priestly ministry and the executive directorship of CFM, Kohler attempted to keep both vocations. In a letter to Pope Paul VI, Kohler wrote, "I ask only that I may continue in the priestly ministry after receiving the Sacrament of Matrimony."[67] To many of the elder CFM chaplains, Kohler's letter was sheer lunacy. Many of the CFM rank and file supported Kohler's position. The Maldoons went so far as to support Kohler's bid to remain as executive director, whether he was a priest or not. Dan and Rose Lucey recommended, "Keep Ed somewhere,"[68] while chaplains Putz and Hillenbrand opted for the total removal of Kohler. Putz advised the Maldoons, "I am sure that you have pretty well lost the bishops . . . [You] will [also] lose the pastors if Kohler remains."[69] Putz concluded that Kohler had to leave both posts at once.

Hillenbrand was not so measured in his response. In a letter to Kohler he expressed his disbelief at Kohler's action. "It is incomprehensible that a priest preparing to be married invalidly on April 22 should want to remain until April 15 as executive director of a lay apostolate movement of the Church. . . . The movement cannot at all afford your occupying the post of the executive director, nor can it afford the trouble and the scandal it will cause for the movement and the Church in the wider arena."[70] In a letter to Putz, Hillenbrand asked, "When will CFM resume its good senses . . . ?"[71]

Hillenbrand also corresponded with Archbishop John Cody, in whose jurisdiction Kohler was working. Cody was less than amused by the crisis, and wrote to Kohler's bishop, "I am not too surprised about Kohler's defection. Unfortunately, these men 'leave the Church', and long before they publicly announce their defection— horrors! if they ever heard me use the word defection."[72] Though it is tempting to offer some commentary on the cardinal's mind-set, it is enough to say that he was delighted when Kohler was removed from his CFM office. He wrote Hillenbrand, "Never before did I consider so personally the trite saying, 'All's well that ends well.' The departure of Father Kohler and the unanimous action of the Board of Directors renews my faith in human nature and also in the wisdom of our good Catholic laity."[73]

Although the Kohler crisis ended with his being replaced, the sequence of events prior to his departure showed that, even with all its problems, CFM was still open to even the wildest propositions. That prudence ultimately prevailed does not negate the tremendous support and loyalty many CFMers offered to Kohler. Even as the movement waned, it maintained its avant garde quality.

1975: THE MOVEMENT AT ITS NADIR

By 1975, the movement was in serious trouble. Financial woes, which had always plagued it, became ominous. For years the movement had been kept afloat by the generosity of the Crowleys and of the Crowleys' angels. In 1974 a director of development was hired to try to place the movement on a firm financial footing. One of the first tasks of the new director, Wilfred Hansen, pastor of St. Stephen's Church of Christ in Chicago and father of seven children, was to assess the image of CFM. His report was not a happy one. He reported, "The image of CFM was poor. CFM was seen as exclusively Roman Catholic, not a religious human care service. CFM was seen as active in many radical and national social causes, not a movement focused primarily on family life. CFM was seen as weak, no longer a vital and hopeful potential influence on family life."[74]

Despite the negative image and despite the decline in membership, CFM managed to survive. And though it has never equaled the popularity it enjoyed during the 1950s and 60s, it continued to help young families and to provide an outlet for deeply committed couples and their children. As of 1997, the movement has close to 2,000 couples. They continue to produce an annual inquiry booklet, and they continue to have national conventions. For all its problems, CFM continues to work on behalf of families throughout the world.

WHY THE DECLINE?

No topic is more energetically discussed by old CFMers than why the movement declined. To most, it remains a mystery. A host of explanations have been set forth, none of them completely satisfying.

Some say CFM's attempt to become ecumenical diluted the movement, undermining its strong liturgical focus, as well as its dependence on Catholic social teaching. Louis Putz believes that when CFM went ecumenical, it lost the support of the bishops, thus harming the movement. And the Adlers, prime movers in CFM's ecumenical push recently observed, "They say we killed the Movement."

Others blame the Crowleys' opposition to the papal encyclical *Humanae Vitae.* They argue that their opposition inspired a contentious attitude toward papal authority and pronouncements and created an anti-authoritarian spirit. In failing to support the papal teaching on birth control, these critics claim, the Crowleys ultimately undermined the movement they had worked so hard to build.

Others claim that it was CFM's unwavering commitment to racial justice that caused many to leave. CFM never recovered from the significant losses it incurred following the 1964–65 inquiry on race.

Still others claimed that it was CFM's lack of attention to the family itself. By constantly stressing social action, it alienated many couples who were in CFM to better their own families, not to change the world. Many pointed to the success and growth of Marriage Encounter as evidence that a family movement could still be popular. However, others complained that Marriage Encounter robbed leaders and members from CFM, and never returned the favor. Marriage Encounter benefited from CFM, but CFM did not benefit from Marriage Encounter.

Others claimed that CFM was a victim of its own success. CFM had fought hard for many of the reforms that were achieved by the Second Vatican Council. With its victory at the council, CFM's reason for being ceased to exist. More importantly, the council called for increased lay participation in parish leadership. Where were these leaders to be found? CFM proved to be a mighty reservoir of parish leaders—parish councils, CCD, finance boards, liturgy committees, all were staffed by CFM. CFM's task of creating lay leaders had been successful. Unfortunately for the movement, the demand for lay leaders drained it of many of its members. In the 1950s, many claimed, CFM was the only outlet for lay activism; in the postconciliar era there were a multitude of outlets.

Others suggested that in becoming so successful, CFM lost its edge. A CFMer from Columbus, Ohio, wrote in 1970, "The final testimony to CFM's 'success' was its welcome into the bosom of parish organization. CFM is now listed along with or next to ladies who clean the altar and sacristy, the men who usher and raise money for the athletic programs, et al."[75] CFM now represented the status quo. Without its avant garde luster, the movement lost its appeal.

Finally, many claimed that the societal change in the role of women adversely affected the movement. In the 1950s, the bulk of CFM work was performed by housewives, women who did not have to look outside the family for work. When women joined the work force in large numbers in the 1970s, they no longer had the time they had previously devoted to CFM. CFM suffered.

It is not necessary to embrace a single explanation and reject the others. All of these explanations provide a partial reason for CFM's decline, and perhaps taken in toto they do explain a number of the stresses that led to the movement's decline. But the most persuasive view is that the movement declined not from any defect of its own, but from the societal and ecclesiastical circumstances of the end of the 1960s. As noted before, membership in CFM was extremely volatile. The average CFMer stayed in the movement for the relatively brief span of 3.5 years. Annually CFM lost between 15 and 20 percent of its members. Thus, the movement had always needed to recruit new members. By the late 1960s, CFM's disciplined and incremental approach to social action seemed too slow to many activists. The Chicago federation reported of younger couples in 1967, "These are couples who want to be involved and involved deeply—NOW—they haven't time to become formed and 'committed'. They simply want an active apostolate."[76] Another CFM couple concurred in 1968: "What is its [CFM's] status? Hated by conservatives, considered a waste of time by many professionals, liberals find it too slow in forming members."[77] A veteran CFM chaplain found the same trouble with young priests: "The family is not an 'in' concept. Person, yes, sensitivity group, yes, civil rights group, yes, family, no. Young guys [priests] go where the action is. It's not in the family at the moment."[78] Many couples and priests thus opted for more exciting activities.

More importantly, CFM was a victim of the malaise that affected Catholics, particularly liberal Catholics, in the early 1970s. CFM did not decline in a vacuum. The Church in the United States was in decline everywhere, if judged by old standards and statistics: Mass attendance was down, vocations were down, priests were leaving the priesthood, sisters were leaving the convent. There was a general disaffection for the Church and things churchly. Andrew Greeley suggests that the main source of dissatisfaction was the birth control encyclical. Catholics had been led to believe that the Church's traditional teaching on birth control was going to be modified. When Pope Paul VI issued *Humanae Vitae,* restating the traditional teachings, many Catholics felt betrayed. Having already made up their minds, many simply ignored the papal teaching, and when people ignored the papal teaching in this area, it became easier to ignore it in others. More significantly, the encyclical shattered the hopes of many that the Catholic Church could change. The encyclical undermined the already ebbing euphoria created by the council. CFMers abandoned the movement and the movement lost its attraction, not because the Crowleys had opposed the encyclical but because of the general disappointment with the encyclical.

This disappointment was compounded by the feeling that the whole thrust of Vatican II was being undermined. The council had promised greater lay involvement ("co-responsibility" it was called), and when it became evident that many pastors had no intention of granting any real responsibility, frustration set in. The Trenton federation reported in 1973 that CFMers "were often seen as radicals by pastors, who had little stomach for the laity and lay priesthood."[79] The inability of many clergy to grasp the new directions inspired by the council resulted in an increasing disillusionment with the Church.

Ultimately, CFM was a victim of the end of the sixties. By the mid-1970s, the nonstop social traumas of the 1960s and the endless changes and disputes within the Church had left most Americans and American Catholics exhausted. There was a general turn away from social action and reform. This was clearly demonstrated within CFM, where the commitment to social action became commitment to the family. CFM was not the only group turning inward; many social activists turned to simpler, less grandiose pursuits. Movements such as Marriage Encounter and Cursillo prospered. CFM's social-action orientation would have to await another era of reform to be revived.

THIRTEEN

Conclusion

In the late 1940s a group of not quite wild-eyed young couples set out to achieve the impractical task of restoring all things in Christ. They set out with little more than a vision and a method. For more than three decades they struggled mightily to bring Christ to their families, their neighborhoods, their communities and their world. Though the movement never exceeded 50,000 couples at any one time, CFM profoundly affected the Church in the United States and Canada.

CFM emerged at a time when the old Catholic ethnic neighborhoods, which had defined the Catholic Church in the United States for more than a century, were beginning to dissolve. A new breed of young Catholic lay man and woman was emerging—middle-class, professional, college-educated, suburban—that sought a new way to serve their Church. They could not be the docile "pay, pray, and obey" laity of the past. CFMers were disturbers of the peace; they were bright, energetic, well-informed Catholics, who learned to "observe, judge, and act." As such, they could not accept the status quo, particularly if it conflicted with the mind of Christ. They sought to change themselves, their families, and the environment and institutions that affected family life. To the dismay of many pastors, CFMers also applied their method to issues within their parish and Church. All things had to be challenged and transformed if a world in which it was easier to be human was to be created.

Over the course of two and a half decades, CFM affected hundreds of thousands of lives. It not only affected the lives of the

246

couples in the movement, it also affected the thousands of people they came into contact with through their actions. Moreover, CFM's effect did not end once a couple left the movement. A common saying among veteran CFMers is, "Once a CFMer, always a CFMer." Even when they left the movement they took CFM with them. One couple wrote that "We 'dropped out' of CFM in 1965—with the sure knowledge that CFM had done its job (for us). We looked on CFM as a vehicle of formation, which, when ripe, enabled CFMers to 'move on' in the Christian struggle."[1] Countless couples moved on to other endeavors. Former Program Committee chair Madelyn Bonsignore noted of CFM, "It's an incubator that has turned out people who are making a difference: mayors; members of legislatures and of Parliament; candidates for the presidency; staff and volunteers for the parish, diocesan and national training centers that are the hope of the Church; artists of every stripe; teachers with vision; writers and publishers with a mission; the moving forces behind homes for the homeless, ecumenical housing projects, innovative programs for the elderly, the hungry, the handicapped."[2]

CFM's effect does not merely end with the efforts of its members; it also extends to the children of CFMers. CFM children were made aware that what occurred beyond their families had immense importance. They learned that they had to be concerned not only with their own welfare but with the welfare of all people who made up the Mystical Body of Christ. The result: CFM children have filled the ranks of Peace Corps and VISTA volunteers, community action groups, missions to Latin America and Third World countries, and countless other service projects. Though many did not become CFMers themselves, they were the tangible result of CFM brought to a new generation.

CFM was the most successful of the specialized Catholic Action movements begun in the United States. As pioneer Father Donald Kanaly once observed, "The work that we've tried to do with YCS and YCW—so much of it seems to have been a work of frustration, a work of failure, a work of discouragement. . . . CFM finally found the formula."[3] And it was Hillenbrand and the Crowleys that made the formula a reality. Hillenbrand provided the vision, but it was the extraordinary efforts and gifts of the Crowleys that made the movement a success. The Crowleys' seemingly endless energy spread the movement to all the corners of the earth. They brought together an extraordinarily diverse group of people and forged a unity that changed the face of American Catholicism. They had the gift of hope, the gift of enabling people to believe in themselves, and in so doing to accomplish things far beyond what they might have thought possible. Though experiencing many disappointments, they did not dwell on them. Instead, they looked to the next challenge, believing that ultimately all things will be restored in Christ.

Typical of the Crowleys, they would not be comfortable with this assessment. Repeatedly, they downplayed their own importance to the movement. In an interview given shortly after they stepped down as the national executive couple in 1970 they gave their own summary of the movement's success. Asked: "Is there anything you would have done differently?" they responded, "That question implies a rational program that has been pursued over the years. That implication would be too much. We have taken things as they have come and more or less moved with them. Our 'philosophy' has been a very simple one, even if maybe we have never really defined it. Looking back, we see that all the great things that may have taken place within CFM have done so simply because some CFM leader wanted them to take place. And he knew that in CFM he possessed the freedom to experiment, to try the untried, and to take a fling at something that may never have worked before. Over these years, we shudder to think of the mistakes that so many of us have made and the ambitious projects that began but were never finished. But some of them were. And they were finished because there was an atmosphere in CFM that said, 'Let's go to it. Let's try it.' If we played any part in that activity, it was merely to encourage people with ideas to go ahead. So we guess we would say, no, we probably would not have done anything differently. Because it wasn't we who did it. Everybody did."[4]

APPENDIX

CFM:
The Second Twenty-Five Years

KAY AITCHISON

Although CFM moved into its second twenty-five years with gusto, the winds of change were stirring. Membership was declining, and CFM leaders were looking for creative ways to recharge the movement and attract new members.

The national leadership explored new avenues for CFM expansion. Ongoing efforts to spread CFM to Protestant denominations bore little fruit, despite the fact that many ministers were interested in CFM's small-group structure and emphasis on action.

Despite the decline in numbers, CFM continued to be a vital force in family life both locally and nationally. In 1975, CFM wrote and pilot-tested a family-oriented drug awareness program, FIND. More than 500 participated in the project which was published by the U.S. Department of Health, Education and Welfare.

The production of CFM inquiry books was also undergoing a change. The CFM Program Committee was disbanded in 1975. After that, the Directions Committee of the board of directors took responsibility for producing CFM's inquiry books. Over the next five years, books were written by area teams or the national office staff. In 1981, a plan was established in which an editor and theme were selected by the Directions Committee, and CFMers from across the country wrote individual chapters.

Another tradition came to an end in 1975 when the site of the biennial convention, which had always been held at the University of Notre Dame, was moved to St. Mary's College in South Bend, Indiana. Convention numbers had declined, and St. Mary's smaller campus was a better fit. About this time, the convention committee began concentrating more effort on the quality of children's and teen programming. The programs at early conferences had been strictly for parents, while teens attending had provided childcare for younger children. Now, parents were more concerned about the total family experience.

In 1977, the summer convention took another turn. That year CFM joined with National Marriage Encounter and the National Council of Churches in sponsoring a family seminar. This nation-wide gathering brought 3,000 to Estes Park, Colorado.

At the CFM board meeting that preceded that conference, a new president couple, Bob and Irene Tomonto of Miami, Florida, took office. The Maldoons had served as leaders of the movement for nine years and went on to become the executive directors. The Tomontos instituted a Service Team, of officer couples, to share the work load.

That fall, there was still another change, when the CFM office left Chicago and moved to Whiting, Indiana. The office building at 1655 W. Jackson Boulevard had become too costly to maintain. Through the years, CFM maintained the building and assumed that it was the rightful owner. However, when the building was sold, CFM received none of the proceeds from the sale.

CFM continued to analyze its membership and its outreach to new families. In 1979, a survey of its membership was conducted. The results found that 97 percent were in their first marriage, and 93 percent were happy with their marriage. Ninety percent had two or more children. The typical member earned $20,000 a year, lived in or near a large city, had some college experience, and was a Catholic about thirty-three years old. Ninety percent said CFM made life more interesting, 82 percent indicated that CFM made life happier, and 73 percent said it improved spiritual life.

In 1979 CFMers became involved in the White House Conference on Families, presenting eight position papers which be-came part of the resource library of the conference. These position papers were written at the local level and then presented and refined at CFM's 1979 convention.

Although CFM was basically a couples' movement, in the late 70s it began to reach out to a wider range of people. Through special programming, as well as annual inquiries, it addressed aging, the widowed, and single parents.

At this same time, CFM's ecumenical thrust was waning. Its last Protestant chaplain for the national team resigned and was not replaced. Eventually, most Protestant groups ran their course and faded away. CFM's appeal to other faiths has been through non-Catholic CFM spouses. CFM has always been a place where the non-Catholic spouse in an interfaith marriage was welcomed and could feel comfortable.

In 1981 Gary and Kay Aitchison of Ames, Iowa, were elected CFM president couple. The national office was moved to Ames so that the new president couple could better work with the day-to-day operations. That year, 1981–82, CFM membership bottomed out with 1,132 dues-paying member families. The office was downsized and rebuilding efforts were begun. The following year, membership had climbed to 1,576. When the Aitchisons completed their tenure as president couple, four years later, the office stayed in Ames, and they continued as executive directors.

One of the benefits of the Christian Family Movement's methodology has been its success in building leaders. Over the years, CFM empowered countless lay leaders to serve the post–Vatican II church. This move to other involvements definitely contibuted to CFM's decline in membership. Even today, one-third of CFM's membership drops out each year and must be replaced just to maintain the status quo.

The 1980s were designated by the Catholic bishops as the decade of the family, and CFM accelerated its efforts to provide programming and projects for the diverse needs of families. In addition to annual inquiries, programs were also published for teens and the divorced and separated. CFM already had a marriage enrichment program for couples and special inquiries for developing families.

CFM's newsletter, *ACT,* had been edited and published for several years by the national office staff. In 1981, an editor outside the office was appointed. The publication took on a new look and a more creative style that has continued to evolve. *ACT*'s ten issues per year provide a link between groups throughout the country.

CFM created its first promotional video in 1985. "Taking the Time to Make a Difference" was produced by a CFM team from southern California. This professional video showed real CFMers meeting together, working on social actions, and enjoying family activities.

As family life was threatened by the changing times and culture, CFMers demanded more family-centered programming. CFM leaders struggled to maintain a balance between family and social-action inquiries. The 1985-86 program, *Peaceworks,* was based on the U.S. bishops' peace pastoral. It was CFM's most controversial book in its second twenty-five years. *Peaceworks* was followed, the next year, by *Family Values in the Marketplace* which dealt with the bishops' economic pastoral. While this was popular with many members, it, too, was criticized by those who wanted something that related strictly to family.

The national office has always had a strong international connection and has long been a resource for CFM groups in other countries. Many groups in Second and Third World countries look to the U.S. for programming ideas and leadership material. United States CFMers have regularly participated in activities of the International Confederation of Christian Family Movements which has groups in fifty-one countries. In July of 1986, U.S. CFM hosted the ICCFM World Assembly of Families in Chicago. At the subsequent meeting in Spain in 1989, Wayne and Sue Hamilton and Father Sam Palmer of the U.S. were elected international presidents and chaplain. They served for six years.

As CFM moved into the nineties, it adapted and changed with the times but continued its commitment to reach out to diverse groups. Programs were published for families in crisis and for middle years and empty-nest families. In 1994, CFM expanded its services to families when it introduced a weekly syndicated column, "Taking the Time to Make a Difference," written by Paul Leingang. By the middle 90s CFM publications had taken on a consistent format and design, and most annual inquiries had both a social-action and family orientation.

In 1991 CFM's biennial national convention left St. Mary's College and began rotating among campuses in the center of the country. Regional conferences were held in off years. CFM's national convention has always been an important force in the vitality of the movement. The convention revitalizes CFMers at all levels by exposing them to stimulating speakers, prayerful liturgies, and outstanding leadership programs. There is also the opportunity to build community with families from all over the country. The enthusiasm that is generated at conventions feeds back into the local groups and helps launch the new CFM year.

CFM has deep roots and is a pioneer among family-life movements in the American Church. CFM has often been invited to provide input to various Church documents, conferences, and projects. The movement has long been recognized for its expertise in developing small groups and supporting families. The U.S. bishops' pastoral, *Follow the Way of Love,* recommended CFM as a way to improve family life. In 1993 the National Association of Catholic Family Life Ministers presented CFM with its special recognition award for enhancing the quality of life for families.

CFM has provided a link between other organizations by maintaining contact and inviting them to participate in conferences and events. When CFM created a World Wide Web page in 1996, it included a number of marriage and family groups on its web page. That same year CFM joined with eighteen other organizations in the creation of the Families against Violence Advocacy Network.

From the beginning, CFM has been a grass-roots movement. The action group has always been the heart of CFM. Today's groups have adapted to the times but bear a strong resemblance to those that launched the movement in the 1940s. Most are composed of about a dozen people, meet every two weeks, and use the annual CFM inquiry to observe, judge, and act on situations that affect their families and neighborhoods. Leadership of the meetings is rotated in most groups. Groups in the early years were made up entirely of couples and a priest chaplain, but today single parents, widows, widowers, and an occasional single are also found. The chaplain of the nineties may be a priest, nun, religious brother, permanent deacon, seminarian, minister, or lay person. He or she serves as a spiritual advisor for the group and participates in the meetings.

CFM programming continues to be written by CFMers and has a history of dealing with cutting-edge issues. CFM inquiries weave the traditional observe-judge-act methodology into current topics and concerns. A new program book is published each year and takes two years to develop.

CFM has grown and matured in its nearly half-century life span. Today, it has a solid membership of 2,000 families. These CFMers are a diverse group and cover a wide age span; however, the majority are married, middle-class Catholics. While a few groups have been together for as long as thirty years, most members have been in the movement only a short time and have young, developing families. The membership is slightly older now, but that is attributed to the fact that couples marry and have children later. Family size is also smaller.

CFM groups today are more apt than in the past to include their children in some or all of their activities. Many of their actions are geared to include the entire family, therefore actions may not be as far-reaching as they once were. Some groups even involve their children in some of the meetings. The 1997–98 program, *Seasons of the Spirit,* included supplemental family and children's meetings to accommodate such groups.

In preparation for the celebration of its first fifty years CFM will publish two volumes of an anniversary inquiry book in 1998-99. These programs will draw from the movement's rich history as they challenge members to look to the future. The books will pair actual meetings from past inquiries with updated fast-forward questions. These anniversary books will serve as the CFM program for the two years in which CFM ends its first fifty years and moves forward into the next.

CFM will return to the site of its early conventions, the University of Notre Dame, to celebrate its fiftieth anniversary on July 1–4, 1999. The celebration conference, "FAMILIES OF FAITH— The Golden Jubilee of CFM—Remembering the Past, Embracing the Future," will have much of the flavor of early conventions. It will bring together pioneer CFMers, former members, and current members.

As CFM moves toward the next millennium, the reins of leadership have been passed to a new generation. Chuck and Jan Rogers were elected copresidents in 1997. It is significant that Chuck is the first national leader to have grown up in a CFM family.

The national CFM office is located at 314 Sixth Street in Ames, Iowa 50010. CFM may be contacted by telephone: 515-232-7432; e-mail: *office@cfm.org;* or visited on the World Wide Web at *http://cfm.org*

Notes

Unless otherwise noted, all collections cited in the notes are located at the Archives of the University of Notre Dame, Notre Dame, Indiana.

INTRODUCTION

1. Interview with Mike and Muriel Dumaresq, October 31, 1997.

2. "Editorial: Dissatisfied—But Happy," *Act*, v. 9, no. 9 (June 1956).

3. Bill and Laura Caldwell to Monsignor Hillenbrand, October 30, 1963, Hillenbrand Papers, Box 10.

4. Jim and Shirley Martinelli quoted in *NOW: Newsletter of Richmond, Virginia CFM* (June 5, 1967), p. 5.

5. William Nerin, "What is CFM?" Xerox copy, CFM Papers, Box 64.

6. 1953 Report, CFM Papers, Box 58.

7. Reynold Hillenbrand, "History of CFM," unpublished paper, CFM Papers.

8. Monsignor John Foudy, 1987 interview, transcript in the Archives of the Archdiocese of San Francisco.

9. "Editorial," *ACT*, v. 2, no. 1 (May, 1948), p. 2.

10. Reynold Hillenbrand, "Man and Institutions," *Catholic Family Bulletin*, n.d., quoted in Mary Irene Zotti, *A Time of Awakening: The Young Christian Worker Story in the United States, 1938 to 1970* (Chicago: Loyola University Press, 1991), p. 161.

11. Reynold Hillenbrand; this quote appears many times—see CFM Papers, "Hillenbrand Speeches."

12. "From the President's Desk," *Act*, v. 1, no. 3 (December 1947), p. 2.

13. "Editorial," *ACT*, v. 1, no. 3 (December 1947), p. 2.

14. Louis Putz, "Mediatrix of Graces," *ACT* v. 10, no. 7 (May 1957), p. 3.

15. Charles Peguy quoted in *Community: The 1954–55 Inquiry Program* (Chicago, 1954), p. 3.

16. Dennis Robb, "Specialized Catholic Action in the United States, 1936–1949: Ideology, Leadership, and Organization," (Ph.D. dissertation, University of Minnesota, 1972), p. 121. Much of the preceding discussion is based on Robb's work.

17. See Kathryn Johnson, "The Ol' Tyrant Can't Get Away With It," *Catholic Historical Review* (forthcoming).

18. See William Halsey, *The Survival of American Innocence* (Notre Dame: University of Notre Dame Press, 1980).

19. "The Chaplain's Corner," *ACT*, v. 3, no. 2 (1949), p. 4.

20. "Catholic Action in Our Daily Lives," *ACT*, v. 1, no. 1 (October 1946) p. 1.

21. Quoted by the Hunts, letter to the Crowleys, 1964, n.d., CFM Papers, Box 28.

22. CFM Papers, Box 80; Louis Putz to Mrs. Richard Frisbee, August 9, 1961.

23. John Kotre, *Simple Gifts: The Lives of Pat and Patty Crowley* (Kansas City: Andrews and McMeel, 1979), p. 54.

24. Ibid., p. 56.

2. THE ORIGINS OF THE CHRISTIAN FAMILY MOVEMENT, 1943–1950

1. Joseph Cardijn, quoted in Kotre, *Simple Gifts*, p. 39.

2. Quoted in Zotti, *A Time of Awakening*, p. 3.

3. Robb, "Specialized Catholic Action," p. 73.

4. Steven Avella, "Reynold Hillenbrand and Chicago Catholicism," *U.S. Catholic Historian*, 9 (Summer 1990) p. 360.

5. George St. Peter, oral history interview by author, July 7, 1996.

6. Dennis Geaney, quoted in Robb, "Specialized Catholic Action," p. 89.

7. Avella, "Reynold Hillenbrand," p. 362.

8. Hillenbrand, quoted in ibid., p. 360.

9. Robb, "Specialized Catholic Action," p. 93.

10. Ibid., p. 93.

11. Ibid., p. 108.

12. *ACT*, v. 1, no. 1 (October 1946), p. 1.

13. Ibid., p. 1.

14. George St. Peter interview.

15. Robb, "Specialized Catholic Action," p. 197.

16. Kotre, *Simple Gifts*, p. 43.

17. Ibid., p. 44.

18. "Editorial: A Beginning," *ACT*, v. 1, no. 1 (October 1946), p. 2.

19. *The Couplet*, v. 1, no. 3 (May 1946), p. 2.

20. Kotre, *Simple Gifts*, p. 44.

21. Ibid., p. 45

22. *The Couplet*, v. 1., no.4 (June 1946), p. 1.

23. CFM Papers, Box 1.

24. Quoted in Zotti, *A Time of Awakening*, p. 148.

25. CFM Papers, Catholic Action Women's Federation File, Box 39.

26. CFM Papers, Box 1, Patrick Crowley to William Paul Brown, January 3, 1949.

27. Hillenbrand Papers, Patty Crowley to Reynold Hillenbrand, September 5, 1949.

28. Patty Crowley interview, July 28, 1995; Rev. Gerard Weber interview, September 25, 1995.

29. Interview with Louis Putz, C.S.C., July 18, 1995.

30. Louis Putz, "Reflections on Specialized Catholic Action," *U.S. Catholic Historian*, 9 (Fall 1990), p. 437.

31. CFM Papers, Box 1.

32. Burnie Bauer, "History of the Christian Family Movement," Bauer papers.

33. Interview with Burnett C. Bauer, July 25, 1995.

34. Bauer to the Crowleys, n.d (but from the text obviously 1948), CFM Papers, Box 1.

35. Zotti, *A Time of Awakening*, p. 295.

36. See Florence Henderson Davis, "Lay Movements in New York City," *U.S. Catholic Historian*, 9 (Fall 1990), p. 401–18.

37. Declan Bailey, O.F.M., "Chaplain Asks Family Union Built Around Catholic Action Groups," *ACT*, v. 2, no. 1 (May 1948), p. 4.

38. Hillenbrand Papers, Box 33.

39. CFM Papers, Box 1, Kate McMahon to Pat and Patty Crowley, January 24, 1948; "West Coast Couples form Catholic Action Sections for Marriage Study," *ACT*, v. 2, no. 1 (May 1948).

40. "Providence Tackles Housing," *ACT*, v. 3, no. 1 (February 15, 1949), p. 1.

41. CFM Papers, Box 79, Scrapbooks.

42. "How Catholic Action Operates in Cleveland," *ACT*, v. 2, no. 1 (May 1948).

43. "Undercurrent," *ACT*, v. 1, no. 3 (December 1947), p. 4.

44. CFM Papers, Box 97. Patty Crowley, November 2, 1951.

45. *ACT*, v. 3, no. 1 (February 15, 1949), p. 3.

46. *ACT*, v. 3, no. 2 (May 5, 1949), p. 1.

47. *ACT*, v. 10, no. 2 (November 1956), p. 7.

48. *ACT*, v. 3, no. 3 (August 15, 1949), p. 1.

49. Ibid., "Conference Highlights," p. 4.

50. Ibid., p. 4.

51. Ibid., "Express Aims of Organization in Wind-Up Talk," p. 5.

52. Ibid., "Delegates Probe Problems," p. 2.

53. Kotre, *Simple Gifts*, p. 69.

54. Quoted in ibid., p. 67.

55. CFM papers, Box 1, Business Men's Federation, June 2, 1947.

56. Patrick Crowley, CFM Papers, Box 79, Xerox from *Today*, December 1950.

57. Married Women's Group, CFM Papers, Box 4.

58. CFM Papers, Box 4.

59. "Cells Study Reading Habits, See Danger in Current Trends," *ACT*, v. 1, no. 3 (December 1947), p. 3.

60. Gerard Weber to Reynold Hillenbrand, April 8, 1949. Hillenbrand Papers.

61. Ibid.

62. Kotre, *Simple Gifts*, p. 61.

63. George St. Peter interview.

64. *ACT*, v. 3, no. 2 (May 15, 1949), p. 2.

65. Consult CFM papers, Box 39, Hillenbrand Papers, Box 33, and "Fall Plans . . . ," *ACT*, v. 3, no. 3 (August 15, 1949).

66. "Summary of Past Conventions," *ACT*, v. 5 no. 1. (Fall 1951), p. 4.

67. "CFM Convention Well-Attended," *ACT*, v. 4, no. 3, (October 10, 1950), p. 3.

68. Crowleys to Hillenbrand, March 13, 1950. Hillenbrand Papers, Box 38.

69. Burnie Bauer, "Pat Crowley: Model Saint for an Affluent Society," *Agape*, v. 4, no. 10 (1975), p. 11.

70. Burnie Bauer to Pat and Patty Crowley, August 25, 1953, Bauer papers.

71. Bauer to Burgraffs, August 4, 1971, Bauer Papers.

72. "Memo to CFM Federation Leaders," (1953), Bauer Papers.

73. Bauer to Father Powers, May 17, 1955, Bauer Papers

3. THE 1950S: FORGING A NATIONAL MOVEMENT

1. All statistics derived from issues of *ACT.* For 1957, see "Annual Reports Show Progress of the Movement," *ACT,* v. 10, no. 10, (September 1957), p. 3.

2. See Robb, *Specialized Catholic Action,* p. 186.

3. J. O'Shaughnessy, "Reactions," 1954, CFM Papers, Box 227.

4. "Letter to the Coordinating Committee by Pat and Patty Crowley, February, 1960," CFM Papers, Box 239.

5. "Letter to the Coordinating Committee from Estelle and Mario Carota, March, 1963," CFM Papers, Box 233.

6. Bill Caldwell, "Report on Structure of CFM to Coordinating Committee," Coordinating Committee Minutes, August, 1964. CFM Papers, Box 39.

7. Definitions derived from *CFM Directions: A Short Guide to the Christian Family Movement* (Chicago: CFM Publications, 1969).

8. Rose and Dan Lucey, "Convention Memories," *ACT,* v. 10, no. 1 (September 10, 1956), p. 2.

9. All these conventions statistics are derived from the *ACT* convention roundup issues.

10. Luceys, "Convention Memories," p. 2.

11. "Editorial: Convention Spirit," *ACT,* v. 11, no. 1 (October 1957), p. 2.

12. Interview with Alma and Peter Fitzpatrick, July 21, 1996.

13. Recap for Coordinating Committee, 1957, CFM Papers, Box 58.

14. 1965 Convention report, CFM papers, Box 59.

15. "Tenth Anniversary Meet Sets Record," *ACT,* v. 12, no. 1 (October 27, 1958), p. 1.

16. Reynold Hillenbrand, Progress Report to Coordinating Committee, 1953, CFM Papers, Box 39.

17. "Proposed Plan for National Organization, 1956," CFM Papers, Box 39.

18. Bill and Laura Caldwell, *Another Newsletter,* no. 5 (July 15, 1965), p. 2.

19. Hillenbrand quoted in "New Inquiries to Stress Oneness," *ACT*, v. 7, no. 4 (February 1954).

20. Hillenbrand, CFM Chicago Federation Meeting, February 6, 1955, Box 39.

21. Donald Kanaly, quoted in *Social Responsibility—Family Finances—Education: 1953–54 Program*.

22. Hillenbrand, quoted in ibid.

23. Weber quoted in Chicago Catholic Family Action Officers' Meeting, June 7, 1950, CFM Papers, Box 39.

24. Coordinating Committee Minutes, August 19–20, 1955, CFM Papers, Box 39.

25. For an extended discussion of Hillenbrand's life and thought, see Steven Avella, *This Confident Church: Catholic Leadership and Life in Chicago, 1940–1965* (Notre Dame, Ind.: University of Notre Dame Press, 1992).

26. Reynold Hillenbrand, "Basic Ideas of CFM," CFM Papers.

27. Reynold Hillenbrand, "Genius of CFM, September, 1952," CFM Papers.

28. Reynold Hillenbrand, "Hillenbrand Speeches, 1952," CFM Papers.

29. Hillenbrand, "Genius of CFM."

30. Reynold Hillenbrand, "A Time for Self-Criticism," *ACT*, v. 11, no. 8 (August 1958), p. 8.

31. "Notes on Monsignor Hillenbrand's Talk to the Coordinating Committee, January 20, 1956," CFM Papers, Box 39.

32. *Social Responsibility . . . 1953–54 Program*.

33. Hillenbrand, "Background: The Economic Problem," *ACT*, v. 12, no. 5 (February 23, 1959).

34. "Notes on Hillenbrand's Talk . . . ."

35. Hillenbrand, "Basic Ideas of CFM."

36. Ibid.

37. Hillenbrand, "Layman Has a Tremendous Job," *ACT*, v. 5, no. 3 (March 1952), p. 4.

38. Hillenbrand, "The Apostle Is Never Stunted," *ACT*, v. 6, no. 3 (February 1953), p. 1.

39. Avella, *This Confident Church*, p. 152.

40. Hillenbrand, "The Mass as Source and Center of the Lay Apostolate," Mimeo, CFM Papers, Box 227.

41. *Parish Life—Education: The 1957–58 Inquiry Program* (Chicago, 1957), p. 2.

42. Reynold Hillenbrand quoted in "National Convention Focus on Parish," *ACT,* v. 16, no. 11 (October 1963), p. 3.

43. Martin Quigley, Letter to the Crowleys, July 21, 1961, CFM Papers, Box 296.

4. THE 1950S: BECOMING CITIZENS OF THE WORLD

1. "Action Highlights," *ACT,* v. 4, no. 3 (October 10, 1950).

2. "To Serve . . .," *ACT,* v. 4, no. 4 (January 1951).

3. *ACT,* v. 5, no. 4 (May 1952).

4. "Prelates, Priests Discuss International Life," *ACT,* v. 13, no. 3 (December 15, 1959).

5. "Guest Editorial: A World to Win," *ACT,* v. 13, no. 11 (August 1960), p. 2.

6. Marcel Fredericks and Paul Mundy, *The Christian Family Movement and Hospitality of Foreign Students* (Chicago: Loyola University, 1979).

7. Interview with Patty Crowley, 1995.

8. 1955 reports, CFM Papers, Box 58.

9. Bud and Marian Girsch, "CFM's Student Committee," *ACT,* v. 12, no. 2 (November 24, 1956).

10. 1959 Report, CFM Papers, Box 78.

11. "Report on Meeting of Coordinating Committee," *ACT,* v. 12, no. 6 (April 6, 1959), p. 1.

12. "Hospitality for Students," *ACT,* v. 12, no. 2 (November 24, 1958), p. 12.

13. "What You Are Doing," *ACT,* v. 10, no. 5 (March 1957).

14. "How Oregon CFM Assisted Refugees," *ACT,* v. 13, no. 6 (March 1960), p. 6.

15. Charles Wilber interview, July 31, 1995.

16. "Letter from Cuba" *ACT,* v. 12, no. 5 (April 6, 1959), p. 3.

17. "Humberto J. Lopez to Crowleys, August 21, 1960," CFM Papers, Box 67.

18. Ibid.

19. CFM Papers, Box 67.

20. "CFM Couples Show Way to Help Cuban Refugees," *ACT,* v. 15, no. 11 (July 1962), p. 3.

21. Crowley interview.

22. Robert F. Clark to Pat Crowley, July 21, 1965, CFM Papers, Box 78.

23. *ACT*, v. 14, no. 3 (November 1960).

24. "Missionary Families on the Move," *ACT*, v. 13, no. 11 (August 1960), p. 3.

25. "Faradays in Africa," *ACT*, v. 20, no. 4 (May 1967), p. 3.

26. See CFM Papers, Box 135.

27. "Mission to Statesboro," *ACT*, v. 15, no. 7 (March 1962), p. 3.

28. CFM Papers, Box 135.

29. CFM Papers, Box 65.

30. Peter and Mary Goulding, "The Good Tree Bears Good Fruit: CFM History—last of four parts," *ACT*, v. 17, no. 13 (December 1964), p. 13.

31. Ibid., p. 14.

32. CFM Papers, Box 81.

33. Ibid.

34. Quoted in Rose Marciano Lucey, *Roots and Wings: Dreamers and Doers of the Christian Family Movement* (San Jose: Resource Publications, 1987), p. 46.

35. Goulding, "Good Tree," p. 13.

36. Lucey, *Roots and Wings*, p. 46.

37. Coordinating Committee Minutes, CFM Papers, Box 39.

38. "FIC's Growth Impressive After Two Years," *ACT*, v. 15, no. 9 (May 1962), p. 1.

39. CFM Papers, Box 78.

40. CFM Papers, Box 189. See also Goulding, "Good Tree," p. 13.

41. *FIC News Notes* (Fall 1972), p. 1.

42. Rose Lucey Papers.

43. *FIC News Notes* (Fall 1972), p. 4.

44. Lucey, *Roots and Wings*, p. 45.

45. Ibid., p. 35.

46. The Carota Family, *Our Moments of Awareness* (Prince Edward Island: self-published, 1973), p. 9.

47. Carotas, *Moments*, p. 9.

48. "CFMers Successful in Lay Missionary Project," *ACT*, v. 13, no. 2 (November 15, 1959).

49. "Report on Your FIC," *ACT*, v. 14, no. 10 (March 1962), p. 4.

50. Carotas, *Moments*, p. 34.

51. Ibid., p. 34.

52. Ibid.

53. Ibid.

54. Quoted in Lucey, *Roots*, p. 36.

5. THE MOVEMENT GOES INTERNATIONAL

1. Patty Crowley interview.

2. "Crowleys on World Trip," *ACT*, v. 9, no. 7 (April 1956), p. 1.

3. Information in the preceding paragraphs based on interview with Al and Lettie Morse, November 10, 1997.

4. See CFM Papers, Box 58.

5. Interview with Bernard and Mae Daly, November 5, 1997.

6. Interview with Alma Sternik, October 30, 1997.

7. Ibid.

8. Interviews with Bishop William Power, October 30, 1997, and Muriel and Mike Dumeresq, October 31, 1997.

9. CFM Papers, Box 29.

10. Leroux notes to author, February 19, 1996.

11. Ibid.

12. Ibid.

13. Interview with Grant and Vivian Maxwell, October 31, 1997.

14. Jim and Pat Cooney, "What CFM Is Doing in Canada," *ACT* (August 1967), p. 22.

15. Alma Sternik interview.

16. CFM Scrapbooks, CFM Papers, Box 80.

17. MFC Report for 1958, CFM Papers, Box 58.

18. "First National Convention," *ACT*, v. 16, no. 8 (July 1963), p. 9.

19. Coordinating Committee Minutes, February 8–10, 1957, *ACT*, v. 10, no. 8 (June 1957), p. 7.

20. "CFM Convention of the Americas Held in Uruguay," *ACT*, v. 10, no. 10 (September 1967), p. 1.

21. "Third Latin American Assembly of CFM," *ACT*, v. 16, no. 8 (July 1963), p. 3.

22. Jaime Fonseca, "CFM's 'Impact' Being Felt in Latin America," *ACT*, v. 16, no. 8 (July 1963), p. 3.

23. Pepe Alvarez Icaza, quoted in Lucey, *Roots*, p. 51.

24. "CFM in Caracas," *ACT*, v. 19, no. 9 (November 1966), p. 10.

25. Ralph and Reggie Weissert to Father John Sheehy, November 25, 1966, CFM Papers, Box 146.

26. Steve and Virginia Landregan, "CFM in Caracas," p. 11.

27. Reprinted in "News from the World," *ICCFM Newsbulletin*, v. 3, no. 1, pp. 6–7.

28. This section on the Philippines is based primarily on Librada I. Coquia, "A Study of the Christian Family Movement of the Philippines" (Master's Thesis, University of Manila, 1973).

29. Peter Sawada, 1953 Report, CFM Papers, Box 58.

30. Pat and Patty Crowley "Guest Editorial: Report on CFM," *ACT*, v. 9, no. 8 (May 1956), p. 2.

31. Lucey, *Roots*, p. 49.

32. "Father Dalmeida Writes," *ACT*, v. 10, no. 9 (July 1957), p. 12.

33. "CFM Around the World," *ACT*, v. 9, no. 11 (August 1956), p. 3.

34. "Report from Uganda," *ACT*, v. 11, no. 3 (February 1958), p. 11.

35. "Example of U.S. CFMers Helps Found Movement in Nigeria," *ACT*, v. 16, no. 9 (August 1963), p. 12.

36. "A Letter from Malawi," *ACT*, v. 21, no. 6 (July-August 1968), p. 21.

37. "International Report," *ACT*, v. 10, no. 10 (September 1957), p. 9.

38. Pat and Patty Crowley, "Message to MFC," August 1968, ICCFM Papers, Box 2.

39. Pat and Patty Crowley, "A Look at the Families of the World," Offprint from *World Justice*, v. 9, no. 2 (1967–68), p. 200.

40. Quoted in Lucey, *Roots*, p. 49.

6. THE MOVEMENT MATURES: SELF-CRITICISM AND CRITICS

1. Donald Thorman, "A Second Look at the Movement," *ACT*, v. 13, no. 7 (April 1960), p. 1.

2. Dennis Geaney, "CFM, 1960," *ACT*, v. 13, no. 10, (April 1960), p. 8.

3. *International Life: 1960–61 Inquiry Program*, p. 52.

4. Burnie Bauer, "Letter to the Editor," *ACT*, v. 13, no. 6 (March 1960), p. 7.

5. Rev. John J. Morgan, "Letter to Editor," *ACT*, v. 13, no. 7 (April 1960), p. 7.

6. Reynold Hillenbrand, "CFM," CFM Papers, Box 39.

7. "The Problems as Described by a Member of the Program Committee," CFM Papers, Box 49.

8. Fred and Norma Moore, "Letter to the Editor," *ACT*, v. 11, no. 4 (March 1958), p. 15.

9. John Garcia, "Letter to the Editor," *ACT*, v. 19, no. 3, (April 1966), p. 14.

10. Dennis Geaney, "CFM in Perspective," *ACT*, v. 9, no. 6 (August 1956), p. 10.

11. John Cogley, "The Religious Revival," *Commonweal* 18 (January 1957), p. 407.

12. George Higgins, "Apostolate Unlimited," *Apostolate*, v. 3, no. 3 (1956), p. 37.

13. *International Life: 1960–61 Inquiry Program*, p. 93.

14. Jim Cockrell, "On 1960–61 Social Inquiry," CFM Papers, Box 64.

15. For the "Communist Crisis" as it was called, see CFM Papers, Box 62.

16. "Editorial: Mother and Teacher," *ACT*, v. 15, no. 1 (September 1961), p. 2.

17. *ACT*, v. 4, no. 3 (October 10, 1950), p. 3.

18. "Editorial: Building a New Society," *ACT*, v. 11, no. 9 (September 1958), pp. 2, 12.

19. "Coordinating Committee Minutes," *ACT*, v. 11, no. 4 (March 1958), p. 1.

20. Ed and Gerry DeCaussin, "Next Year's Inquiry Program," *ACT*, v. 12, no. 10 (August 24, 1959), p. 7.

21. "CFM Objective," *ACT*, v. 12, no. 6 (April 6, 1959).

22. "Coordinating Committee Holds Denver Meeting," *ACT*, v. 14, no. 1 (September 1960), p. 1.

23. "New York Holds Annual Meet," *ACT*, v. 11, no. 2 (December 1957), p. 8.

24. George Kelly, Letter to Crowleys, September 12, 1961, CFM Papers, Box 62.

25. George Kelly, "The Family Apostate of CFM," CFM Papers, Box 62.

26. George Kelly, "Is CFM Truly a Family Movement?" CFM Papers, Box 62.

27. Reynold Hillenbrand, Hillenbrand Papers, Box 10.

28. Louis Putz, "Social Leadership Through CFM," CFM Papers, Box 64.

29. Laurence Kelly to George Kelly, January 1, 1962. In possession of author.

30. Ibid.

31. CFM Papers, Box 49.

7. THE COUNCIL AND THE 1960S

1. "Editorial: Years of Change—and Hope," *ACT*, v. 17, no. 13 (December 1964), p. 2.

2. Bernard Daly, CFM Papers, Box 39.

3. CFM Papers, Box 65.

4. Quoted in Xavier Rynne, *The Fourth Session: The Debates and Decrees of the Vatican Council II, September 14 to December 8, 1965* (New York: Farrar, Straus and Giroux, 1966), p. 89. My thanks to Grant Maxwell for supplying me with this reference.

5. Rynne, ibid., p. 89.

6. De Roo quoted in Rynne, ibid., p. 89.

7. Rev. Donald Campion, in Walter Abbott, s.j., editor, *The Documents of Vatican II* (New York: The America Press, 1966), p. 189.

8. Coordinating Committee Minutes, August 1966, Box 39, CFM Papers.

9. Bill Morhard, quoted in Executive Committee Minutes, February 10–13, 1966, Box 39, CFM Papers.

10. "Program for Renewal," CFM Papers, Box 49.

11. "A Meeting in Toronto," *ACT*, v. 19, no. 6 (July-August, 1966), p. 18.

12. CFM Papers, Box 65.

13. Ibid.

14. Executive Committee Minutes, January 1–February 2, 1964, CFM Papers, Box 39.

15. Forrest Macken, *ACT*, v. 10, no. 8 (June 1957).

16. Gustave Weigel, s.j., "The Role of the Layperson," *ACT*, v. 14, no. 5 (January 1961), p. 6.

17. Joseph Fichter, s.j., "Family and the Parish," *ACT*, v. 11, no. 1 (October 1957), p. 10.

18. Leo Brown, o.f.m., "What CFM Means to a Chaplain," CFM Papers, Box 64.

19. John Coffield, interview notes, January 17, 1984, Rose Lucey Papers.

20. Executive Committee Minutes, June 22–23, 1966, CFM Papers, Box 39.

21. James Halpine, May 1964, CFM Papers, Box 78.

22. François Houtart, "International Responsibility," *ACT,* v. 18, no. 7 (September 1965), p. 16.

23. Father William Thompson, Coordinating Committee Minutes, June 23–26, 1966, CFM Papers, Box 39.

24. Chicago Area 8 Report, CFM Papers, Box 192.

25. Rev. Robert Daugherty, "CFM's Liturgy Survey Report," *ACT,* v. 17, no. 9 (July–August 1964), p. 3.

26. Coordinating Committee Minutes, June 1966, CFM Papers, Box 39.

27. Larry Ragan, "An Informal Conversation about the Liturgy of the Eucharist," *ACT,* v. 24, no. 9 (February 1972), p. 3.

8. CFM AND RACE

1. See John McGreevy, *Parish Boundaries: The Catholic Encounter with Race in the Twentieth-Century Urban North* (Chicago: University of Chicago Press, 1996).

2. Kotre, *Simple Gifts,* p. 52.

3. CFM Papers, Box 1.

4. Kotre, *Simple Gifts,* p. 52.

5. Ibid., p. 53.

6. Henry V. Sattler to Pat Crowley, June 26, 1946, CFM Papers, Box 1.

7. *CFA Semi-Annual Inquiry 1950* (Chicago: Catholic Family Action)

8. *CFM Semi-Annual Inquiry 1951* (Chicago: Christian Family Movement)

9. Interview with Peter and Alma Fitzpatrick, July 21, 1996.

10. *Social Harmony: 1956–57 Inquiry Program* (Chicago: Christian Family Movement, 1956), p. 3.

11. McGreevy, *Parish Boundaries,* p. 86.

12. "Archbishop Outlines Christian Race View," *ACT,* v. 10, no. 1 (September–October 1956) p. 1.

13. "A Report of Actions" *ACT,* v. 10, no. 5 (March 1957), p. 7.

14. All activities cited are reported in the issues of *ACT* for 1957.

15. *Louisville CFM Bulletin* (January 1957), p. 2, CFM Papers, Box 56.

16. Rosemary Myers, CFM Papers, Box 56.

17. *ACT,* v. 10, no. 6 (April 1957), p. 8.

18. Crowley to Hillenbrand, 1963, CFM Papers, Box 62.

19. 1963–64 Program Survey, CFM Papers, Box 49.

20. Caldwells to Hillenbrand, October 30, 1963, Hillenbrand Papers, Box 10.

21. Green Bay Report, June 30, 1964, CFM Papers, Box 26.

22. Grand Rapids Report, June 27, 1964, CFM Papers, Box 26.

23. "CFMers Tell of Efforts To Further Interracial Justice," *ACT,* v. 16, no. 11 (October 1963), p. 7. The following examples cited in the text are drawn from this article.

24. Cardinal Albert Meyer quoted in McGreevy, *Parish Boundaries,* p. 148.

25. This paragraph is derived from McGreevy, *Parish Boundaries,* p. 148.

26. "National Conference on Religion and Race Held in Chicago," *ACT,* v. 16, no. 5 (March 1963), p. 9.

27. Executive Committee Minutes, January 16–18, 1963, CFM Papers, Box 39.

28. Interview with Joe and Madelyn Bonsignore, August 8, 1995.

29. "National Convention," *ACT,* v. 16 no. 11 (October 1963), p. 20.

30. "Civil Rights Bill," *ACT,* v. 17 no. 6 (April 1964), p. 16.

31. "Letter to the Editor," Mrs. M. E. Casserly, Westport, Conn., *ACT,* v. 17, no. 8 (June 1964), p. 12.

32. Flyer on Politics and Race, CFM Papers, Box 87.

33. *Encounter in Politics and Race: 1964–65 Inquiry Program* (Chicago: Christian Family Movement, 1964), p. 12.

34. Bob Senser, "Race and Science: How Colored Are You?" *ACT,* v. 18, no. 2 (March 1965), p. 9.

35. *Encounter in Politics and Race,* p. 7.

36. Hillenbrand was so impressed with the book that he wrote a note to the Bonsignores: "In all the years since 1938 this is the first beautifully written program I have read. . . . It will serve, I am dead sure, as the one to point to for a long time to come." Note in author's possession.

37. *Encounter in Politics and Race,* p. 6.

38. Interview with Reggie Weissert, August 4, 1995.

39. Quoted in "People React to the Race Theme," *Milwaukee Witness* (Fall 1965), p. 3, CFM Papers, Box 53.

40. Albert de Zutter, "Find Home Visit Program an Ideal Racial Icebreaker," *ACT,* v. 15, no. 6 (February 1962), p. 2.

41. "CFMers in Interracial Visits," *ACT,* v. 17, no. 13 (December 1964), p. 6.

42. "Evaluating 'Race and Politics,'" CFM Papers, Box 39.

43. "What CFM Is Doing Here and Elsewhere," *Chicago Observes,* CFM Papers, Box 53.

44. "Comment: How We Can Work for Fair Housing," *ACT,* v. 18, no. 4 (June 1965), p. 8.

45. See CFM Papers, Box 157.

46. Michael Ambrose and Charles Moran, "We Were Sent to March in Montgomery: A CFM Report," *ACT,* v. 18, no. 4 (June 1965), p. 2.

47. William Nerin, "Witnessing in Mississippi," *ACT,* v. 17, no. 9 (July–August 1964), p. 6.

48. Maryann and Joe Parus to Fr. Jerome Fraser, April 20, 1965, Jerome Fraser Papers.

49. Sallie Troy, "Letter to the Editor," *ACT,* v. 18, no. 5 (July 1965), p. 12.

50. Bill and Laura Caldwell, *ACT,* v. 18, no. 6, p. 2.

51. "Evaluating 'Race and Politics,'" CFM Papers, Box 39.

52. Quotes from 1965 report. CFM Papers, Box 59.

53. Rev. Peter Sammon to Crowleys, September 15, 1964, CFM Papers, Box 26.

54. 1965 Survey, CFM Papers, Box 64.

55. James B. Strenski, "How One City in Illinois Enacted a Fair Housing Law," *ACT,* v. 20, no. 9 (November 1967).

56. Box 145, CFM Papers.

57. "New York Federation," *ACT,* v. 21 , no. 2 (March 1968), p. 2.

58. *Chicago Observes* (July 1967), p. 3.

59. "We Need the Inner City Parish," *ACT,* v. 20, no. 1 (January–February 1967), p. 6.

60. Executive Committee Minutes, August 22–24, 1967, CFM Papers, Box 39.

61. "Black Power," *ACT,* v. 20, no. 1 (January–February 1967), p. 16.

62. "Life in an American Ghetto," *ACT*, v. 20, no. 3 (April 1967), p. 9.

63. "Has Time Run Out for the White Man?" *ACT*, v. 21, no. 6 (July–August 1968), p. 13.

64. *South Bend New Life* (May 1970).

65. Milwaukee CFM Papers.

66. "People React to the Race Theme," p. 1.

67. Ibid., p. 3.

68. Ibid., p. 3.

69. CFM Papers, Box 53.

70. Quoted in Dan Patrinus, "Don and Mary O'Connell—Activists in Milwaukee," *ACT*, v. 21, no. 1 (January–February 1968), p. 17. Also cited in Lucey, *Roots and Wings*, p. 69.

71. Area 7 Report, March 12–13, 1966, CFM Papers, Box 61.

72. *CFM Observes* (August 1967). CFM Papers, Box 147.

73. Ibid.

74. "Grapevine," *ACT*, v. 21, no. 7 (September 1968), p. 7.

75. Tom Fox, "Hope Always Focus of Detroit Priest," *National Catholic Reporter*, v. 33, no. 33. (July 4, 1997), p. 2.

76. Jerome Fraser, "Fragments of Our Yesteryears," Unpublished memoir. Copy in author's possession.

77. Ibid.

9. BECOMING ECUMENICAL

1. *The Layman's Role in the Church: 1955–56 Inquiry Program* (Chicago: CFM, 1955), p. 47.

2. *That All May Be One: International Life, 1960–61 Inquiry Program* (Chicago: CFM, 1960), p. 33.

3. *The Family: Center of Social Rebirth: 1961–62 Inquiry Program* (Chicago: CFM, 1961), p. 30.

4. "Suggestions for Interfaith Dialogue," *The Parish Leaven in the Community: 1963–64 Inquiry Program* (Chicago: CFM, 1963), p. 64.

5. Ibid., p. 67.

6. Quoted in Jim and Pat Cooney, "The Grapevine," *ACT*, v. 18, no. 3 (April-May 1965), p. 12.

7. "The Dialogue Coffee House," *ACT*, v. 19, no. 9 (November 1966), p. 12.

8. "Episcopal CFM," *CFM Syracuse Newsletter*, September 1966.

9. Interview with Don and Margaret Jones, August 22, 1995.

10. Adlers to Chuck and Stella Lundquist, December 26, 1967, CFM Papers, Box 46.

11. "Living Room Dialogues," Press Release November 18, 1965, CFM Papers, Box 46.

12. "Dialogue in the Living Room," *ACT,* v. 18, no. 10 (December–January 1966), p. 12.

13. Jim and Pat Cooney, "The Grapevine: Advice for Interfaith Groups," *ACT,* v. 21, no. 10 (December 1968), p. 14.

14. Quotes from meetings 19 and 20 taken from *For Happier Families: An Introduction to CFM* (Chicago: CFM, 1967), pp.68–72.

15. Joe and Jody Adler, "Interfaith CFM Proposal," CFM Papers, Box 159.

16. *Building Community: 1967–8 Inquiry Program* (Chicago: CFM, 1967), p. 13.

17. Adlers, "Interfaith Meeting," August 25, 1967, CFM Papers, Box 159.

18. CFM Papers, Box 46.

19. Adlers to Harry Belgum, September 7, 1967, CFM Papers, Box 57.

20. Adlers to the Executive Committee, October 31, 1967, CFM Papers, Box 46.

21. "Jews and Christians," *ACT,* v. 21, no. 9 (November 1968), p. 3.

22. "Resolution on Ecumenism," *ACT,* v. 21, no. 4 (May 1968), p. 3. Also reprinted in the 1968–69 Inquiry Program.

23. *Shalom: Peace in the City, in the Family, in the World* (Chicago: CFM, 1968), p. iv.

24. Donald Jones, "We Are An Ecumenical Movement," *ACT,* v. 22, no. 9 (February 1970), p. 4.

25. Ibid., and Donald Jones to Reverend Walter S. Mitchell, December 8, 1969, CFM Papers, Box 159.

26. *People Are . . .* (Chicago: CFM, 1969), p. ii.

27. Jones's Letter, mimeo., CFM Papers, Box 159.

28. Louis Putz, in "Collected Notebooks of Federation Chaplains, March 1969 (8?)." CFM Papers, Box 133.

29. Ed Kohler, in ibid.

30. "Ecumenical Groups," *ACT,* v. 21, no. 2 (March 1968), p. 4.

31. "CFM Ecumenism in San Diego," *ACT,* v. 23, no. 4 (July–August 1970).

32. Rory Johnson, "Something Called the Agony," *ACT,* v. 23, no. 10 (March 1971), pp. 3–4.

33. Report, CFM and the National Workshop for Christian Unity, CFM Papers, Box 118.

34. Katherine Burgraff, "Christian Unity," *ACT,* v. 23, no. 3 (June 1970), p. 1.

35. Interview with Ed Kohler, July 12, 1996.

36. Quoted in Rick Casey, "CFM Shows Undefiant Independence of Church," *National Catholic Reporter,* v. 7, no. 39 (September 10, 1971), pp. 1, 22.

37. Executive Committee Minutes, January 15–18, CFM Papers, Box 190.

38. Jones interview.

39. Many of these responses are present in CFM papers, Box 163.

40. "Official," September 26, 1971, CFM Papers, Box 163.

41. Quoted in Casey, "CFM Shows Undefiant . . . ," p. 22.

42. "Celebrating Reality," reprinted in *ACT,* v. 24, no. 5 (September 1971), p. 2.

43. Dorothy Maldoon, quoted in Casey, "CFM Shows Undefiant . . . ," p. 22.

44. Jones interview.

45. Maldoons to Louis Putz, January 23, 1972, CFM Papers, Box 133.

46. "A Step Forward for Ecumenical CFM," *ACT,* v. 24, no. 8 (December–June 1972).

IO. GENDER AND SEXUALITY

1. Walter Imbiorski, ed., *The New Cana Manual* (Chicago: Cana Conference of Chicago, 1957), see pp. 74, 160–61.

2. Ibid., pp.161–62.

3. "Three Big Advantages of CFM Told," *ACT,* v. 7, no. 4 (February 1954), p. 2.

4. The quotes from the Crowleys are taken from an essay by Kathryn Johnson, in the author's possession. Original quotes from Pat Crowley, "Christian Family Living Day by Day, Year by Year, Part I," in Sister Mary Ramon Langdon, ed., *The Catholic Elementary School Program for Christian Family Living* (Washington, D.C.: Catholic

University of America Press, 1955), pp. 22–23, and Patty Crowley, "Christian Family Living Day by Day, Year by Year, Part II," p. 28.

5. Forrest Macken, C.P., "Must a Wife Obey Her Husband?" *ACT*, v. 11, no. 3 (February 1958), p. 6.

6. "The Husband's Role in CFM," *ACT*, v. 10, no. 7 (May 1957), p. 2.

7. Lettie Morse, "Woman's Role in Next Year's Program," *ACT*, v. 15, no. 11 (July 1962).

8. "Husband's Role . . . ," p. 2.

9. Quoted in Bob Senser, "How They Changed Their Neighborhood," *ACT*, v. 12, no. 6 (April 6, 1959), p. 7.

10. "Women Pledge Apostolate With Home Church as Center," *ACT*, v. 1, no. 3 (December 1947), p. 3.

11. *Civic Responsibility—Work—Recreation: 1952–53 Inquiry Program* (Chicago: CFM, 1952), pp. 66–67.

12. *Family Life and Economics: 1958–59 Inquiry Program* (Chicago: CFM, 1958), p. 95.

13. *Christianity and Social Progress: 1962–63 Inquiry Program* (Chicago: CFM, 1962), p. 88.

14. Ibid., p. 89.

15. Interview with Alma Sternik, October 30, 1997.

16. Interview with Isabelle Leroux, August 31, 1996.

17. Thanks to Isabelle Leroux for the last two notes.

18. Interview with Fran Muench, July 28, 1995.

19. Mrs. James Anderson, "Reflections on the Life and Death of CFM in Portland," CFM Papers, Box 101.

20. CFM Papers, Box 40.

21. Trudie Barreras, "Career or Family," *ACT*, v. 20, no. 7 (August 1967), p. 20.

22. William D'Antonio, quoted on back cover, *ACT*, v. 20, no. 9 (November 1967).

23. Sidney Callahan, *ACT*, v. 20, no. 4 (May 1967), p. 2.

24. *Building Community, Through Religious Life, Through Politics* (Chicago: CFM, 1967), pp. 70–71.

25. Madelyn Bonsignore, "Role of Women," CFM Papers, Box 62.

26. *People Are . . .* (Chicago: CFM, 1969), p. 10.

27. *Quality of Life: 1971–72 Inquiry Program*, (Chicago: CFM, 1971), p. 22.

28. See especially, "Women and the New Feminism," *ACT*, v. 24, no. 8 (December-January 1972), p. 5.

29. *For Happier Families*, 5th edition (Chicago: CFM, 1957).

30. "Is It Time To Take Another Look at the CFM Symbol?" *ACT*, v. 24, no. 8 (December–January 1972), p. 4.

31. See "Letters to the Editor" *ACT*, v. 24, no. 10 (March 1972).

32. "Familia '74" *ICCFM Newsletter*, v. 5, no. 2 (Spring–Summer 1973), p. 2.

33. "African Safari, Part III," *ACT*, v. 27, no. 9 (November 1974).

34. "The Woman in the Church," *ACT*, v. 26, no. 9 (November 1973), p. 6.

35. *International Life: 1960–61 Inquiry Program* (Chicago: CFM, 1960), p, 105.

36. *Political Life and the Christian Family: 1959–60 Inquiry Program* (Chicago: CFM, 1959), p. 94.

37. Quoted in Robert McClory, *Turning Point* (New York: Crossroads, 1995), p. 46. Original quoted in "Birth Control: Viewpoint of a European Bishop," *ACT*, v. 16, no. 7 (June 1963), p. 8.

38. Executive Committee Minutes, August 24, 1967, CFM Papers, Box 39.

39. John Noonan, "Catholics and Contraception," *ACT*, v. 18, no. 5 (July 1965), p. 4.

40. Walter Imbiorski, "What We Should Ask Ourselves," *ACT*, v. 18, no. 5 (July 1965), p. 4.

41. Ibid., p. 5.

42. "Love and Contraception in Marriage—A Response," *ACT*, v. 18, no. 6 (August 1965), pp. 10–11.

43. Trudie Barreras, "Let's Rid Ourselves of Negative Theology," *ACT*, v. 18, no. 8 (October 1965), p. 8.

44. See "Letters to the Editor," *ACT*, v. 18, no. 8 (October 1965), pp. 11–13.

45. "Letter to the Editor," *ACT*, v. 18, no. 10 (December–January 1966), p. 9.

46. Letters to Editor, CFM Papers, Box 41.

47. "Editorial: Birth Control and *ACT*," *ACT*, v. 18, no. 10 (December–January 1966), p. 2.

48. Letter to Larry Ragan, September 12, 1965, CFM Papers, Box 41.

49. "Letters to the Editor," *ACT*, v. 18, no. 10 (December–January 1966), p. 9.

50. Weisserts to Father John Sheehy, March 30, 1966, CFM Papers, Box 146.

51. Sheehy to Weisserts, April 9, 1966, CFM Papers, Box 146.

52. "Birth Control Delay," *ACT*, v. 19, no. 10 (December 1966), p. 4.

53. "The Encyclical—Populorum Progressio" *ACT*, v. 20, no. 4 (May 1967), p. 3.

54. Crowleys to Bernard Haring, September 6, 1965, CFM Papers, Box 57.

55. Larry Ragan, "Editor's Notebook," *ACT*, v. 20, no. 8 (September–October 1967) p. 2.

56. "Letter to the Editor" *ACT*, v. 19, no. 1 (February 1966), p. 14.

57. "Letter to the Editor," *ACT*, v. 20, no. 3 (April 1967), p. 21.

58. See Robert McClory, *Turning Point.*

59. Crowleys, CFM Papers, Box 200 +.

60. Statement by Patty Crowley, September 25, 1968, CFM Papers.

61. "A Matter of Conscience," *ACT*, v. 21, no. 6 (July–August 1968), p. 5.

62. Quoted in Ragan, "Editor's Notebook," p. 2.

63. "End Birth Control Fight," *ACT*, v. 21, no. 10 (December 1968), p. 7.

64. CFM Papers, Box 57.

65. Quoted in McClory, *Turning Point*, pp. 107–8.

66. Quoted in Ibid., p. 126.

67. "Area Conventions," *ACT*, v. 16, no. 1 (November 1962), pp. 4, 8.

68. "From Chicago CFM," *ACT*, v. 23, no. 11 (April 1971), p. 2.

69. Larry and Marry Little, "Thou Shalt Not Kill," *ACT*, v. 25, no. 5 (September 1972), p. 6.

70. See CFM Papers, Box 168.

71. "Here and There," *ACT*, v. 27, no. 3 (April 1974), p. 2.

72. "Letter to the Editor," *ACT*, v. 20, no. 6 (July 1967), p. 18.

73. *The Family in a Time of Revolution: 1970–71 Inquiry Program* (Chicago: CFM, 1970), pp. 76–77.

74. "Letter to the Editor," *ACT*, v. 25, no. 7 (November 1972), p. 8.

75. Dan and Rose Lucey, "The Important Resource—CFM," *ACT*, v. 26, no. 8 (October 1973), p. 5.

76. Petra Schwartz in *ACT,* v. 25, no. 8 (December-January 1972).

77. The Muraskis, "Natural Family Planning: One Couple's Experience," *ACT*, v. 27, no. 5 (June 1974), p. 4.

II. ICCFM: THE INTERNATIONAL CONFEDERATION OF CHRISTIAN FAMILY MOVEMENTS

1. See Michael Tangeman, *Mexico at the Crossroads: Politics, the Church and the Poor* (Maryknoll: Orbis Books, 1995), p. 49.

2. Jose Alvarez Icaza, "Mexico and Marxism," *ACT*, v. 21, no. 10 (December 1968), p. 6.

3. Tangeman, *Mexico at the Crossroads*, p. 53.

4. Ibid., p. 6.

5. Pepe and Luzma Alvarez Icaza, "Alliance for Understanding," *ACT*, v. 15, no. 3 (November 1961), p. 5.

6. "Confederation Agreement," CFM Papers, Box 147.

7. Ibid.

8. *ICCFM Newsletter*, v. 1, no. 1 (December 1967), p. 1.

9. Much of the remainder draws on the essay by Vernie Dale, "By Our Roots We Know Ourselves: An ICCFM History" offprint, n.d.

10. Ibid., p. 2.

11. ICCFM Papers, Box 2.

12. Crowleys to the Alvarez Icazas, March 23, 1967, ICCFM Papers 13.

13. ICCFM Papers.

14. For reports of the La Prée meeting, see *The Christian Family in Today's World* (Chicago: Foundation for International Cooperation, 1968), which contains the papers presented at the conference.

15. Executive Committee Minutes, ICCFM, CFM Papers, Box 161.

16. Reggie Weissert, quoted in Dale, "By Our Roots . . . ," p. 4.

17. "Five Year Plan for MFC-CFM," *ACT*, v. 25, no. 8 (December–January 1972), p. 8.

18. "Tarrytown Meeting" *ICCFM Newsbulletin*, v. 5, no. 1 (Winter 1972).

19. "Resolution for Family Action," *ACT*, v. 25, no. 6 (October 1972), p. 3.

20. *ICCFM Newsbulletin*, v. 5, no. 2 (Spring–Summer 1973), p. 2.

21. Ibid., p. 2.

22. See Dale, "By Our Roots . . . ," p. 5.

23. Ibid., p. 5.

24. *ICCFM Bulletin*, v. 5, no. 2 (Spring–Summer 1972), p. 2.

25. *ICCFM Bulletin*, v. 6, no. 1 (Fall–Winter 1974), p. 1.

26. From "A Team Report," in "Familia '74," *Risk*, v. 10, no. 4 (1974), p. 18.

27. Ibid.

28. Ray and Dorothy Maldoon, "Christian Family Safari, Part II," *ACT*, v. 27, no. 8 (October 1974), p. 4.

29. *Risk* , p. 19.

30. Ray and Dorothy Maldoon, "Christian Family Safari," *ACT*, v. 27, no. 7 (September 1974), p. 4.

31. Maldoons, "African Safari, Part III," *ACT*, v. 27, no. 9 (November 1974).

32. "Latin American Delegation Report on Population," from "Position Papers of Theme Groups," copy in author's possession.

33. Dale, "By Our Roots . . . ," p. 5.

34. Pat and Patty Crowley, quoted in Dale, "By Our Roots . . . ," p. 3.

35. Ibid., p. 2.

36. This section on Marriage Encounter relies heavily on the work of Robert White, who wrote a thesis on the history of Marriage Encounter entitled "The Origin and Vision of Marriage Encounter." Copy in possession of author via Patty Crowley.

37. Quoted in White, "Marriage Encounter," p. 117.

38. Donald Hessler, "CFM Rediscovers Its Spanish-Speaking Friends," *ACT*, v. 21, no. 10 (December 1968), p. 8. White cites the Spanish team as consisting of fifty-one couples and seventeen priests.

39. "Marriage Encounters," *ACT*, v. 21, no. 9 (November 1968), p. 3.

40. White, "Marriage Encounter," p. 127.

41. Jerry and Joan Whaley, "Our Marriage Encounter: Painfully Honest Dialogue," *ACT*, v. 21, no. 4 (May 1968), pp. 19–20.

42. "CFM People Are 'Into' Marriage Encounter—And Love It!" *ACT*, v. 25, no. 1 (April 1972), p. 3.

43. Whelans to CFMers, January 29, 1970, CFM Papers, Box 189.

44. White, "Marriage Encounter," p. 126.

45. 1973 Federation Reports, CFM Papers, Box 168.

46. "ME and CFM," *The Spirit* (Christmas Issue, 1972), p. 4.

47. Whaleys, "Our ME . . .," p. 20.

48. See "First International Meeting of Marriage Encounter," *ACT*, v. 26, no. 8 (October 1973), p. 1, and "International Marriage Encounter," *ACT*, v. 26, no. 10 (December–January 1974), p. 2.

49. See "CFM Cares: South of the Border Activities," *LA News Notes* (January 1968), p. 3.

50. See "Annual Reports," *ACT*, v. 11, no. 9 (September 1958), p. 6, and "Our Migrant Neighbors," *ACT*, v. 12, no. 3 (December 15, 1958), p. 3.

51. "CFM Leaders Form Group to Help Spanish Americans," *ACT*, v. 13, no. 5 (February 1960), p. 5.

52. "Report from Saginaw," *ACT*, v. 16, no. 5 (March 1963), p. 5.

53. Tim Murnane, "Gonzado's Children Have Hope Thanks to Pope John and CFM," *ACT*, v. 17, no. 3 (January 1964).

54. Terri Mudd, "The Sad Story of a Migrant Farmworker," *ACT*, v. 20, no. 2 (April 1967), p. 18.

55. "Marriage Encounters," *ACT*, v. 21, no. 9 (November 1968), p. 3.

56. Reynold Hillenbrand, Executive Committee Minutes, August 22–24, 1967, CFM Papers, Box 39.

57. Norbert and Vivian Langer, January 23, 1969, CFM Papers, Box 182.

58. Most of this information was culled from CFM Papers, Box 182.

59. MFC, National Executive Committee Resolutions, June 25, 1970, CFM Papers, Box 190.

60. *ACT*, v. 24, no. 6 (October 1971), p. 8, and "MFC Has Come Into Its Own," *ACT*, v. 25, no. 5 (September 1972), p. 4.

61. Don Hessler to the Crowleys, February 9, 1969, CFM Papers, Box 167.

62. Press Release, CFM Papers, Box 167.

63. News Release, CFM Papers, Box 182.

64. CFM Executive Committee Meeting, August 1971, CFM Papers, Box 192.

12. THE END OF THE SIXTIES AND THE DECLINE OF CFM

1. For instance, see Robert Martin, "How Some of Us Have Been Acting," *ACT*, v. 19, no. 6 (July–August 1969), pp. 22–23.

2. *Chicago Observes* (November 1969), p. 4.

3. Gordon Zahn, "Catholics, War and Pacifism," *ACT*, v. 20, no. 8 (September–October 1967), p. 7.

4. Gerry Stafford, "Letter to the Editor," *ACT*, v. 21, no. 2 (March 1968), p. 13.

5. CFM Papers, Box 57.

6. "Convention Report," *ACT*, v. 22, no. 7 (November 1969), p. 5.

7. Lucey, *Roots*, p. 79.

8. "Statement of La Vie Nouvelle" *ACT*, v. 26, no. 4 (May 1973), p. 2.

9. *ACT*, v. 20, no. 2 (March 1967), p. 4.

10. Lucey, *Roots*, pp. 75–76.

11. Pittsburgh Federation Report, 1969, CFM Papers, Box 134.

12. Elmer Zinn, *Newsletter*, 1967, CFM Convention, CFM Papers.

13. "1971 Convention," *ACT*, v. 24, no. 5 (September 1971), p. 2.

14. Coordinating Committee Minutes, July 1968, CFM Papers, Box 39.

15. Executive Committee Minutes, February 7–9, 1971, CFM Papers, Box 190.

16. National Staff Report, February 15, 1975, CFM Papers, Box 192.

17. EC Meeting, February 7–9, 1971, CFM Papers, Box 190.

18. "The Measure of CFM Commitment," *ACT*, v. 25, no. 2 (May 1972), p. 2.

19. San Francisco, "Federation Chaircouple's Column," January 1971, p. 3, CFM Papers.

20. "Executive Committee Meeting," *ACT*, v. 26, no. 7 (September 1973), p. 2.

21. Hillenbrand Papers, Box 10.

22. Nerin to Morhards, January 4, 1965, CFM Papers, Box 70.

23. "Discussion Corner: The Future of CFM," *CFM in Louisville* (August–September–October, 1966), p. 4.

24. William Nerin, "Purpose of CFM," Family Life Bureau, NCWC, reprint. First published in *Apostolate*, v. 9, no. 2.

25. William Nerin, "Status of CFM in Oklahoma," CFM Papers, Box 61.

26. "Discussion Corner . . . ," p. 4.

27. Ibid., p. 4.

28. CFM Papers, Box 62.

29. "Thoughts of John and Dorothy Drish after last Executive Committee Meeting, 1966," CFM Papers, Box 125.

30. "From John and Dorothy Drish" CFM Papers, Box 62.

31. Executive Committee Minutes, January 26–29, 1967, CFM Papers, Box 49.

32. Reynold Hillenbrand, Hillenbrand Papers, Box 75.

33. Reynold Hillenbrand, "The Ideas That Animate Us," *ACT*, v. 18, no. 6 (August 1965), p. 7.

34. Caldwell Letter, Executive Committee Correspondence, February 5, 1964, CFM Papers, Box 39.

35. Crowleys to Morhards, October 8, 1965, CFM Papers, Box 70.

36. William Nerin to Crowleys, February 4, 1964, CFM Papers, Box 39.

37. See Notre Dame Study, CFM Papers, Box 65.

38. Crowleys to Maiolo and D'Antonio, February 23, 1970, CFM Papers, Box 65.

39. For Crowley response, see CFM Papers, Box 65, and "Young People and CFM," *ACT*, v. 23, no. 1 (August 1970), pp. 1–2.

40. "Editorial: A Matter of Prudence," *ACT*, v. 10, no. 7 (May 1957), p. 2.

41. "Editorial: CFM and a Public Stand," *ACT*, v. 13, no. 7 (April 1960), p. 2.

42. See letters to the editor, *ACT*, v. 18, no. 10 (December–January 1966), pp. 10–11.

43. Larry Ragan to Executive Committee, February 7, 1968, CFM Papers, Box 61.

44. "The Issue Policy: Who Speaks for CFM?" *ACT*, v. 21, no. 4 (May 1968), p. 6.

45. Press Release, *Our Sunday Visitor*, December 7, 1969, p. 6.

46. Hillenbrand Papers, May 26, 1966, Box 75.

47. Executive Committee Minutes, August 22–24, 1967, CFM Papers, Box 39.

48. Philadelphia Federation Newsletter, May 1969, p. 3. CFM Papers, Box 134.

49. Federation Reports, 1967, CFM Papers, Box 40.

50. "Letters to Editor," *ACT*, v. 21, no. 2 (March 1968), p. 14.

51. *People Are . . . : 1969–70 Social Inquiry Program* (Chicago: CFM, 1969), p. 2.

52. Kohler-Olsen Report, June 1970, CFM Papers, Box 159.

53. Gary, Indiana, Federation Response to CFM Program 1970–71: *Revolution*, CFM Papers, Box 132.

54. June Smith, Letter to Program Committee, March 13, 1969, CFM Papers, Box 132.

55. "CFM of the Future," *ACT*, v. 23, no. 10 (March 1971), p. 5.

56. CFM Papers, Box 158.

57. Ibid.

58. Executive Committee Minutes, February 2, 1972, CFM Papers, Box 181.

59. "Highlights of CFM Executive Meeting," *ACT*, v. 25, no. 8 (December–January 1973), p. 3.

60. Maldoons to Board of Directors, January 17, 1974, CFM Papers.

61. "New 1973–74 Inquiry Books," *ACT*, v. 26, no. 6 (July–August 1973).

62. "Project FIND," *ACT*, v. 28, no. 1 (February 1975), pp. 1–2.

63. Joe and Madelyn Bonsignore to Program Committee, November 7, 1974, CFM Papers, Box 168.

64. Program Committee Meeting, September 1974, CFM Papers, Box 168.

65. "Mission Statement," 1974, CFM Papers, Box 192.

66. Letter to CFM History Committee, February 24, 1994.

67. Kohler to Pope Paul VI, February 4, 1972, CFM Papers, Box 192.

68. Luceys to Maldoons, February 4, 1972, CFM Papers, Box 192.

69. Putz to Maldoons, January 27, 1972, CFM Papers, Box 192.

70. Hillenbrand to Kohler, February 15, 1972, CFM Papers, Box 159.

71. Hillenbrand to Putz, February 15, 1972, Hillenbrand Papers, Box 11.

72. Cody to Leo Byrne, February 7, 1972, Hillenbrand Papers, Box 11.

73. Cody to Hillenbrand. February 29, 1972, Hillenbrand Papers, Box 11.

74. National Office Report—Financial Development Program, February 1975, CFM Papers, Box 192.

75. Jim Schmidt, "The Future of CFM," *Columbus Ohio People Are* (February 1970), p. 2.

76. Chicago Federation Report, 1967, CFM Papers, Box 40.

77. Jim and Eunice Saum, 1968 Survey, July 3, 1968, CFM Papers, Box 64.

78. Laurence Kelly, CFM Papers, Box 133.

79. Trenton Federation Report, 1973, CFM Papers, Box 168.

13. CONCLUSION

1. Chuck Fisher to Dr. Maiolo, December 12, 1969, CFM Papers, Box 65.

2. Madelyn Bonsignore, "Generation to Generation: The CFM Challenge," July 1987. Copy in possession of author.

3. Father Donald Kanaly, "Speech," CFM Papers, Box 39.

4. "An Interview with Pat and Patty Crowley," *ACT*, v. 23, no. 8 (December 1970–January 1971), p. 6.

Index